Autism and Other Adventures: Lucy's Story (Naught to Nineteen)

Lucy Blackman

Published by Lucy Blackman Books, 2024.

While every precaution has been taken in the preparation of this book, the publisher assumes no responsibility for errors or omissions, or for damages resulting from the use of the information contained herein.

AUTISM AND OTHER ADVENTURES: LUCY'S STORY (NAUGHT TO NINETEEN)

First edition. April 13, 2024.

Copyright © 2024 Lucy Blackman.

ISBN: 978-0975634592

Written by Lucy Blackman.

Table of Contents

Prologue | April 1992 – June 1993 1
Chapter 1 | Little Lucy: Taste, Touch and Tantrums 6
Chapter 2 | Little Lucy: Vision and Voids 31
Chapter 3 | Little Lucy: The Glass Carillon 51
Chapter 4 | Little Lucy Goes to School: Age 4–9 72
Chapter 5 | Big Lucy 1982–1986: Age 10–14 96
Chapter 6 | Language Without Speech: Age 14 122
Chapter 7 | Life With Typed Language, 1987: Age 14 148
Chapter 8 | The New Me, August 1987 – June 1988: | Age 15 174
Chapter 9 | More About Me, High School 1988–1989: | Age 16–17 201
Chapter 10 | Family Matters, Summer 1989–1990: | Age 17 225
Chapter 11 | School Matters, 1990: | Age 17 241
Chapter 12 | Curriculum and Communication, 1990: | Age 17 258
Chapter 13 | Typing and Talking, 1990: | Age 17–18 275
Chapter 14 | A Question of Touch, 1991: | Age 18 291
Chapter 15 | Looking To the Future, 1991: | Age 19 315
Chapter 16 | Going to America, | October 1991 – January 1992 338
Chapter 17 | Earphones and Reggae, | January 1992 355
Chapter 18 | An Exciting, Frightening Journey, | January–February 1992 375
Chapter 19 | Mapping My Enchanted World, | February 1992 397
Chapter 20 | The Lens Of the Kaleidoscope, | March 1992 412
Afterword to Lucy's Story. 1999/2001 edition | Tony Attwood, Ph. D. 428
Glossary 435

Lucy's Story was originally published by Book in Hand in 1999 and distributed to markets outside Australia by Jessica Kingsley Publishers (2001). This re-issue has been retitled to make it easier to find on-line. The text is largely unchanged, but there is a new layout to help you better understand Lucy's world.

***

AUTHOR'S DEDICATION
This book is dedicated to all those people who have played a part in my life, whether or not they appear in the events which feature in *Autism and Other Adventures: Lucy's Story*.

***

FOREWORD (From *Lucy's Story*. 1999 Edition)
Tony Attwood (whose "Afterword" to the 1999 edition appears at the end of this book) wrote in the Foreword to the First Edition:
Lucy provides the point of view of someone with autism who has never used speech. I first met Lucy in 1990, and she taught me more about autism than any academic text.

Professionals who specialise in autism will be interested in how her descriptions are consistent with our theoretical models and the research literature.

They will also be interested in her response to specific programmes and how to adapt the strategies to other children and adults with a similar expression of autism.

(For more details, go to Tony's *Afterword* at the end of this book).

***

www.lucysautismstory.com[1] will bring you access to other writing, illustrations and free downloads, together with occasional blogs about, and links to topics related to this book

Follow us on Facebook[2] (Lucy Blackman's Autism Story: Jay's Page)

---

1. http://www.lucysautismstory.com
2. https://www.facebook.com/profile.php?id=61557061335763

Prologue
April 1992 – June 1993

I came to language late — about twelve years too late.

Another five years on I was nineteen and I was enrolled in a literary studies course at University. I wrote a story in which I showed how personal experience could enrich fiction, even when all the characters and settings were imaginary. The central character was a small child much like my memories of my silent self.

Because of what was going on in my life in that Year of Grace, 1992, I called this invention *Flat Reflections in the Round*. Here is a part of my completed tale. This book is my account of how that story came to be written.

Nappies on the hoist whirled against the blue sky, carrying hopes and flashes of fear and delight. The lines were parallel yet circular streaks and angles cut the space that cried to the eye as a void that was also a containment. Round and round and round again.

The fat white cloud came to break the sky and her safety started to go as nappies and cloud and single strangling silver wires melded and flew. The voice called and saved her, but she did not turn.

Hands from behind gripped firmly, carrying the sensitive body to the other part of her world where her ears and eyes registered safety and the wildness of existence was bearable.

***

The dishes were on the firm surface of the table, and the unyielding wood caught the shock of the metallic crash of the spoon swirling downwards in the chubby hand. She felt the food with her other hand, testing the texture, then dipping her face to sniff it before the spoon came across and dextrously shovelled to her mouth.

LUCY BLACKMAN

Around her came her family's laughter. She could now link the words 'climbed over the fence' with her scratchy flight to freedom that had been spurred by the noise of the kindergarten.

The challenge of the food absorbed her again, and the peanut butter jar started to take on an obsessional importance as a longing for the texture and taste wiped all else from her mind.

Her hair and face smeared with brown, and the short hair became spiked with the same colour. An aroma of peanut engulfed the family.

***

The water hurtled from the tap to hit the white enamel. Screaming, the struggling child passed from anguish to blind terror. The towel loomed, and the rough threads stood out in serried shattering ranks.

***

... The piggybacked burden did not grip, so [the woman] clasped her hands below her daughter's legs. That left a body that swung back, and swayed to each movement while the arms flailed purposelessly. The mother put the child down, but carefully retained a full grip on both wrists before handing an arm to her son. The hands starred outwards and did not clasp. There was no desire to cup another's hand, no revulsion but no urge ...

***

...The swing moved, running on grooves of air. The rush and dip gave depth to the world and anxiety receded ... till the call to move. Her headlong joyous scamper ended in still rapt contemplation of the straight soaring triangles linked by the parallel loops of buzzing wire that strung across the green belt. Under the angles, the child stood rapt and alone ...

AUTISM AND OTHER ADVENTURES: LUCY'S STORY

***

The horns before her held no fears. But below, the eyes, large and insistent, demanding she meet them if only for a moment. There was no escape but stillness. So she sat, soles of her feet pressed together and head turned sideways to shut out the vision she could not flee.

The policeman handed the small damp figure to her mother ... The screams started to rotate as threshing arms and legs fought for freedom ... Over her head and through the fury of her restraint, the little girl heard the voice, 'Well, that's autism for you.'

(Extracts from Assignment, Deakin University, April 1992.)

The little girl in that tale was an invention, though the way that she saw her world was mine. The characters were not based on my own family alone.

There were other families in my life, friends whom we visited over the years and a galaxy of after-school care-givers while my own mother worked, all fully furnished with houses, memories and scents, but no faces — or at least not in my mind.

My own mother was a feeling and a presence, but not a visible person until a couple of years ago. And yet of course I recognised her and all these other people when we actually met, though usually I would seem to glance through them as if they were inlaid in a plexiglass screen.

Barely was I aware of myself as an individual until my twenties, and then intermittently.

***

Little Lucy inhabited a magic world that was mine alone, but it was enriched by four older sisters.

We tumbled together on the carpet in front of the television in the ramshackle granny-flat that served as a play-room. Here was a secret world where my sisters read from wonderful books, 'Hardy

LUCY BLACKMAN

Boys', *The Story of Christmas* and illustrated fables of Unicorns and Mermaids. They talked about the equally fabulous world of 'real school' and tolerated me as playmate and poltergeist.

***

As the character of that imaginary little girl built up, I lived again my first four years of life as a composite of memories rather than an accurate chronology.

Yes, I was still autistic, dependent on others and without useful speech, but as I wandered around the labyrinth that had been my life, I began to have some inkling of why this might be so.

It became important to ask people how they remembered me at different stages of my life. I started with my four big sisters.

Jenny, who was the nearest to me in age, was press-ganged to invite the whole family to her home one wintry afternoon. My mother, now known as Jay, was firmly in tow. Along with a keyboard, she clutched a tape recorder

So two decades later the family conclave was back in session, my typewritten draft being passed from hand to hand. Jenny-the-adult and Jay-the-Mum sat with a bottle of wine between them, read, and then disinterred their own memories.

Hayley and Val, looking extremely self-conscious, kept glancing behind them at Val's toddler son being caressed and tumbled by Shay, Kara and Aaron, Hayley's little pre-school monsters. Kay, five months pregnant, leant stoutly forward to press the tape-recorder button.

I was hoping that the tape of their comments would help me fill in the gaps and that they would not be offended by my idiosyncratic world view.

They turned to the typescripts with all the enthusiasm that I remember in a Friday afternoon English test at school. The paper shuffled and shifted in their hands.

AUTISM AND OTHER ADVENTURES: LUCY'S STORY

Dad had been born in Jersey Channel Island, the only part of the British Commonwealth to be occupied by the Axis forces in Hitler's rampage east and west in Europe. When civilian rule was restored to the island in 1945, one of the unclaimed orphans was a three-and-a-half-year-old boy called David.

We understood clearly that we were loved and missed by my father's adopted family in South Africa. Our sense of belonging to extended families was strong. However, in everyday life there was just us, our parents, new friends, baby-sitters and school.

***

My parents were inveterate hoarders, so when they moved a third of the way around the globe, they naturally brought the matinee jackets and booties given to each of my sisters when she was born, as well as a lacy wool shawl which features in Jay's own baby photos of 1942, wrapped around her bald head and placid face which even then had a suggestion of the grin which later in life was to be her insurance against taking herself too seriously. So, I was tenderly wrapped in these heirlooms — but not for long.

The adults did not realise for many years that I found all fabrics irritating, and some intolerable. However, they did notice that I was never cold, even in winter. In my case a T-shirt was warm enough for most winter days. That first summer thin jackets or just a nappy were the order of the day.

This was the first obvious sign of my sensory peculiarities. For many years summer was like a hot sauna, and in winter I was always in demand to jump into one of my sisters' beds as a kind of sibling-cum-hot-water-bottle, only to be evicted as a chronic wriggler.

For another peculiarity that my family had noticed when I was small was that, in any situation, it was a fight to make me tolerate any kind of clasp or hug.

LUCY BLACKMAN

***

The other children and I grew into a very cohesive group. With only two bedrooms between five children, we shared in various combinations, learning to rely on each other for support as my parents slowly adjusted to a new country, and then moved towards a reconstructive divorce.

As all babies are handled and cuddled, in spite of struggles so was I, because, unlike anxious mothers, a two- or four-year-old sister is totally persevering in the face of resistance.

Look at any family kitten in the arms of a child. Surely, if the child is not scratched to ribbons, the cat is strongly desensitised and even knows how to relax in its predicament.

Years later as an adult when I unexpectedly suddenly lost some of that tactile distress at being caressed, I realised that I had not developed an affectionate reaction because I simply had had no opportunity to learn how.

I had a collaborator in this discovery, a tiger-striped kitten named George. Rescued from some unknown fate, he had been delivered up to the untender but loving arms of Hayley's brood.

By the time he was an adult cat, he would drape himself over the linked arms of a staggering two-year-old who was barely taller than George's own stretched length, paw-to-paw.

Dangling much like an old fox-fur stole with its stuffed head intact, George would purr as if this was his ultimate mission in life, while his handsome feline face had an expression of simpering bliss.

As his rear paws thumped dangling in the wake of his porter, I suddenly was able to draw the obvious conclusion that I had never felt my body comfortably in someone's embrace. My skin response had been as much a barrier as a wire cage. I had learned to endure, but not enjoy.

***

AUTISM AND OTHER ADVENTURES: LUCY'S STORY

However, in adolescence I was able to learn to tolerate localised touch on my hand, arm and wrist while I made intelligent controlled movements that related to visual language processing.

This type of touch was effective because it made some parts of my visual processing coordinate with my self-image, so I knew where my moving hand was going or when it had just paused to rest on, or point to, a symbol. After years of working this way, I began to enjoy the sensation of this kind of touch.

In childhood, though, being held in a hug by an adult was not pleasant, and the limitation on my freedom was horrible because I felt uncomfortable unless I was able to move. The world felt out of control. I now realise this was because of some kind of abnormality in vision and balance.

***

The family read the original draft of that passage, and started to look bored. Kay released the pause button on the tape recorder. I was the first person to say anything, though on the recording it is Jay's voice that speaks my words one by one, with the sound of a tiny grating click behind her voice:

DO// YOU// FEEL// THAT// I// CAN// MAKE// SLIGHTLY// HUMOUROUS// REFERENCES// TO// US// AS// A// FAMILY?// DID// WE// DO// THINGS// VERY// ODDLY// BECAUSE// OF// ME//?

Jenny: *Do you want us to tell stories?* - (giggling) *why not, it was a bit strange!*

Kay (slightly pompous with embarrassment): *Lucy remembers she was often in demand as a hot-water bottle. Of course, as the youngest and cutest, she was probably the most popular choice as a real-life doll.* (Perhaps we should have hidden the tape recorder, because she sounded like someone reading a statement).

Jay: *You weren't much bigger than she was, Jenny. What happened if you tried to hold her wrist?*

Jenny: *She would just wriggle free, except when we were playing games. I can remember as a young kid being taught a game in which two people do a rocking boat action, sitting on the floor opposite each other, and holding hands while saying, 'Slowly, Slowly, Fast, Fast, Faster ...'*

Lucy was the only one who would do it with me because I liked playing it for hours and hours on end. You see, I also liked the sensation! (I notice that she still lisps!)

Jay: *By fourteen months old she climbed up and over anything, swarming up the side of the timber cot. So, I moved her into the bottom bunk.*

When she was about a year and a half, I saw her climb up the end of the bunk set, hand-over-hand. That was the end of her sleeping on the bottom bunk.

Jenny: *Yeah, I can remember being furious. I was four, and I loved lying on my back so I could put my grubby hands and feet up onto the ceiling and make wonderful patterns. When Lu took the bunk over, I was not very impressed with the idea.*

Jay (officiously trying to bring the conversation back to me): *Once she could walk, she just headed in the opposite direction. Then in her second summer we went to the beach on the Bay. She walked into the sea, and was still walking several feet after her face had first gone under water. We then picked her up, and she did not seem to have realised that anything had been different ...*

(Audio recording of family meeting, June 1993).

***

I remember that day, but I remember also that a few months later I had a short period when I was frightened of water.

AUTISM AND OTHER ADVENTURES: LUCY'S STORY

I wrote that into *Flat Reflections* as if the child were frightened of water's splashing as it hit the tub, because I have the impression that most people assume that a child would find this alarming, and I was writing the story to be marked by a university tutor who presumably did not have autism.

However, in real life the splash was not a problem. It was seeing the water shooting from nowhere as it poured from the tap, and the sound of the fluid rush through the air that terrified me. Water in general then became a monster in whatever guise I encountered it.

But the following summer I played with abandon in the small, one metre deep, above-ground pool. Somehow in the neck-high density of the water my tactile response was different, and I could laugh at and with the other children.

The reduction in gravity may have cancelled out the difficulties in balance and body-awareness that I was later to recognise, because even now I can rarely act as spontaneously as that unless in a swimming pool.

***

My very first memory must be from very early babyhood. I had a recurrent sensation of a distasteful trickle in the back of my mouth, and now recognise it as the flow of formula from a baby-bottle. This discomfort on my soft palate may explain why I would push the bottle away with my tongue and turn my head away.

My parents thought that I was a 'difficult feeder'. As all my sisters had been conventionally gluttonous, Jay had no idea that my feeding behaviour was more odd than that.

They would either keep jiggling the bottle because otherwise I did not seem to know what I was supposed to do with it, or rest a finger on my chin to create a reflex. It sounds like giving tablets to a cat, but it seemed to work — I certainly thrived.

LUCY BLACKMAN

***

When I came to finger foods, I acquired the habit of stuffing my mouth with enormous quantities of food, and then gulping the congealed mass down in a python-like convulsion. That way I could avoid that unpleasant sensation at the back of my throat.

My other solution was to force a banana down my throat in one unbroken arc. That really was a conversation-stopper if we had guests. Not surprisingly my mouth was not stimulated, nor did my jaw movements really develop into a chewing motion.

When my second teeth came through, they were to remain serrated for many years as they did not have the abrasion of chewing to wear them as I continued to bolt my food. If the texture of a food was repulsive, I simply could not swallow if the flavour did not give me some kind of urge to do so.

Without an automatic trigger, I never learned to make my throat or mouth move on command without someone making the movement for me to model.

Of course, this was a mystery to the people who tried to make me eat such horrors as boiled or fried rice. In some strange way these foods, and a good many others, became embedded in my language processing as general terms for anything totally repulsive.

***

My main approach to food was formed by vision and touch. I was completely in the thrall of flavour and colour. I could not resist anything that was sweet, brightly coloured and very widely advertised.

My aversion for certain foods and my obsession with others was not the only abnormality. I constantly tried to make my tummy have that comfortable feeling of being full.

AUTISM AND OTHER ADVENTURES: LUCY'S STORY

I don't think this was hunger. It was just that my intestines, and all the other bits and pieces that food churns through, never felt quite right unless I was what Granny Joy called 'FTB' (full-to-bursting).

***

If the effects of migration and settling into a new culture had been tempestuous for my family, the early years of my life must have seemed like a constant hurricane. I was not diagnosed as having autism until I was six years old.

So it was as a chaotic mystery that I cut a swathe through the fridge, oblivious to the budgetary deficits in the wake of my consuming four litres of ice-cream or an entire cake in one successfully completed foray.

I think it might be kindest to describe Jay's housekeeping as eccentric, though this was probably aggravated by our fairly low income in the early years in Melbourne, and her chronic distaste for all forms of cooking.

As a cherry on the top, she had to work around my constant foraging for ice-cream, sweets, cookies, fruit, savoury finger foods, and things like carrots and radishes which felt crisp and fibrous. I did not grow out of this until I had nearly finished my university degree.

At various times food was hidden around under beds or in the back of wardrobes so that the weekly family marketing had some chance of lasting from pay-day to pay-day. In my worst stages the fridge was secured by a large chain.

When I learnt that it was possible to slip a tiny groping hand into the slight slack that was unavoidably left, Jay moved all food, including the refrigerator, into the laundry outside the back door.

***

In time Jay came to realise she was not as nutty as she thought. She eventually was to meet the parents of other children like me. While they gossiped, I would loiter or run in circles, apparently without understanding a word that was being said.

By the time I was a teenager, I had come to the conclusion that families of children with autism have an ongoing obsession with the binge-eating or semi-starvation of their offspring — that is when they are not chasing after them or telling horror stories of escapes and police searches.

***

I was a skilled escapee myself. The model for the little girl's encounter with a cow in *Flat Reflections* was my disappearance from a plum-picking barbecue in the hills near Melbourne. It certainly was not the last or the first.

The whole family had very definite opinions about my behaviour on that day, and had no hesitation in expressing them:

Kay: *We held onto her wrists like a vice. She never held our hands and it was fatal to let go. You know how she would just disappear! At all barbecues and picnics Lucy seemed to take delight in escaping. That wasn't the only time she went for miles.*

The most embarrassing times were when she took all her clothes off, and she didn't mention in that story that she sat in that cow paddock stark naked!

Another reason that 'plumdinger' was so awful was that the other people were all strangers, and thought we were panicking unnecessarily.

Jay: *Funnily enough I had expected the plums to be the problem that day because she was so obsessed with the ones that grew in our yard. Remember the plum tree round the side of the house?*

Hayley: *And you sorting through Lucy's 'droppings' to count the stones to see how many she had eaten?*

AUTISM AND OTHER ADVENTURES: LUCY'S STORY

Jay: *Forty-one!*
Jenny: *The worst was when she ate the whole four-kilogram bag of apples, and was as high as a kite. She was running up and down the corridor singing to herself ... we could only look, and think 'I hope she comes down soon.'*
Jay: *How did she get a whole four kilo bag?*
Jenny: *Oh, you know how she sneaked food! 'Whoops - oh, that apple's gone!'*
Kay: *Most people have the same compulsions. But most people, even children, don't steal or raid from other people's plates, glasses or pantries to satisfy their craving. Lucy never had any qualms about stealing food wherever she was.*
Jenny: *I remember my friend Michelle being really mortified once. Lucy was about ten and was drinking tomato ketchup from the bottle. Michelle said, 'Put down the Ketchup bottle, Lucy.' Lucy just took another swig, and squelched her cheeks in and out a few times while looking at Michelle. It was so funny!*
Val (with memories of similar episodes dripping off her voice) *Oh, yeah?*
Kay: *She liked beer even more. Until very recently Lucy would grab someone's beer glass from under their nose, and scull it.*
Hayley (laughing, probably at the memory of a startled friend of her husband's only a couple of years before): *... and weren't they surprised!*
(Audio recording of family meeting, June 1993).

***

So, from babyhood the whole of my life centred round food and movement, but food took priority. I would dash into a group of children and grab snacks from their hands as naturally as I drew breath, and a lot more spontaneously than I scratched myself. The movement of food to my mouth was the answer to a need; that is, I did not consciously pick up food and open my jaw to receive it.

I did move efficiently sometimes, but I do not think that my vision and my sense of touch were sufficiently integrated for my body parts to learn from experience exactly what they had just done.

In the first version of this segment, an earlier sentence had read, 'the movement of food to my wasted mouth'. 'Wasted' was a response to a sudden flashback to facial muscles that were not to develop properly because they were underused, or not used in the way that most toddlers' mouths are. My memory must have been so immediate that my facial muscles felt as unstimulated as they did when I was a toddler.

***

My autism was not caused or aggravated by lack of interaction in any way. My own lack of interaction was innate.

However, watching the development of my sisters' children from the day of their birth, I speculate on the view of oneself as a person and the capability of that person to be complete if interaction with others is impaired, not only in one or two modes, but very slightly in all.

For I never spoke, except for occasional random unshaped phrases and syllables. Now I think that the use of speech and of other sensory activities that are normally lumped together as 'communication' are themselves a kind of sensory exploration.

One's sense of oneself as a person is augmented and developed in that process. The spoken environment is a peculiarly human invention, and like all other environments is learned by experience, both as a receiver and as a speaker.

AUTISM AND OTHER ADVENTURES: LUCY'S STORY

But for me all was distorted and unpredictable. It was only as an adult aunt that I learned that both the babbling of a baby and adolescent gossip are an essential part of learning and exploration.

I did make sounds of course. All my life I have cooed and chanted vaguely and hummed happily, and so drawn a sense of awareness of myself from my own voice.

***

The rest of the family was less than enthralled by my habit of night-time formless monologues. (They were to have their turn later when they acquired trumpets, recorders and guitar-playing boyfriends. Trumpets and electronic amps I could cope with, but plastic recorders must have been invented in Hell. Actually, I am told that no sone likes plastic recorders, but most people don't try to toot on one and block their ears at the same time, as I did when Jenny later tried to teach me to play it.)

***

I had other ways of making myself content. I would move my hands a few inches from my eyes for hours on end, and feel at one with the leaves fluttering against the white pergola.

In time the movement became a form of self-expression, so that even as an adult woman, when I feel very content, my fingers twitch in a formalisation of that movement.

However, originally the finger movement gave me a means of analysing near and far, and could lend coherence to light and shade, much as a spinning peep-show did in a nineteenth-century fair booth.

***

This was not an attempt to communicate. For me, successful 'social' contact depended on someone else interpreting my own signals.

Some of my attempts at communication were fairly conventional, as when I put my arms up towards a person with my hands stretched up because I desperately needed to be picked up or lifted over an obstacle.

However, Jay noted that if I turned my hands outward when I put my arms up to her, I was asking for a boost for a somersault, rather than some help in climbing up. If she interpreted wrongly, things could get very noisy.

***

My family was never into keeping a journal, but for some weird reason Jay used me as a subject for an exercise on 'Consistent and Meaningful Communication Signals in a Pre-school Child' when she undertook a teacher training course shortly after my third birthday. So I have been able to read a description which my mother wrote of me sitting on the toilet:

During the long hassle of toilet training, her gestures of resistance eventually became stylised to two. First, she held both hands above her head, with the fingers stiffly stretched, often for a very long time, usually accompanied by crying or niggling.

Then she would drop her shoulders slightly, and allow her arms below the elbow to drop inwards with her hands dangling down. I interpreted this as a sign of resignation.

After this she usually did what was required - that is once she had understood why she was sitting there, which took several months for her to learn. She used these signals for a very long time, and each family member had reacted before we compared notes and discovered they were consistent and meaningful.

AUTISM AND OTHER ADVENTURES: LUCY'S STORY

Once she became proficient at toileting, if she wanted to say she did not wish to 'go', she would say 'Ah-goo', which then I interpreted as 'I've been', whether she had or not.'

(Mary Jane Blackman, April 1976.)

Two things at once shone out to me. My gestures were a stylised derivative of a tantrum, so the early toileting sessions must have been wild.

Also, even that young, what speech I had was not filling a normal role. 'Ah-goo' was an echo of 'Have you gone?', not an attempt at 'I've gone'. I could not yet answer a query, truthfully or otherwise.

I had interpreted and processed the question as a release from durance, and so my spoken expression was linked to a consequence, and not to language I developed internally.

***

Even when I knew what I should do when I was placed on the toilet, I was not able to demonstrate when I needed to go until I was rather older than many children. This was not so much because of my communication difficulties as because of the slight confusion between 'now' and 'soon', 'past' and 'later' that permeated my personal awareness (and I think still does) and is paralleled in body awareness and anticipation.

Then, one day for the first time I had asked to 'go', though not in speech. Jay had been in the process of changing from casual, hourly-paid work as a cataloguer to a regular job as a librarian in a state High School.

On this day she had to drop off copies of her various qualifications at the Victorian Department of Education offices in the centre of the city. She always tried to cut down on child-minding expenses, but was not prepared to drag me unrestrained into the central business district — think of the little fictional girl as a walking companion!

Our own family pushchair had long since disintegrated under my bouncing and the weight of any older sister who had been inserted behind me in the seat if she did not walk fast enough.

So, on this occasion Jay borrowed one from the people who lived over the road. They had an elderly and portly corgi, which was occasionally taken for a walk in a small canvas pushchair in which a little human passenger would sit facing the person holding the handle.

We were moving over the slightly irregular paving stones, with the unsprung frame allowing my whole body to feel the vibration, when suddenly I clasped my hands very dramatically between my legs, my feet shot forward, my mouth moved soundlessly and my eyes met my mother's with unaccustomed intensity.

Of course, this did not mean that I had 'learned' something that I would do consistently, but that, under that particular stimulation, my body had got its act together sufficiently to make the signal surface at the right moment.

The message was clear. We dived into the nearest public toilet, which seemed infested by elderly ladies wearing little beaded hair nets. In the rather muted and eminently respectable conveniences Jay clasped me onto the threatening chasm of an adult toilet which threatened to devour my writhing bottom-end.

When I had finished, she tucked me together, and, my wrists circled by her hands, whirled me round and round next to the hand-basins, squawking in her virtually tone-deaf voice *Happy Birthday to You* and *Pop Goes the Weasel*, because that was the only communication from her, other than rewards of food, that as far as she knew gave me any pleasure.

***

AUTISM AND OTHER ADVENTURES: LUCY'S STORY

Kay: *Lucy's autism doesn't faze me at all! In fact, sometimes I find her less embarrassing than Jay. (Then hastily building bridges). Of course, we all used singing to get through to Lucy. We used to sing one song to her, which I suppose will always sum up what Lucy is to me.*
'Lucy, you're my darling ...'
Jenny: *Oh, yes. That song was really made up to shut her up on long car trips. She was sick and 'carrying on', so we started singing to her. At the end of each verse she would say, 'Loosy, Yoor awl ri". The first time she sang it, we thought, 'This is a really good song,' but really, she was pissed off, and sang it in a really aggro way. Then we thought, 'Well, there wasn't much point in writing this!'*
Val (huffily): *It was me who made up that song for Lucy before we went on that holiday.*
Jay: *I'm so glad I was an only child. (Her usual response when sibling rivalry got too much for her).*
(Then five flattish voices came on line, singing roughly to the tune of 'Charlie, you're my darlin''').
'Lucy, you're my darling
Specially when you are smiling.
And when you're in the kitchen stealing Vegemite
I know everything's a-a-a-ll right.'
(Audio recording of family meeting, June 1993).

***

In spite of everything, my father had fairly old-fashioned views on child rearing, even for the Seventies. We had an organised routine, which revolved around my father's priorities. I remember these as leaving for work in the morning and his extensive social life. Except when we were at group barbecues and parties, we seemed to be visiting other people, or, more commonly, having visitors streaming in and out of our living room.

'Darling,' he would say to Jay. She would sigh and put down her book. He would continue exuberantly. 'Phone So-and-So. We need company.'

As a result, we seemed to be inundated with visitors, which I suppose was a reasonable solution to the constant problem of his incurable need for a social life and my unique qualities as a guest in other peoples' homes.

***

When there was no one else there, he would sit in a chair reserved for him alone, with a cigarette in his hand, reading a favourite novel or the evening paper, while we kids sat with him, watching the programme that he had chosen. We would already have eaten and be ready for bed.

This evening ritual was to have the most extraordinary effect on my life some ten years on. In the short term it ensured that, although I certainly leapt to my feet, turned somersaults or lay on my back giggling, I eventually learned to sit relatively still in adult company in the midst of my sisters, though when I was small the monochrome screen was pretty meaningless.

Earlier in the day while *Sesame Street* was on, I could see the letters and mathematical shapes better than the people and puppets who flickered among them.

In the same way I gleaned a great deal of fragmented information from the news and current affairs each night, as well as quiz programmes favoured by Dad, because there were clear words shown on the screen which the announcer or presenter emphasised.

In gaps between her rather haphazard housekeeping, Jay occupied another chair. When she wandered off to attend to something that could be postponed no longer, on the seat which she had vacated there would be a thriller thrown down. Where her feet had rested was the sheaf of broad sheets of the evening newspaper. In big, clear letters the same words that the news anchor had emphasised were splashed blackly.

When she was entrusted with a junior history class, there would be a scruffy manila folder spilling completed assignments she had brought home to mark. They were enthusiastically illustrated by their twelve-year old authors with sketches, whole photocopies and diagrams of lethally sharp stone-age axes, or the Sphinx and the Great Pyramid. I can remember quite clearly that they fascinated me whenever they came to my notice.

***

As these continually growing paper middens showed to anyone who was reasonably intuitive, Jay was a human being badly in need of personal space, which was a pretty rare commodity in our neck of the woods. She simply muddled through, so her approach to parenting was a lot more laid back than Dad's and she attacked problems on an *ad hoc* basis.

Her tactics were not always dignified. It could be argued that creative problem solving gave her an amusing hobby, and that without me it would have lacked that special spice. On occasions she would imitate or mirror me, especially when I was running around happily.

My movement would suddenly have meaning and I could change direction to imitate her as she turned briefly away. However, once my frantic pleasure in being chased evaporated, the world fragmented and I was adrift. I stopped in my tracks if I was expected to follow any further.

***

She had developed a tantrum inoculation which was fairly effective even with Little Lucy, though unfortunately unusable once over our own threshold.

One day she happened to be looking at me as the first angry flush of a two-year-old tantrum began to spread behind my eyes. Even as I flung myself backward, and raised my buttocks to arch between my head and heels, she stretched on the carpet beside me.

She looked into my wide eyes and shrieked at the same tempo and pitch as I did. As my heels drummed, so did hers. As my head (suddenly more sensitive at two than it had been when I was a staggering fourteen-month-old) thumped rhythmically on the floor, so crashed hers. Then she sat up and laughed at me.

My sensory system was still so stirred up from the falling and rocking that I felt the same effect that I got when I was chased. I briefly interpreted this extraordinary activity on the part of an adult as completely unseemly.

Jay still remembers the wounded dignity with which I sat up and glared at her in amazement. Another couple of similar efforts, and I learnt that tantrums at home were likely to be unproductive, though in horribly stressful moments I would shriek and howl with the best of them.

Along the way my mother's and sisters' wacky sense of humour seemed to penetrate my isolation. I not only learned to dislike being laughed at when I was being intentionally uncooperative, but also being ribbed gently for my involuntary behaviours by the people I loved best occasionally gave me some kind of acceptance and understanding of my difference.

Unfortunately, my own sense of humour, which secretly coexisted with my autism, was rather less kind and later fed off the ludicrous spectacle of other people coping with the odd way that I acted, a sure-fire recipe for undermining many attempts at behaviour modification.

AUTISM AND OTHER ADVENTURES: LUCY'S STORY

***

The baby in a big family may be kept over-protected in some ways, but she certainly is expected to dress herself and do some chores. No one expected me to be an exception, but they were about to embark on a sharp learning-curve.

I was taught, and then taught again, and yet again, to dress myself by being partially inserted into garments, day after day, month after month, year after year. However, motivation was a problem.

There is a memory I have of sitting on the floor at the time I was learning how to put simple garments on, as long as they were offered to me in the obvious position. My head was covered by a soft woven, ribbed and striped T-shirt. My arms were above my head, and my hands dangled free from the ends of the short sleeves.

I did not like the feel of the fabric, nor the colour of the stripes, nor the confusion that I felt when there were several of us dressed the same — this T-shirt was a remnant of a number of matching outfits my mother had bought when the three oldest were small.

So, I sat there, flaccid and uncooperative while my parents got crosser and crosser because all I had to do to settle the garment onto my shoulders and over my spine was to wriggle and shrug.

For what I now think was most of the normal children's cartoon time on television — about an hour and a half — the battle of wills went on, the normally mobile presence that I was, stubbornly sitting in the main thoroughfare of the house, draped like some mysterious sculpture.

There was a victory for neither party. I wore the T-shirt, but my mother had to pull it down so it fell naturally into place.

If one disregards my determined sabotage, this is a pretty effective technique. Because my next movement would have guaranteed success, (in theory) I could not fail.

The next step would have been to have held the T-shirt in front of me so that the hole at the end of the sleeve-tunnel would have been clearly visible through the trunk section, concertina'd as it would have been in someone's hands.

A sweet or an apple held just the far side of the cuff would probably have brought greedy fists straight into the trap. So, there I would have been, back in the original scenario, two hands sticking up out of two sleeves, and my head ready to pop through the neck welt.

After an eternity of variations on this theme, I was eventually able to dress myself in simple pull-on clothes when they were handed to me one-by-one, or laid out before me in the exact sequence I would don them, because they involved my own self-space and the areas of that space which were within my visual field. The family had far more limited results when they tried to teach me to perform tasks which were not of my own personal dimension.

***

In the opinion of my sisters, I got away with murder. Jay decided that I had to perform at least some token chores. For me drying the dishes was a failure, because I honestly did not understand the purpose of stroking the plates with that little towel. As soon as the person looming over me relaxed her attention for a single second, I departed for greener pastures.

Dish-washing was an obvious choice, because I loved water and froth. However, in the same way that I did not understand that the purpose of drying up was to remove water, so did I not realise that I was meant to get at least some of the discarded food of the plate. That is understandable in a four-year-old, puzzling in a six-year-old and infuriating in someone in her teens.

AUTISM AND OTHER ADVENTURES: LUCY'S STORY

In the short term my share became the fun of pulling the plug out of the drain-hole, which was a first step in my doing the washing-up by myself as an adult — at which I was quite competent, as long as no one minded a rather contoured surface to their dinner plate.

***

From the first I was confusing to parents and siblings. I swooped with instant recognition on whatever my visual memory had categorised as important — mainly snack foods, but also things like the earrings dangling from Jay's ears, or the more precious and fragile of the other girls' personal possessions.

Apart from the rather unpleasant scenes which followed each discovery of a dismembered doll or shredded book, I luxuriated in the complaints about the mess that I caused in the bedrooms that I shared over the years.

Inevitably the family tried to teach me to make a bed. The first stage, as with the washing-up plug, would have been to place the pillow on the tucked-in shape of the mattress.

This was easy as long as I was dragged to the bed, and my unresponsive hands placed on the bottom of the pillow, and then raised so that the pillow could be tipped into approximately the right area.

However, right until I was grown up, I could not string the preceding segments of how to make a bed together, and I really think that this was because I could not process 'cause-and-effect', as I was to see my sisters' children do in their simplest play.

I had no idea that putting the bedclothes on the mattress and tucking them in resulted in the neat shape that I then saw. The transformed blankets did not even seem to be the same items as the tumbled shapes on the floor, though I had seen them picked up and smoothed over the sheets.

Each time I was introduced to this kind of practical skill by new baby-sitters, and later by teachers, it was as if it were the very first time, because the concrete movement in my own body was in a completely different universe from the world of chaotic artefacts which I was expected to place in some kind of arbitrary order.

In the fullness of time some of these tasks became comprehensible, but this did not mean that I was motivated to perform the jobs that all these people considered important. Once my universal view began to expand as I got older, I found their irritation satisfying.

So, in the first years of my life, I was able to keep the world at a manageable distance by enduring in ferocious complacency the sanctuary that my strange sensations created. I remember the world of my childhood as people moving on distant and interlocking orbits. These orbits occasionally collided with mine.

Some of these collisions I remember as enchanting with 'tickles' and 'chasing', and some as distressing, like hair-brushing and being made to stand still. But they were not initiated by me except when I was under severe stress or wanted something very badly.

***

Possibly that was because I was often tossed in a sensory maelstrom, so that skin sensation was so unbearable one minute, and yet completely unfelt the next.

This might not have been a problem on its own, but sometimes I had a crossover effect where real sound flashed through my brain from what my eyes had picked up and what my skin had sensed.

This was a two-way phenomenon. Chaos in my visual processing has always been linked to sound. Even today continuous motor noise makes it impossible to interpret my environment or the people in it. Hearing certain sounds gave me more of a skin- than a brain-response.

AUTISM AND OTHER ADVENTURES: LUCY'S STORY

Extraordinarily some sounds are still processed in both areas, and others only involve what I call 'sound-feeling'. 'Sound-feeling' may come from sounds other people cannot hear. The rules seemed to very slightly shift all the time, as my own response and interpretation changed.

'Feeling', which is a word which peppers my typed language, is nowhere as abstract in how I intend it to be understood as I think it is for some people. When I type, 'I feel foolish', or 'I feel good', the emotion is sensory and on a par with how my organs register comfort or hunger.

***

As a little girl I was coping in a world where other people effectively realised nothing of that. I reacted to all this bombardment and confusion with those physical movements, silence and strange sounds which are generally lumped together as 'autistic behaviours'.

All the other children saw when they looked at me was a non-communicating and distant child, who could be roused only by food or by being grabbed and pushed and pulled into a certain position.

Yet they stumbled onto some very useful ways of helping me develop some sensory integration. Jenny's rocking game was one of the best, and when we were doing it, I had no sense of the giddiness and floating feeling that happened when I sat completely still without something to focus on.

Sometimes they would literally stand on me, or sit on top of my tantrumming, heaving body when I was completely over the top. As Hayley pushed on my shoulders and Val plonked her buttocks on my thighs, I would struggle, but slowly relax as they applied pressure. I could then feel my own distress melt away as my skin and flesh, bone and balance, reassured my brain and nervous system that all of me was a united entity.

LUCY BLACKMAN

***

They also tinkered with 'operant conditioning', as I am sure older brothers and sisters have since the beginning of time. The girls might be reading an Enid Blyton book or playing a game of make-believe, or might simply have been told to keep me quiet.

I would coo and wail happily, feeling the vibration of the tissue behind my mouth, but not really understanding that the other part of the sensation, that which we call 'sound', went off through the space around me, and was strumming on the ear-drums of my companions.

'Shut up, Luce.'

'Be quiet!' Getting crosser.

'Stop that noise!' By now two or three would be yelling, but they had still not penetrated my own world of enchantment.

Then a slight breach, an airborne teddy thumping on my chest. And, if that did not have the desired effect, a couple of other soft toys with a little more force. By the time the first sneaker hit the bean-filled vinyl under me, my attention had been focused and I was concentrating on their instructions.

Now I can see myself, perched in the cup of the Bean Bag on the multi-stripe carpet emerging from the magic forest of my wails of glee, and I can recapture the conscious awareness that I had made a noise.

I had some sense that when I stopped that pleasant sound, I had done what they wanted. Praise and applause might follow. At the least they would stop throwing things.

From all this I began to get some experience of interactions other than those which resulted from my own immediate bodily needs. So, fleetingly, I started to learn that my name, which I recognised as the word that people tossed in my direction, was also a person, and that person was me — Lucy.

Chapter 2
Little Lucy: Vision and Voids

There was a knob and a shiny rotating shaft. If I pushed on the knob, the shaft went round and round. I had no idea that this fascinating silver thing was connected to the glass that was keeping me from moving out of my seat into the fast-moving scene beyond.

'Lucy. You leave that alone!'

I obliged. The glass stayed half-down, so I could feel the wind on my face. I moved through this crack to adventure until there was a yell behind me.

'Lucy!'

Jay also heard it, and looked in the rearview mirror to see Jenny and Kay clasping one ankle each. My body rested on the roof of the station wagon, which was hurtling down the freeway.

I was hauled back furious. This fury would have been made worse by a pair of arms round my shoulders or hands on my wrists. I don't think they were ever rough with me, but I hated them holding me like that.

I certainly learned early on when they were all angry with me, though I could not yet interpret adult scolding unless it was very loud or resulted in other immediate physical discomfort.

I was terrified of being smacked. It was the noise of my parent's palm on the palm of my own hand that punished me. I only realised much later that it was meant to sting.

On the rare occasion that Jay felt that I had to realise that something I had done was dangerous or too destructive, I was even more terrified, because even a tap on my bottom meant being caught and held immobile downwards on her knee. I honestly do not think that I ever felt the smack.

Love was as terrifying and worse. I did not realise that I was expected to enjoy cuddles. Mercifully Jay preferred kissing her babies on the back of their fluffy little skulls where there was less chance of a lipful of regurgitated food. This was love which might have been tailor-made for me.

***

I was not repelled by this maternal nuzzling as I was by the 'good-night' kissing sessions that we worked on in the year before I started school. A small furry teddy was the villain of this piece. In the future Edward Bear was to be known as 'Kissing Teddy'. He would sit propped on Jay's lap.

'Good night, Lucy,' she would say, and kiss this revolting little gingery icon. It would then rest lightly on my face as she said, 'good night, Teddy.' He would be turned to deposit my 'kiss' back on Jay's face.

Eventually I learned to lean forward and move the whole of my face towards his nose. Later my crafty mother dispensed with Kissing Teddy's services by inserting her own face in place of his at the last moment, so that her pursed lips met my mouth or our cheeks brushed.

He still shadows me, stored in a large cardboard box with a shaggy collection of unsorted photos. Whenever Jay scrabbles through this lot for some lost snapshot, she drags out this weird relic and embraces him sentimentally. How embarrassing! — yes, I do feel embarrassment, though I express it rather oddly even today.

***

But in my world, I really wanted love to come from behind. For me this was real love. I would walk backwards towards Jay when she was watching television, and lean against her knees, waiting for a feathery kiss on the back of my head where my sensory alarms seemed to be more dozy. If she were standing up it was a more hit-and-miss procedure. I would lean slightly in her direction while looking the other way.

'Wanna be loved, but please don't hug,' I might have been saying. With any luck she might receive the signal in the midst of feeding five other people, two dogs, and however many cats were milling around at the time.

If I did not get an immediate response, I would wander off in my own sphere again. I simply had no idea that being loved in return was a social thing, and that she had to know that I was there to give it to me.

***

When I sat on Jay's lap I was poised for flight, but she found I could be made more compliant if I were slowly rubbed and stroked up and down my spine as if I had been an enormous cat. I delighted in this after I had learned not to fight it. To this day if someone strokes me like that, I feel real affection towards them, much as other people do when they rush to embrace a close friend.

For me hugs were torture, but there is no way that one of five small children can avoid close physical contact, and some was quite rewarding. Jay's voice would call us as a group.

'Hayley-Val-Kay-Jenny-aannnd-Lucy!' There would be a stirring among the children around me under the acacia tree that dropped purple petals like confetti in the area between the washing hoist and the back fence. Depending on the time of day that yell could mean Snacks, Lunch or 'Tea'.

The girls ceased to be part of the background against which I wiffled my fingers, or playmates rocking me back and forward on a tricycle which I could not pedal. They were transformed into a thumping and totally inconsistent mass. The last two of the thundering herd would halt and grab my wrists. My hands had yet to learn that they could grasp another's.

***

Of course, we might have been called for something apart from food. With any luck it involved a trip in the car. I loved the car. When the adults sat in the two bucket seats in the front, we would sit five in a row in the back seat of the six-cylinder station wagon. We were squashed together with me in the middle, and that did not distress me. I felt comfortable when the vehicle was moving.

Outside the windows, the world was moving too. So was my body. So being touched seemed more tolerable. My escape bid had been an aberration. If Jay were on her own, one of the older ones would sit in the other front seat, which had given me a little more wriggle-room.

From then on, we sat firmly wedged, and, as our radio seemed to be out of order more often than not, amusement was provided Karaoke-style by our own singing. This had the added advantage in Jay's eyes that, when five children are made to sing *Old MacDonald had a Farm* and *The Ants Came Marching One by One*, they cannot argue or ask questions of the driver.

Not only a pretty face, our Jay-Mum, but a veteran survivor — her fault entirely that we must be the only family under the sun to believe that *One Hundred Green Bottles Hanging on the Wall* is the authorised version of that old favourite!

By the time I started school, I had a good grounding in most popular kids' songs, but I could not sing at the same time as someone else, because the sound of the other voices cut off my urge to vocalise. Although I could sing the songs in tune with a wavering version of the vowel sounds, all became distorted when the others joined in. (Consonants were an uncharted wilderness into which I rarely ventured.)

AUTISM AND OTHER ADVENTURES: LUCY'S STORY

As their notes reached me, I could not hear my own voice, so I did not know where my song had gone. I truly thought that my voice had got lost somehow. I remember feeling vaguely scared as part of me was not there anymore, and my lips would close tightly as I went quiet. I could no more 'sing-along' than I could fly.

***

I wonder how I would have developed if I had not been a member of that herd at some hours each day. I had such difficulties in even remotely understanding what other people meant when their faces curved, wrinkled up and smoothed out, or when their bodies turned away, let along all the other social signals.

When I was moving in a group surrounded by my own family noises and shapes, some of my sense of being adrift in a great noisy fluctuating tide seemed to abate.

***

From the time I was eighteen months old, I had other people in my life. Jay worked during school hours, and Jenny and I were 'minded', first by the mother of one of Jenny's kindergarten friends, and then by a lady known to me as Tim's Mum.

Tim's Dad worked for the Railways, so Tim lived in a little house belonging to the station in our suburb. I was fascinated by the noisy space over their back fence. Jenny remembers my being hauled inside unceremoniously one day, and Tim's Mum being very upset.

After a few months the two Mums, mine and Tim's, seem to have decided that neither of them could stand the stress of my being so close to this busy commuter line. Then there were three or four years with Cricket, a woman with a commanding presence and a tiny house full of children.

She largely supported herself by being what was known as a 'backyarder', which in that context meant an unlicensed care-giver. Once again, I had ended up in an environment where I had plenty of other small people around me, though I was still a bit confused about being a person in my own right.

As far as I was concerned, only I could experience my own sounds, and I could not initiate a game or make an approach to another person unless they had already established real eye contact.

***

'Ball!'

Kay had held up a plastic sphere, and spoken. There was a vague connection between whatever Kay was showing me and the sound she was speaking, but there was no sense of immediacy.

The concepts did not rub together, and I had yet to learn that I was meant to show some understanding, in the same way that in my bedroom at night, I was to learn to offer my frozen little face for my mother to kiss. In any case, toys were of little significance unless they could cater to my view of what was important in my world.

There were some toys that I was attracted to. Jay had long brooded over her own disappointment at being given a doll's pram for her sixth birthday. She was determined none of her daughters was going to feel so let down. So, when maternal little Jenny turned six, she received a bright yellow tip-truck.

Jenny waited another ten years before she could bring herself to say what she thought of being the victim of what she saw as Jay's childhood frustrations. That might have been because the words that she would have liked to use were definitely on the banned list at the age of six. She went bonkers in the play-room though.

The truck may not have been much use to her, but I loved it for its four rough-tyred wheels. It sat upside-down on the carpet, and my little hands span the black and yellow disks. The whirr of a wheel in my hand caught the edge of my vision as a flicker. If I had rolled that truck over the carpet, I would have had no sensory feedback from it to make my world a comfortable place. There was no point to it.

In the same way, to hold a doll had no meaning for me, because to be held myself was like a hot prickling if the restraining touch did not respond to my reactions.

Actually, the idea of turning a doll into a pretend-person created an image that could be described as alien. People moved in relation to me and talked to me, but, as far as I can remember, I did not reciprocate.

I do not mean that I did not move, but that my movements concerned me and not others. I did not mean to be as uncooperative as I was, but, because I did not see other people as being able to interact with me, I treated them as something to be manipulated.

Colliding head-on with how they were trying to make me act was one form of self-assertion. However, doing nothing, like the time that I refused to wear that striped T-shirt, was just as effective, because eventually people responded by doing something themselves.

***

I cannot remember any time in my childhood when I thought of myself as being similar to other people in how God had constructed me, in spite of the way that I could make use of someone else mirroring my own movements to understand the movement of my own body.

I sat on the orange upholstery in Cricket's living room, surrounded by little shapes who did not realise that they simply were not there. When Michael, who was a little older than I, cried,

I did not see him as sad but that his face had changed and that his noise hurt my ears.

I did not understand that he was experiencing what I did when I was upset. I felt disoriented rather than sympathetic. I was confused when the cornerstones of my world, these familiar, coloured shadows among whom I lived, acted in an inexplicable way. As I was in the centre of a world which had neither cause or effect, this left me without a rational frame.

***

My weird sound environment, and my enchanted world of light and sudden gaps into which people and objects moved, affected the way that I processed my fellow human beings, and may have been part of the reason I could not interact.

The space against which we all move and the words that other people juggle so adroitly had little meaning for me unless the object that they encapsulated was concrete, and fixed in that immediate minute in time.

This took me ages and ages to work out, mainly by contrasting the way I am today with the way that I remember myself as a child and adolescent. These changes I then measured up against how I saw my nephews and nieces grow during the time that I tried to turn my experiences into narrative.

In my first attempt to describe my early childhood, I wrote: *The difference in inversable* [sic] *and tunnelled appearance and small actual spaces was horrifically pleasurable*

(July 1992).

That is still the most accurate way that I can describe my visual perception in my youth. My response to people was either very dead, or emotionally extremely excited. Sometimes I ran in circles, or just lay on my back and laughed when I was not allowed to move far away.

AUTISM AND OTHER ADVENTURES: LUCY'S STORY

I could not just stand there and endure. I wonder if it would have been less terrifying if I had realised that the chaos was within myself, and not in what I observed.

***

No one guessed that my eyes picked up different signals from the light, shade, colour and movement that passed into the retina and thence to my brain. I basically emphasised folds and depths. The other children seem to have discarded these in their visual sorting, because these shadows are only background in the world view of most human beings.

So, I perceived people, especially their faces, but also their bodies, as slightly distorted. This was not only in shape, but also in the composition of the components of their bodies in my visual imagination.

I seem to have lived in a world where depth was not a factor. I now realise that my sense of perspective did not develop properly. If something moved from one point in space or time to another, I sometimes did not realise why it was no longer visible in one spot and then suddenly was in position in another.

As a corollary people did not move through space. They arrived in a certain point within their own space, which supplanted the space that was already there.

I think that is why I still draw figures which seem to have a long veil which flows from above where their head would be, to somewhere approximating their elbows.

***

In my pre-school years I did not draw. People would put a pencil or felt-tipped pen in my hand, and I would twiddle it endlessly, feeling its movement in my fingers. My sisters and Jay would move my fist so that the point scrawled on a piece of scrap paper.

Later Jay created an enormous chalkboard in the playroom, and I would scrawl my lines on that, over and over, back and forward. At school, of course, I was to be taught to draw shapes, houses, faces. Eventually stars, triangles and rudimentary letters were to be speckled haphazardly on my board.

However, the faces my teachers trained me to draw had nothing to do with what I conceptualised as a face. I had no idea why the face I was expected to draw had a circle as its starting-point and two smaller circles in the top half, with a horizontal line or curve below.

Though I learnt to label these strange shapes as 'faces', I knew that faces were not like that.

Faces consisted of shadows. A pair of small circular shadows inside the eye. More important was the pair of long mouth-to-inner-eye shadows which ran along the nose.

When not moving in speech, laughter or fury, the mouth was a comfortable slit-shaped shadow, not much wider than the base of the protuberance above. The rest of the space — eyeballs, forehead, cheeks, eyebrows, lips, chin — was not shadowed enough to catch my visual processing system.

So, in turn it did not jerk the string which triggers the mechanism by which one member of the human species relates automatically to another, and develops the social awareness to keep that relationship between normal bounds.

***

I think that it was when I was about seven that I could work out the purpose of drawing sufficiently to put my human world on paper. The faces of my private universe were uncontoured, without the slants and slopes and little curves which accompany eye, ear and mouth movements.

I do not even today draw a human being as others do. Although I now see faces nearer to the way they appear on photos, movies and television, my original childhood version of people has stayed imprinted on the drawing part of my brain.

One of the images that I still reproduce endlessly in scrap pads with ball-point pens is in outline like an old-fashioned nun, or rather like Darth Veda, with his snorting muzzle set apart from his face-mask by a pair of bends in the metal from which it is made.

***

Like many of my autistic peers, I also had far more impact from peripheral vision than most people. This gave a sort of 'wide screen' effect, rather than a narrower and deeper comprehension of the world that I scanned. So, things might overwhelmingly engulf my analysis.

What a ponderous expression! It came to me one afternoon when I was perched on a bank of seats in a big-top, watching a three-ring circus.

Suddenly as an adult, I realised that the performance I was then trying to process was a pretty fair parallel for the world through which I rushed and drifted as a child. The centre ring was in front of me with a cage of rather bored assorted Great Cats, as I tried to co-ordinate tumblers, horses and a performing dog in each end ring.

The centre ring had less impact when I was aware of the side acts, even if my eyes did not move. I lost the finer details in my memory though my vision would have processed it. Though I had seen the cats move with my eyes, I was mildly surprised to see the lion where the lioness had been, and that the tigers had already started to move to the exit.

This was similar to how I could not make head nor tail of the other children's games when I was a little girl. As a grown up, I had changed just enough to understand that my childhood use of peripheral vision, together with its corresponding loss of detail when I seemed to look in front of me, had given me a world view that shaped all my social responses.

This may have been a result of my inability to process anything too close to the centre of my vision, or it may have caused the problem.

***

Whatever the reason, I felt instantly unwell and sometimes terrified if I were face-to-face with a person, or even a thing like a wall or a chair. I would sit and be aware of my father's presence, marked by shoes or bare feet resting on the carpet near where I sat. I identified him by the smell of his cigarette, his voice and his glasses. Then he would speak.

'Hello, Lucy,' and then add, 'Look at me.' Once I knew what was expected, I would face him briefly, but I had to blur my vision if I looked at his face for any length of time.

To look at any face fixedly from a social distance was intolerable, not for any reason connected with love or withdrawal, but because I had too much impact from the complexity of depth, movement, colour and smell from any human being.

***

One continuing memory of my childhood and adolescence is of regular visits to a friend of Jay's. Eileen was the mother of Michael, the little boy I spent time with in Cricket's noisy living room.

We would walk into their kitchen-family room. On arrival my glance had apparently shot around the room, before I dashed to investigate and guzzle the contents of the fridge, or to perch on a swivel chair at the kitchen table, by preference the one which had a missing foot, so that it rocked and jiggled, driving everyone crazy.

I would stare at Eileen as if attentively listening, and the whole of the centre of my vision over the table would be a wonderful pattern of moving earrings and eyes and her strong and distorting spectacles.

'Hi, Lucy,' she would say. 'You look happy!' and smile widely at my beaming face.

'Lucy,' said Jay. 'Say 'hello'!'

'Ewwo,' I would say, thinking that this was the noise that I had been taught.

The affection that I felt for her and her family was real, but had she only known it, I expressed it by sitting contentedly, and listening and watching while apparently quite self-absorbed. My frenzied smiles when face-to-face and my enthusiasm were the result of the twin attractions of the environment — food and the face that I smiled at.

An onlooker would have seen two people locked into a frenzied gaze, because either I could not look at another person's eyes at all, or I had to latch on to them.

This kind of thing was described later as 'good' eye contact, which it certainly was not. For a human being, other than a young baby, it was completely unnatural in social terms, and made the other person either embarrassed, or frightened or angry.

***

By the time I was an adolescent, I knew that when I looked fixedly at people, they got a bit weird, but I only realised that the reason was my own eye contact when an autism professional raised the topic at a small meeting at my High School when I was sixteen. At the time things were going comparatively well.

'Oh,' said LO, who was only to cheerfully bounce into my life about Chapter Eight, 'Of course, Lucy isn't very autistic, is she?'

Chris (the autism expert) and I would have exchanged glances if that had been possible. Chris drew a deep breath, and pointed out some of my mannerisms, then directed their attention to my comparatively wooden face and strange eye movement. Embarrassed, the meeting moved on to the next item on the agenda, and broke up fairly quickly after that.

But I was delighted, and very glad that we had decided to co-opt someone who could be so frank. I simply had not known till then exactly what it was about my face and eyes that spooked other people. Of course, at that point I could not have changed, because the underlying causes of my immobile but excited face and unnatural gaze were still a mystery.

***

As a child, at least sometimes I appeared to be looking more or less in the direction of what I saw. Later I met children with autism who always avoided gazing. Their eyes seemed never to flick in the direction where they were expected to look.

As a result, I think I may have been less impaired than some of these, and that this may be why I acquired some simple self-help skills. I learnt to do up easy buttons, and to put plates on the table. By the time I was ten, I could do some concrete things like making sandwiches or tying laces.

My hair though remained an abstract quality, carrying as it did a separate existence that I could feel, but not see. A mirror could reflect my image, but by the time the reflection had reached my mind it was in multiples, and inhabited some kind of undifferentiated void, even though my eyes could see it much as my sisters did their own reflections. So, styling my hair was always beyond me, much as washing-up and bed-making still were.

AUTISM AND OTHER ADVENTURES: LUCY'S STORY

***

In time I was able to realise that I also had problems which were more important than how I saw myself in a mirror. At first when I tried to drag a pencil over paper, I only made vague swirls, but graduated to those dark, sinister Darth Veda figures which littered my imaginary world.

I did not see them as sinister, of course, but my family must have wondered what morbid thoughts I harboured. However, most of the pencil drawings which I was to churn out while Jay and Dad watched television were of me.

I went for what I thought was a realist approach, a tiny pointed cone, which the tip of my finger resting on the apex of my skull told me was the shape of the top of my head, a square block which then was how my body looked when viewed from above, and my view of my hands, two thalidomide flaps on the top corners of my body, with a stump or two for fingers.

I seemed to have no concept that the arms that hung from my shoulders and stretched upwards from my wrists had any existence in the area between these extremities.

As I drew my self-portraits I sat on the floor, the paper in front of me, and my legs stretched out straight on each side, directly below my uninteresting square little torso. Reality started and ended with my legs. They stretched out hugely on my drawing, clad in what seemed to be long, flared pants, whether I was wearing shorts or fitted jeans.

Below them a couple of mounds showed that I had noticed my feet, or at least my toes. I was a toe-walker. I would guess that, although I was aware of my heels, and had learned to label them along with cheeks and shoulders and other inessentials, my felt-body and my seen-body did not intersect at the point where my legs took a right-angled turn to become my feet, and so in my world view they were unimportant.

***

In the same way I had not quite distinguished the difference between seeing and touching other people. If my hand reached to another person, the movement that I made was a kind of extension to my sight, like a feely-touchy-eye. This made me look very odd to strangers, because where someone else would give covert glances, I would caress or poke.

My earliest memories of this kind of thing bugging my family were of the hypnotic delights of hair-stroking, not only my own hair, but any smooth shiny head which came within reach.

I can see myself sitting behind Hayley with her short, straight cap of blonde silk, and drawing first one, and then the other palm over her head. The strands were melded smoothly into a silk-like surface under my hands.

At that moment what I felt was what I saw, not a series of strands, but a surface not unlike that in a poorly produced picture-book. I have the same problem with denim jeans, as they are very comforting in a tactile way.

When I was about four, we got our first colour television set. When I looked at the screen, the moving shapes occasionally made sense.

Shortly after that there was a spate of advertisements for jeans that highlighted the shape of the stitching on the back pockets, and the weave of the material. I would sit by the hour and draw denim jeans, row after row of sloping hips and shaped pockets, in lines on notebook paper.

Jay still has to be alert when we walk past those jeans shops which had been advertising at that time when I was starting to absorb a little of what happened outside my own body.

AUTISM AND OTHER ADVENTURES: LUCY'S STORY

The shop assistants are slightly bewildered if they rush forward to forestall shoplifting under the guise of offering assistance, only to discover an adult woman stroking the banks of children's jeans, or feeling the stitching in the adults' sizes. I console myself with the notion that at least the 'normal' clientele of a jeans shop is an alternative one.

***

There are more embarrassing applications of touch-sight. Occasionally I would grab a wrist, a finger, or some other bit attached to someone else's body, and examine it by touch or smell or vision.

Holes like mouths or ears fascinated me, but, though I can remember opening someone's mouth to look inside, I do not think that I realised that I was constructed the same way, though I certainly had all the usual baby games played with me.

I also fiddled with bits of my own body, including places that are usually taboo, often to the acute embarrassment of teachers and friends in years to come.

They did not realise that touching myself in some sensitive places was not necessarily having the kind of effect that most people get. Sometimes the rest of my body was so dead in terms of how my skin felt, that I had to make some part of me feel that I existed.

***

I played with toys much the same way, by integrating what I felt with my hands with what my brain extracted from what my eyes had gathered. Lego blocks were not a tool from which I constructed something which my mind had pre-planned.

As a small child, the feel and symmetry of these plastic interlocking blocks was all absorbing, and all I understood of their function was that they made patterns in long rods.

So, as a four-year-old I leapt across the intervening space to grab the plastic cubes from in front of another child, only to place them into some meaningful-to-me arrangement. I did the same as a twelve-year-old. At eighteen I would play with Shay's toys as if I were also a toddler.

Even in my twenties if I saw Lego blocks, and even somewhere like a doctor's waiting room, the direction of my eyes was riveted, and I could hardly make any effort at self-control. The need to touch, and to incorporate the feedback from touch and to establish a visual pattern, is like a thirst.

***

Food obsessions came into the same category in some way. Embarrassingly, for the whole of my life visual stimulation and the craving for food have been related.

Strangely enough, being given something that mimics an extremely desirable junk food can be an effective reward. For example, coloured cotton-wool balls in a transparent plastic bag still give me a feeling of comfort as they resemble fairy floss.

I still try to sneak away from whoever takes me shopping, so as to find the little cards that are displayed below the hair-colour tubes in supermarkets and pharmacies. From these cards project tiny, glossy, smooth loops of coloured nylon hair which I finger and stroke.

I stand there in the aisle, stolidly blocking the way in both directions. The shopping public little know that in front of them is a traveller in time and space, cradled in the blissful sensation of her own fingertips.

AUTISM AND OTHER ADVENTURES: LUCY'S STORY

'Lucy!' As sharp as a piece of space debris — Jay or my sisters or someone else. I sigh and turn. There will be another chance soon, whether it be in this shop at the display of coloured sweets in plastic bags, or further down the mall, where early Christmas shoppers are being tempted by a range of shiny baubles. The key to my magic wilderness has never really gone away, though I have been able to control its use to some extent.

I saw the same things so many times when later I spent time with other small children with autism. The non-autistic onlooker would jump nervously as there was a sudden flurry of movement.

A vibrant hand reached forward, and no minor distraction could relax the tense little body that was totally concentrated on the desired object.

It might have been a clothes-drier, food, a certain toy — and that toy only, not even a duplicate would do — and until the two, the child and the obsessional object, occupied the same sensory orbit there was no relief for anyone.

That orbit might have been in space, as created by taste or touch, but it might have been in some dimension beyond that, regulated by memory and sound.

So, the little person had to make a special noise or say a certain phrase in a ritualistic litany which brought that object into what the brain has constructed as true, immediate reality.

***

This personal-world-reality and the world-as-processed-by-the-eyes are continually confused.

From the comments around me, I gather that this is not a problem for the person whose visual field is fine-tuned to the space and speed common to most humans: but to me, and I think to others like me, it is a source of constant misunderstanding.

I was an adult before I could explain to anyone the dreadful instability of a scene that could sparkle one minute, and simultaneously have some components in a pastel haze.

I would have done so sooner if I had realised that human sight was not like that, and that as a result most people positioned each movement of their bodies in a space that was not unstable.

Seeing that my eye movements were not as apparently random as those of some other kids with autism, I then wondered whether they saw themselves in relation to others even less effectively than I did.

***

Whatever the real reason, the next minute in time was not a comprehensible picture during my childhood.

So, a game of 'catch' was someone chasing *me*, and I had no understanding that my stretching out and reaching would result in my catching her, no matter how often my hands were held in the right position and I was clapped and cheered. That in some way was connected with the unpredictability of my environment.

There were times when I was physically stimulated when I was closer to how I now think other people see. I loved being tumbled and twirled, because then my self-awareness was much clearer.

In 1975 colour television came to Melbourne. In 1976 we hired a colour set for the Olympics. The rushing runners and flag-waving crowds had nothing to hold me. They were as foreign as the people I passed in the street, but unbelievably across the screen came images of my own movement, twirling and tumbling, those wonderful little flying gymnasts, streaking over a mat to music and applause. So, I turned, sat — entranced.

Chapter 3
Little Lucy: The Glass Carillon

Somewhere in my brain there was a Bermuda Triangle where my vision went adrift but much of my visual processing was on target — in fact too much on target. I fixated on those items which I did notice. When I think about these visual processing oddities, it is not surprising that my hearing abnormalities remained a mystery to everyone, and that included me.

I can remember my first hearing test clearly. I can remember the darkened room, and the dramatically illuminated puppets that were intended to focus my attention.

The idea was that I would be so attracted to them that I would swing my head in the direction of the lighted booth every time I heard a noise that indicated that the display was about to function.

The first couple of challenges from the loud-speakers riveted me. For the rest of the session, I continued to make patterns with the toys on the little table. Once seen, those puppets were etched in my memory. The actions that were meant to fascinate were like a little play, so they were as meaningless as any other social scene.

Frustrated, the audiologist recognised that in my stillness was awareness and non-interest. She correctly assessed me as hearing all the sounds that had engulfed me in that dreadful room.

However, she would have been startled to know that some of the sounds she had played loudly I had processed as soft, and that some of the tones that I heard best were soft when they left the loud-speaker. Also, in some frequencies specific noises deafened me at some degrees of loudness, and were not clear at slightly *greater* volume.

***

In my childhood I felt sight and sound as an almost identical sensation, but one which had the translucence of a slightly transparent glass chime. I regret that I did not understand the not-usual nature of this charmed view of the universe.

On the good days, my world was one of time and 'feeling' and light and movement all in one, but fear or other unpleasant sensations fragmented my surround, so I relied on activities such as swaying, humming and running in circles, which defended me against uninterrupted exposure to my sound-environment.

For all my life when I feel nervous or ill, or when the noise is horribly outside my area of tolerance, I have had a sensation between vertigo and pain.

***

When I was little, the fluctuation of sound was continual. The distant noises on the main road that ran about sixty metres from our house were always present. They sloshed against the day-to-day sounds of my own home in a sort of wave-on-the-shore effect.

I could feel the sensation of cars and a heavy-laden truck pass, and also feel my own physical response to the noises that the vehicle made from its tyres, its engine and the wind of its passing. That wind could suddenly drown out a nearer sound, but not consistently.

Other people learn to make social decisions from ongoing and consistent stimuli. I have not been able to make instinctive social judgements based on prior experience in a reliable way, because the incoming signals were switched often enough that I did not learn to untangle those shadowed moving faces and their inconsistent voices.

***

AUTISM AND OTHER ADVENTURES: LUCY'S STORY

Real and extraordinary fluctuations in all sensation were a part of daily life. I could not understand that this was a problem not of my own making. The way that my sisters, who were only slightly older, reacted to other people's speech seemed to indicate that the discrimination of sound and its translation into meaning was a skill that could be learnt, because the differences between us in most ways seemed to me to be so slight.

I think I was about three when I realised that I was being given instructions, but that the individual words were blurring into the fluctuations around me, and sometimes being overtaken by following or preceding sounds. As I came to accept that auditory differences were part of my life, I became confused that others did not understand that this was one of my problems.

***

Actually, I did not know for another fifteen years what those differences were, but I did know that I was hearing differently from the rest of the world. Over the years I lost some of the confidence that I should have had in my own family and the teachers of my various schools as this ignorance continued to puzzle me. However, I simply could not indicate this. Later when I did acquire expressive language, I could not explain it because I just had no concept of how others heard.

My family did work out that I had some kind of sound problem, because when I was about five, I started to put my fingers in my ears when some loud noises sounded. I do not think that I had realised that I could use my hands this way till then.

I had only recently worked this out when some psychologist told Jay that it was me withdrawing from reality, and should be discouraged. Talk about dense! I would have thought it was obvious that it was the sound outside me that needed plugging, rather than the spirit within.

***

I was hearing differently from the rest of the world. So what? One would think that that must be better than being profoundly deaf. The person who is deaf from childhood has problems in some areas far worse than mine. However, the hearing world has the imagination and the information to be somewhat aware of the plight of someone who grows up with little or no hearing.

No one dreamed I was having these auditory problems. In time I was to watch Hayley's eldest daughter, Shay, become reliant on consistent signals, and then develop through the 'terrible twos' to become a social person in her own right.

However, as a small child I would stand and wonder why something was happening, but could not ask, 'Why?' Then someone would release some spoken sounds in my direction, but, unless I already knew what they were trying to say, I floundered because only part of the speaker's intended information package got through.

***

I must have known that there was something wrong very early. I remember sitting at the table in Tim's Mum's kitchen. At the most I would have been two and a half. This is my first real memory that involves a scene outside my own body.

I remember sitting there with Jenny and Tim, and the train roaring past on the track behind the house, and the stupid frustrations of not being able to blurt out the excitement that its wondrous passage brought with it. And then in rushed Jay, late as usual, and hustled me, still silent, into the car. I think that I was ready to talk, but the rest of me just had not caught up.

***

AUTISM AND OTHER ADVENTURES: LUCY'S STORY

I also remember the first time that I realised that other people thought I was not developing properly. I was sitting on a potty on Cricket's kitchen floor because I wanted something to eat.

Why, one might ask, sit on a plastic pot instead of pointing? Poor Cricket had started minding me at the most dramatic and sodden point of my toilet training, so, unknown to Jay, she would bribe me to sit there with food.

Now I could use the toilet by myself, but I still could not rest my nose on the 'laminex' table and whine with the other kids that I wanted a second (or fourth) cookie. Sitting on that immaculately scrubbed pot in that position had become my equivalent communication strategy.

There were two people sitting at the table. I could see Cricket's feet. The other pair probably belonged to a neighbour who popped over for a chat most days. I would guess the conversation was something like this.

'I see Lucy doesn't run in circles all the time now.'

'No.'

'Does she still climb up and run across the top of that old piano?'

'Not if I can help it! I still almost have a heart attack when I think how she used to jump off the top. I wish the mother had told me she was a climber when she first came.' (Of course Jay hadn't. She was not stupid, and she needed that childminder very badly).

'But she's still not talking, is she?'

'No, and she's so behind in other ways ...'

***

I can't guarantee that this is an accurate word-for-word re-creation of what was said, but I do link my first memory of knowing that I had developmental problems with Cricket's kitchen and people sitting down to a cup of tea.

However, I do not remember being conscious of being without speech in my own home at that time. This may be because my family seems to have learnt to bridge the communication gap effectively.

I confirmed it when we uncovered Jay's rather unflattering notes on 'Consistent and Meaningful Communication Signals in a Pre-school Child'. Goodness knows what her lecturer had thought of this:

Communication with Lucy is most effective when reinforced with signals which are almost over-dramatic. It is possible to communicate with her almost by mime. When she was younger this was the most effective means to make her understand something.

(Mary Jane Blackman, April 1976.)

She listed that I pulled people by their hands in the direction of something that I wanted very badly, and that I held up my arms if I wanted to be lifted away from a situation which I could not climb out of myself. This was not affection:

She shows affection by jumping up and down with a teasing smile. The 'pickup' signal means 'let's play tickles', or 'I would like to be picked up, swung around, stroked, etc.'.

To confuse the issue further, I had an almost identical signal that was an urgent request to be boosted into a somersault. The only difference between the two was that the somersault signal involved my hands being out-turned, rather than in a straight line with my arm.

***

Jay had also noted my still, leaning requests for affection while I was standing up. Funnily enough, she had not added my walking backwards when I wanted really to show love, though I still remember that so clearly. Perhaps she had thought that I had not initiated this interchange, and that she had just taken advantage of my presence, not realising that I was not there by chance.

***

She also said that I 'tried out' as a way of asking questions. By that she meant that I would start to grab a piece of food, or to move away, as a way of asking if I were allowed to have a snack or be freed from sitting still.

I only did this if there were someone there on whom I could fix my gaze to gauge their response. The second Jay or Dad turned their backs, I did it anyway of course. Jay had finished up her list with an interrogation technique which was a particularly ineffective attempt at mime:

Examining pointed finger, which was sometimes cradled in the other hand. This was followed by her looking at her slightly cupped palm, while querying her mother [i.e. Jay] *with eye contact.*

(Mary Jane Blackman, April 1976.)

This peculiar sequence of gestures originated in the out-thrown arm and pointing finger of Cricket, who had trained in opera. She would fling her arm out towards a small transgressor and wag her large forefinger dramatically.

This sign was great from my point of view. I could understand the movement clearly, and could focus on the projecting digit, without allowing myself the feeling of disorientation which would have come from looking at her face and trying to make sense of her confusing voice-sounds.

The only bit of Cricket's scolding that really had been imprinted on my brain was her finger. I held my finger because I was showing it to myself through sight-touch. I had no idea that the other person had to see and decode what I was showing them.

My parody asked two questions, 'Have I been naughty?' and, if Jay nodded, it also doubled as, 'Is it only a small badness?' I rarely had to go on to the second stage, which could be translated as, 'Is it a smackable offence?'

Queerly that was entirely symbolic. It did not exactly mean, 'Am I going to be smacked?' I certainly did get smacked occasionally, but I can remember that I was more concerned with whether what I had done was going to totally drive my family up the wall.

***

I know from watching Shay & Co. that little children learn this slowly, but I really never worked out at all why I was such a terrible nuisance.

I can remember standing in the kitchen door, waiting for the answer, peanut butter warmly in my mouth, my palm warm with the slight weight of my first finger, and Jay, with a huge pile of sliced bread lying next to the school lunch-boxes, peering into a nearly empty jar, and not able to stop laughing.

I suppose life with me was a little Pythonesque. Of course, if my family had always been serious and consistent about my zigzag progress through their daily routine, it would have been a pretty humourless home, and I would have been a lesser person for it.

***

I did not always understand that people were cross or pleased with me because of what I had just done. Therefore for many years 'cause and effect' was very much a mysterious and variable phenomenon. In fact, people's emotions and praise simply did not impact on me at all.

I wonder, had my sensory deprivation been greater, would I have lived in chaos that would have been even more disabling? In me the confusion was aggravated because, except for very exceptional instances like my idiosyncratic gestures about naughtiness, I could not ask for explanations.

***

I sat in a chair. Jay squatted in front of me. Her lips pressed together, then opened, then were pressed together again. A humming rumble came from her face. I extracted from this the sound that my sisters used to get her attention. She touched me and spoke.

'Lucy.'

I remained silent. She touched herself.

'Mum!' Jay's voice again. I tried to escape, and she gave up that day. Eventually I learnt to label her in a wooden, gruff little voice, but I was seven or eight before that sound suddenly surfaced for the first time spontaneously in a moment of crisis.

'Mummy-i-y!' That was the only time for years that I used a spontaneous inflection. Now, seventeen years later, I can remember it as if it were yesterday, and the spot of dead silence in my head which came just at the moment before I screamed. I had few of these windows, though, and for the most part I saw the family's efforts to encourage me to speak as unconnected with whatever I expected of them.

***

Eventually there were more words, and some worked certain miracles, delivering cookies more reliably than any potty-sitting, though my enunciation remained wooden.

Naming parts of my own body came to be a bed-time ritual, but these personal bits and pieces were not really connected in my mind with the sounds which gave such satisfaction to the person who was playing these inexplicable games with me.

Someone would laugh, and touch my face, and make speech-sounds. I was aware that if I touched the protuberance above my mouth, and said the sound I know now as 'nose', there would be applause and praise.

However it was years before the idea penetrated that if I used that sound to another person, it would cue her to look at that part of my face.

When I growled 'Sore nose' (which I pronounced 'dore no'), they thought that I was complaining of a bump or a sinus attack, but in reality, it was a kind of monologue which had happened to take place in their presence.

I was not reaching out. I was simply showing off my skill in making that sound in the presence of those I loved best.

***

My family seems to have been obsessed with my lack of speech. In fact, they almost willed me to talk, which was reasonable in view of the alternative — screams, tantrums, singing and giggling.

Here Jenny took a hand. It started, as do so many family dramas, with a permission form brought home from school for our parents to sign. Jenny had been identified as a child who needed speech therapy.

In the event the speech therapist did not get rid of Jenny's lisp, and even today Jenny says she has a very mild version of the problems I have in moving my mouth precisely enough to make the sounds that are shuffled like a deck of cards between the front and back of the tongue.

She was less sympathetic in the playroom when she tried to drill me in what I guess was a travesty of the speech therapist's methods.

'Ba-ba-ba-ba-ba-ba ...' We faced each other, and our eyes met. I felt my lips bump together and apart as I mirrored her.

AUTISM AND OTHER ADVENTURES: LUCY'S STORY

That noise I could hear even when my back was turned, and, if I had been able to work all this out, would have realised that other people used it in front of the word I pronounced 'nana'.

Then, as now, I was essentially confined to three or four sequential sounds in a word, and the uninflected syllables washed away in the rest of the whirling sound-chaos that I lived in.

I saw her making the same movement, but sound from her mouth did not reach my brain. I realise now that she must have said, 'Pa-pa-pa-pa-pa-pa.'

'Ba-ba-ba-ba-ba-ba …,' I said, the same as I did before.

'You see,' said Jenny to the others. 'She can say the heavy sounds but not the light ones.'

'Now try a back sound,' said Hayley.

'Ge-ge-ge,' the face in front of me said. I mimicked that too.

'Look at that,' said Jay, who was wandering around ineffectually in the background, slowly picking up the worst of the debris of the day's activities. 'You see what I mean. She isn't deaf, because she does not need to lip-read.'

'But,' my little blonde teacher said. 'She can't say 'ke'!' The others nodded.

***

I was a mystery in their midst. I sometimes could model the tone of a voice with parrot-like accuracy. Real speech, though, was my downfall. My wooden intentional words took so much cross-referencing that I could barely manage single vowel sounds, and those were ground out woodenly when they could surface to my mouth.

'I sometimes think that it is just that she doesn't want to 'give out',' I was to hear Jay say later to some visitors, a contradiction in terms, because the sounds I had learned from Jenny flowed and bubbled from my mouth as I ran back and forward and round and round — 'Da-da-da-da-da-da', 'Ba-ba-ba-ba-ba-ba', Ee-ee-ee-ee-ee-ee', 'Um-um-um-um-um-um'.

It drove them all nuts to hear me playing with these sounds, as uselessly as I spun wheels or made patterns with Lego. Frustrating for me too! And yet satisfying, in a malicious kind of way, that we all could not solve the puzzle.

All this sisterly tuition seems to have reinforced some of my two-year-old communication mannerisms, metaphorically almost as if I had been pulling a face when the wind changed. Even in High School, years later, I would behave as a small child if someone tried to treat me as a friend.

***

This saddened me, but angrily I would play on the situation, or become even less socially competent. The strange thing was that I could see the ridiculous and comic scenario in my mind's eye, but I could not alter the behaviour. As the other person got more and more embarrassed, I became more and more 'autistic'.

Once when I was eighteen, I was walking home from school. An elderly lady stood next to me at the pedestrian crossing. I assume she was concerned at my odd movements. She asked me if I were all right. Confused by the fact that she expected me to respond, I started running in a little circle.

When Jay came to find me nearly half an hour later, I was still describing ritualistic circles, and my would-be benefactor was standing aghast, with the attitude of an affable bird mesmerised by a newly hatched snake.

***

So, my own weird social overtures (for that is what that behaviour was) created inappropriate responses in others. This made it even more difficult for me to respond appropriately in return. I still do not turn and speak or sign when someone speaks to me.

I know that I should say, 'Goodbye!' to the speaker after these one-sided conversations, but cannot spontaneously look at someone and speak. Instead, I glance sideways and walk off, or wait for someone else to tell me that this is the moment to say farewell.

Then I flap my hand in a vestige of the wave that my sisters instilled in me with so much effort, and mutter, 'Bye-bye,' as woodenly as twenty years ago, my eyes often flashing back to the person who has reminded me of what to say, and on whom I am relying for timing and reinforcement.

Occasionally when I am very relaxed and pleased to see someone in a place where I am comfortable, a wonderful flash of enchantment takes over.

'Hello, So-and-so,' I will say conversationally when the door swings open.

'Hi, Lucy,' they say. 'Nice to see you again.'

However, it is just a matter of luck. I am equally likely to grab at any food that is laid out, or do something my friend probably thinks pretty bizarre, such as pouring a cup of coffee into a waste-paper basket, regardless of whether it is solid plastic or woven wire. This is a far more effective greeting than simply calling out, 'Hi!' If I really get them to notice me, I feel I have shown them how thrilled I am that we have got together.

***

When I was a child, my family and carers assumed that it was my intention to communicate, and in some instances, they were right, especially when food was involved. Because of my difficulties with consonants, Jay eventually learned to offer me two or three food items with very different vowel sounds, but not to show them to me in case I just grabbed towards one, while chanting the name of another.

'Do you want an Apple, or a Pear, or a Banana?' she would say, and frantically tried to exhume the appropriate bag from a hiding place she hoped would remain a mystery to me for as long as possible. Really, I must have been a very stimulating house mate then!

***

The language that I developed internally could not get past the barrier of what speech I did have. I did not understand that the words I did produce were unintelligible to others. I thought I was sounding as they did, but of course I was not.

Apart from indistinct sounds, I used echolalia, not as much as more fluent autistic children, but still enough to confuse the issue. I used to repeat single words to say that I agreed, because I did not use the 'y-e-s' word then.

A second reason for echoing was that I did not understand. I still do that, not with a nice questioning lilt, but with a panicky flutter in my voice which is the forerunner to real stress. These days background sound in quiet places is less disorienting, so I can see this panic starting up and control it, but in places like city streets or offices full of computers and air conditioners it erupts without warning.

The third reason for my echolalia has gone, thank goodness. This urge to speak spontaneously was always preceded by a patch of internal silence and I simply dared not leave a vacuum in the sound that I felt within my head, because I felt the word as if it were part of me and not something said by me.

***

AUTISM AND OTHER ADVENTURES: LUCY'S STORY

By and large I was mute. My morass of chaotic thought, which I suspect changed in Hayley's children as they heard the language of their own voices discipline and organise their wishes and ideas, changed in me only in response to movement and peace in the sound environment. Of course, those kids had much more conventional thought patterns than I did to start with.

My family struggled with my incomprehensible and idiosyncratic articulation. The sound processing problem that caused this was responsible for another difficulty.

I often caught the gist of offers of food, of affectionate murmurs or of growls of displeasure, because they were connected with fairly concrete episodes in daily life.

However, instructions wandered through a maze that I now see as undeveloped loud and soft discrimination, and the jarring of patches of silence.

So, I could not do what I was told, because I could not connect my own activity to another person's string of words and then project the result into even the instantaneous future.

The spoken word had little impact, compared with the immediate comfort of a full mouth, the rapture of swallowing and the reassurance of taste. All this showed up as a wide-eyed stare and a complete disregard of any other person's needs.

***

By the time I was four, I think I was under the impression that I must just not be using sound right. That is a funny way to put it. The difference in my response to music, television and speech, compared with that of my sisters, seemed to be without reason.

As I mentioned, the possibility that I could not always hear the same noises was an early memory, but that did not mean much to a small girl. I seem to have got the idea that stability in the world of my hearing was something I could develop. There seemed to be a lack of a skill that my sisters had learnt, but I could not.

Now I see that the words that someone else spoke were not an explanation as far as I was concerned, but a source of confusion. So, I did not intentionally use speech to tell other people what they wanted to know.

Neither did I point at what I wanted, nor beckon to anyone to show them that there was something they should see in the next room.

I did use gesture, but it was completely related to how I interpreted the feeling that engendered it. The onlooker had to enter a new culture to be able to interpret it.

***

When as an adolescent, I started typing, other people thought that I would express myself as if I were using the keyboard as a substitute for speech. However, never having used so normal a path for my thoughts, I had not made any tracks linking problem-solving and language, nor understood the complex ways in which other children had constructed their understanding.

Not only had I no practice at using description, but I had no inbuilt mechanism for the process.

Now when I start to write a concrete visual account of what I see, I can almost feel two unmeshed gears. When I try to do the same thing into the void of trying to conjure up a scene to someone who was not present at the time, I seem to be completely free-wheeling.

***

When my spontaneous spoken words did appear on the scene, they related to what I remembered rather than what I had been taught, in the same way that my Cricket gesture had. That kind of thing continues to dominate what speech I have, especially in relationship to memory, fear, happiness, or when I am disorientated by sound.

That seems to cover most situations in daily life! Anything to do with the past, including an imaginary episode, is simply not encoded properly in my speech thought.

For example, for years I have used the spontaneous word, 'Bertie!' to say how I feel. Although 'Bertie' the word is flourishing, Bertie the long-haired dachshund dog has been dead for about fifteen years — a problem, as no one apart from my family remembers him. 'Bertie' underpins several emotions, and the other person has to understand exactly what his link with the present is to be able to respond meaningfully.

'Bertie!' I will snarl at Jay when I think she has been neglectful or unsympathetic towards anyone (not just me). She struggled unsuccessfully with Bertie's summer eczema for years before she had him put to sleep. I am simply having a memory-jerk into the mood that I personally was in when I saw him being led out of the door for the last time.

'Bertie' is also my generic word for canine. That is the second use of the word. 'D-o-g' is an exotic import which has only recently come easily to my lips, though I had been taught it for many years. So if I see a dog my mouth flaps, and I speak.

'Bertie.'

When I stand without distress, and gaze over a large walkway flooded with people and completely dogless, one would think that this should be a 'Bertie'-free zone, but the furry long dog is still floating around somewhere in my speech processing.

'Bertie.' My tone is interested, conversational even. Across the furthest corner I have spied a slightly built, dark-haired man with horn-rimmed glasses. What I am saying is, 'Oh, is that Dad? No, it can't be, but he is very similar to how Dad looked when I was small.'

This was true of course of how Dad was when Bertie, his little mate Alex and, for two brief enchanting seasons, luscious litters of sausage-shaped puppies competed with Dad's feet, Jay's discarded reading matter and us five girls for space in front of the gas heater. (This blasting warmth was almost silent to the rest, but bombarded me with hissing jets and continuous vibration from the fan.)

To understand the word 'Bertie' in all its glory, one has to be an initiate, much as Jay was when she interpreted my cradled finger which would not have been explicable to anyone who did not know Cricket.

***

Even today I will suddenly imitate the sounds of Cricket's house, or her rather distinctive voice. That occurs when what I call 'small memory' surfaces, such as taste or even a passing feeling of regret that has gone almost before I can recognise it.

This sensory trigger that releases the speech relates to the emotion I was experiencing at the time when I first processed the sound. When these odd squeaks and syllables come from my mouth, I feel out of control, which is pretty scary.

***

As a child there were other unpleasant consequences of my words and actions being a reflex to my own thoughts. These activities often got me into a lot of trouble. That was sometimes deserved, because my rather angelic expression was beginning to hide the emotion that later I was to describe as 'fury' but which really was a kind of burning resentment.

AUTISM AND OTHER ADVENTURES: LUCY'S STORY

Even if I really wanted to do what the others could and I could not, at least I was in control when I was non-compliant. There were many occasions when my autistic behaviours and obsessions were nothing but a very real source of satisfaction.

That does not mean that the tantrums, screams and running around were intentional activities, or that I could control them, because, without understanding of my different world, there was no tool to prize my tentacles loose from my personality.

A spoken vocabulary of nouns which no one understood (not even me on some occasions) was neither useful nor satisfying to me and my family.

***

These isolated and blurred naming words that I speak are still an inconvenience, even when spiced with a few verbs and adjectives. There are strange differences between the way I use typed language and my spoken lack of syntax. That is because of the separate ways in which I acquired typed and spoken expression. For there is another form of human communication which uses words, and which remains uncorrupted by body language and intonation.

Although I was not to make my first total sentence till my teens, and that on a keyboard, the safe and coherent language of the written word was with me from an early age. This started as the other girls brought home simple reading from schools. I must have been very young because I think I could understand some of the words in Jenny's very first reader, and she started school when I was two and a half.

A picture of a ball and the four letters that were below it came together in a completely synchronised way, but I know that until I was a lot older, I never connected those symbols with the huggable plastic sphere I could hold in my hands. I never developed the urge to follow a written or symbolic instruction, and I never became automatic in speaking a written word. So, no one knew I could read.

At that stage I would not have seen any point in showing that I could. I still have problems making an instinctive move towards something I am supposed to identify by picture or word.

It is not only a matter of reading, because, although I obviously know I am a girl, I have to be reminded to go into the public toilet identified by the little skirted icon, rather than by the one representing a man, and be watched until I actually push the door open, in case I get confused on the way.

***

I was old enough for kindergarten. Far in the future I came to write a poem:

The safe womb and the joy of the rushing birth
Gives way to reality and diagnostic discipline.
The eternal child grows beard and breasts
And not the assertion grasped by others.
The care is a prison and the skills of handicap
Grow to fit the cell of love.
The need, massive and unseen, becomes a man and not a cradled babe.
At the craving the world can pity
But not give with generosity
The freedom and the risk
To be the perpetual fool.
The pointed cap lurches over the laughing fearful face.
(Fools Feeling. June 1991).

This was me at about five or six years old, as my nearly adult mind remembered it. I had to challenge because all children do that, but my ways of challenging were so confused, and my chaos so enveloping, that I imposed on my world nothing but a need to protect me from it and it from me. To live anything approaching a normal life, my family had to acknowledge and accommodate my abnormality.

Chapter 4
Little Lucy Goes to School: Age 4–9

Spring 1975. Jay sat in a doctor's office in Melbourne's Royal Children's Hospital. I would have been flipping around somewhere in the background. Jay had filled in forms and waited through a number of tests, then sat with me for an eternity in an overgrown corridor filled with other mothers and their relatively co-operative children to have my head measured and X-rayed. That I do not remember, but my mother still tenses at the memory so I guess that restraining my head motionless under an X-ray machine was fairly nerve-wracking.

The doctor came into the room. Jay was temporarily distracted by the chore of greeting him. I shot out of the unclosed door. Her face probably took on the stereotypical expression of the over-anxious mother world-wide.

'Don't worry,' said the paediatrician. 'She will come back.'

'She won't,' thought Jay, her confidence in the profession starting to erode.

I did not come back. She retrieved me, and tried to concentrate on the face in front of her explaining the results of the tests, but all she could remember by the time we got back to the car was a voice saying, 'She's about two years behind, but don't worry. Special schools are very good.'

I was just past my third birthday.

***

The only tangible result of our tortured hospital appointment came out of the blue a year later. Jay answered the phone, and to her amazement found out that my name was on a list of special-needs children who were to be offered a place in a pilot pre-school group in a Special School just outside our own area.

We fronted up for an assessment at what was then the local 'Psych. and Guidance' Centre of the Education Department. Jay went through the ritual of saying hello, and trying to fit my peculiarities into the questions asked. The psychologist and Jay looked at me. I was turning somersaults on a chair.

'So nice to see such an active child,' said the psychologist.

'Yes,' said Jay. 'She turns somersaults a lot,' and a little more proudly, 'She loved watching the gymnasts in the Olympics.'

By this she had meant that by paying attention to the television I had achieved something I could not do before, but from the typed report it is clear that the psychologist thought she meant that I had learned to do somersaults by imitating what I had watched, which is rather misleading.

***

I was given various tests, and the psychologist noticed that when a brick tower that I had constructed came crashing down I showed no reaction to the sound or to the destruction of my creation. That was probably because the sound was one that did not impact on my hearing.

Building that tower would have been for the pleasure of the pattern, and the edifice itself would have had no meaning. So, its loss was no disaster to me.

Then the two adults had another chat.

'You know, Mrs. Blackman,' said the psychologist. 'Lucy is much too dependent on you. She was watching you all the time. Does she always do that?'

Jay was stunned. As far as she knew I paid no special attention to her. In one sense she was right. If I had been there with Hayley or Cricket or Dad, I would have used each of those just the same, as concrete auditory and visual markers in a strange place.

The upshot of all this was that six months after my fourth birthday I got to attend not one, but two pre-school programmes — that is for as long as the 'normal' Kindergarten and I remained compatible!

***

I was to attend here for the standard four two-and-a-half hour sessions per week, which was not working-mother friendly. I was also spending alternating sessions in the pre-school group at the Special School.

The way that I remember my introduction to the wider world was as one of a large group of children, all the same size as me, in an enormous bright and noisy room which was really a church hall. This was the four-year-old group at the local Kindergarten which Kay and Jenny had attended before me.

The hall was familiar to me from the times that my mother had taken a morning off work to perform the obligatory rostered 'kinder-duty', to clean the toilets and to peel the fruit sent in each child's bag. I had toddled around then in double quick-time, enjoying the freedom as an eighteen-month-old. It was different if I was expected to join in.

The Directress must have been concerned about me from Day One. I imagine myself, self-contained, mobile and reaching avidly at the plates of quartered apples and oranges set out to be shared in the mid-session break.

The final decision to terminate the experiment was probably precipitated by my attempt at the Great Escape. The little girl that I tried to sketch in *Flat Reflections* scrambled over a scratchy fence that I visualise as the normal unfinished timber paling fence of most Melbourne back yards.

AUTISM AND OTHER ADVENTURES: LUCY'S STORY

I was a lot more desperate, though whether from sound sensitivity or boredom, I cannot remember. The staff retrieved me from the adjoining locked tennis court, which I had entered by the most direct route, a ten-foot wire-mesh fence.

I had been rescued from Kindergarten. Alleluia! I had not been unhappy there, but I certainly had been confused. Full-time enrolment in a group of about seven children was bliss by comparison.

***

I started to travel by the bus that was contracted to gather up the Special School kids. Other state school students in Melbourne had to get to school on their own. There was general approval in the family for this school bus arrangement, because it meant two hours in the day that we did not have to worry about child-minding. Also, I *loved* being in a vehicle.

***

At the beginning of the day, after dropping Dad at work, Jay would wait with me in the car at a predetermined spot at the beginning of the one-hour bus run. I scrambled up the rubber treads gleefully, and onto a shiny, worn seat with delight.

Now that I have changed slightly in my understanding of balance and I am less tolerant of continuous vibration and moving scenery, I realise that my pleasure was in the same category as using playground equipment and being swung around.

The big, badly-sprung blue monsters lurched around the suburban streets on a familiar route, and filled with faces that eventually also became familiar. Lots of children have so much less.

I was content as long as the bus ran to time. But, of course, often it did not. I ran up and down the pathway, and round and round in a screaming bundle of anxiety. Every now and again I would try to jump on the road.

***

In the afternoon the bus-interception routine was reversed. After collecting me, Jay then flung the station wagon across a couple of suburbs to where Dad would by now be waiting with his face screwed up with impatience, then home, where the other four girls would have let themselves in, and where Jay would serve cottage pie, spaghetti, or one of her two culinary specialities, GOK (God Only Knows) and MOK, which was a variation on GOK, and stood for Mother Only Knows.

Friday was a highlight as we had fish and chips. On Saturdays Jay cooked macaroni cheese, which she did very badly. However, she was trapped into this ritual as her mother-in-law had always served macaroni on a Saturday. I can only assume her macaroni cheese was more palatable than Jay's.

Sunday, we had roast, part of which I suspect was recycled into Jay's large yellow cast-iron cauldron as the basis of GOK.

***

So, the first school that I attended was a Special School for mildly and moderately intellectually disabled children. At this stage I was there for five terms.

In retrospect I see that the whole philosophy and teaching method of this kind of school were completely inappropriate for me, because the teachers taught through encouragement, and we were grouped for instruction rather than having extended periods of working one-to-one. As a spoken instruction did not engage an automatic response in me, the way that I operated in a class — even one of 'special needs' children — was not very satisfactory.

AUTISM AND OTHER ADVENTURES: LUCY'S STORY

I still could not conceive of myself as an individual, so much so that my teacher, Mrs. Church, remembers my refusing to let her out of my sight, even accompanying her to the staff toilets. Eventually she managed to train me to wait for her in the hand-basin area, rather than cramming myself into the cubicle with her.

***

Because other people's sound processing was alien to me, I had no idea that sound should not be like a pressure-cooker lid. I put my hands to my ears for loud sudden noises, but the continuous clamour of everyday life was only relieved by movement.

Even in the classroom there was visual stimulation and noise, which combined with my own breathing and a buzzing effect that I think was my own inner ear. I rocked, swayed and scampered, even though I knew how to sit in one place and that it was expected of me.

I could provide my own stimulation by running round and round the little tables, pursued by my exasperated teacher. Mrs. Church remembers on one horrific occasion scrambling along the tops of the tables in an unsuccessful attempt to intercept me. When she started to jump off the end table to force me to stop, I did not even seem to notice her, and she was in imminent danger of squashing me.

What an interesting news headline that would have been, 'Mobile Menace Flattened by Frenzied Teacher!' I gather no harm was done. I remained my own unsquashed and irritating self.

As the next report from 'Psych. and Guidance' said, I needed 'a structured programme of academic and social skills' if I were to come down from my own personal orbit.

***

So, I was moved to a four-student Social Adjustment Unit (SAU). I had been diagnosed as having autism some months before, but for some reason no one told my parents that there was an Autism Centre that offered a specialist programme.

The SAU teachers noticed that I could function at a reasonable level of competence, but only if I had someone's undivided attention. They established that I could recognise written words and could try to voice them. I think this was a phonics programme, and also was my first experience of formal operant conditioning.

From my point of view, it was heaven, as they used Smarties for reward and reinforcement. This also worked with speaking and matching numbers and shapes. I succeeded so well at these tasks that during this time I achieved my first cavity, which a very nervous dentist filled while I was under a general anaesthetic.

In spite of my enthusiasm for working for chocolate beans, my total inability to communicate anything that related to real life meant that it was unlikely that I would graduate from this programme to an ordinary primary classroom of twenty-five children.

***

Apart from academics the teachers had to contend with the realities of life. They wrote:

Lucy has acquired a very strange set of behaviours, such as a high-pitched scream, running around or out of the room, or putting her hands over her ears. These behaviours had a most disruptive effect on the rest of the children in the room.

The only direct approach from Lucy toward another person over the past eight months has been for toileting, to obtain a reward, and one other time when she was unable to undo her trousers.

Most of her time in the playground would be spent alone on some piece of play equipment (usually the monkey-bars), quite detached

AUTISM AND OTHER ADVENTURES: LUCY'S STORY

from the other children. She also spent a good deal of time going through rubbish bins, trying to obtain treats from the canteen, and even going through other children's bags for food and things
(From Social Adjustment Unit Report, Mid-1979).

***

The student-teacher ratio often worked out to 'three children and one teacher' and 'Lucy and the other' as I was incapable of following an activity without constant input from someone else. I cannot remember feeling more competent and in control for another eight years. Of course, there was a price in terms of the environment for the other students.

The Social Adjustment Unit was a very happy spot in my memories, but I wonder if my attendance was for the teachers. If my memory is correct, during my time the door had become a portcullis, as a hook was reinforced in turn by a piece of string, a lock and a clanging bell.

The obsessional activity that I craved on the other side of that door was to whirl and spin up and down the polished lino of the corridor. The clearest memory that I have of that school is the whirr of my feet and the smell of polish. The effect of this strong spinning motion was a kind of integration of sensation.

It was not until I was an adult that I experienced dizziness from movement, although walking slowly down a slope could make me feel nauseous because my body image was so unreliable. However, height itself was not a problem at that time, which is why I would perch on the monkey bars so as to be slightly removed from the hubbub of my peers.

***

The circling motion of my body, whirring legs and flailing arms gave the reassurance that I could not get from a warm hug, because it made the moving scene co-ordinate with my own movement.

The same good effect came from concentrating on balance, which is why I still lean back and rock on chairs at a table. I cannot imagine how a person interviewing or assessing a woman in her twenties can be very impressed by a balancing act which suspends my body in the slope of a chair poised on its back legs as a triangle on its apex, so that the interviewer has to address most of his remarks to the toe-caps and soles of a pair of much-loved sneakers.

I am not sure, but I suspect that I toe-walked because that also threw me off-balance, and in trying not to droop forward I was really exercising my vestibular system and essentially making my eyes, ears and general proprioception a little more alert. I do remember as a child the sensation of almost floating on my in-turned toes, and how that was different from how I felt slightly stressed and almost inert when I walked with flat feet.

***

By the time I left the Social Adjustment Unit, family outings were becoming almost unbearable if I went along. In an unfenced area I was a swooping, moving entity.

I ran haphazardly, my feet toeing in, my arms, which are short in relation to the rest of me, waving randomly, and my back not co-ordinating with my stride. My rather large head swung from side to side, which I think was a way of giving myself a high, because I remember sensations when running which were rather like the blessed relief of clutching a rail when overcome with vertigo.

It was also exciting to run away, because once my escape had been noticed, there would be the exhilaration of being chased, although I dreaded my struggle against being brought back.

AUTISM AND OTHER ADVENTURES: LUCY'S STORY

When Jay and I waited each school day by the side of the road for the bus, she would clasp my hand. In an endless maypole action, I ran round and round Jay as she transferred my open hand from each of her own hands in turn, behind and in front of her body in an endless ratchet to allow me a constant movement.

***

There were Jaycee barbecues, work picnics, and each year at least one Christmas party where Santa, well wrapped up in wintry red and a false beard, would swelter under the summer sun either on a beach or in a large sports area full of opportunistic flies.

Then there was a very amateur Rugby Union football club, at whose matches the teams refreshed themselves at half time with port from a flagon, rather than Gatorade or water. My father took us to watch this, so here, against a background of popping beer cans and enthusiastic families, I was lured by food and the open space of the playing field as I was at all the other gatherings.

To survive, Jay took me for long walks [round the outside of the field], or my sisters were coerced into a kind of herding posse. I loved being near other children, especially sitting at the top of a slide, and looking down at the kids clustered at the foot of the ladder.

I could see no reason why I could not sit up there for the whole of the picnic, enjoying the presence of the increasingly restive mob waiting below me. To my disgust my custodians would move me away because they were embarrassed by this, by my food stealing and by my habit of standing around tearing up eucalyptus leaves.

Of course, I disregarded such unimportant social graces as taking turns. More than once I clambered onto an occupied swing and wriggled the other child out of the way. As my bottom settled on the seat, the swing and I became one. I did not have the problem with leverage and momentum which made slipping down the unresponsive slope of a slide so terrifying.

***

On the first Sunday of each month, Noah's Ark Toy Library, which lent toys to children with disabilities, threw open its welcoming doors for members whose parents could not bring them in business hours.

I could not play with orthodox toys in an orthodox manner, but they had an enormous range of large and delightful plastic-covered padded shapes. My sisters would romp like toddlers with me on these, and then we would choose a five-foot long rocking shape or a gigantic yellow and blue cylinder and somehow squeeze it into the station wagon.

Behind Dad's chair there was space for me to play on these. I could extend my own movement as I seesawed and balanced, suspended on an upended four-foot cylinder, my body forming the cross piece to the upright of a 'T' with my chest and abdomen pressed into it as a hinge on a seesaw.

Not that I realised that this was balance as I watched the floor rise and recede into my field of vision. All my sensation was concentrated in the pleasure of movement, and the sound my mouth would make was a direct complement to the pleasure.

As this happened, I felt in control and completely happy, and the slight stress of being still would go. That was not dissimilar to floating on water, and the sight of the floor coming up towards me did not worry me, though as I grew older and more careful, I could not climb down from the heights I could scale.

***

AUTISM AND OTHER ADVENTURES: LUCY'S STORY

Until my teens I continued to climb upwards fearlessly, and was retrieved from roofs, power pylons and other people's fenced backyards, but I could not bear the uncertainty of walking slowly down a slope, because I perceived the space below me as extending far further than my foot actually travelled with each step to reach the ground.

There was less pleasure for me in jumping from furniture and generally being as nerve-racking for others as I had been. I suppose the rest of the world thought it was an improvement, but I still miss that wonderful feeling of flying through the air.

***

Noah's Ark also ran camps. I would go away with a group of other disabled children and an equal number of volunteers to many parts of Victoria, where we swam, swung, bush-walked and ate enormous quantities of hamburgers and hot dogs. These were times of unadulterated bliss for me, and for my parents and sisters I think a tantalising glimpse of a Lucy-free existence.

***

I was not really benefiting from the Social Adjustment Unit the way the psychologist had hoped I would. By chance Jay had seen a newspaper article on a Centre for young children with autism and when my enrolment came up for review, she asked if I could be accepted there. So, my case was turned over to another set of professionals.

This move involved the usual assessment, interviews, form-filling-in and copious reports. That I know because I had a chance to read them after I had roughed out the original version of this section.

From the psychologist's comment on the withdrawn child who would not play with dolls, to Jay's response to a version of the standard autism questionnaire, these documents are the bare bones of my more detailed memories.

The Centre staff also had paid us a home visit before I was accepted. They seemed to think that as a family we were managing well. That may have been so, but I certainly was not managing in anything but my own world, and on my own terms.

I still had all the same problems with processing what was going on in the space around me, which is why this programme suited me in some ways.

***

By using teachers and trained volunteers, the Centre was to teach in a one-to-one partnership without which even as an adult I find that my ability to function in any reasonably complex way is negligible.

That is because my perceptual difficulties blur the divisions between cause and effect, not only in concrete outcomes, but in the minutiae of social interaction, and of time and space.

I can perform a sequence of tasks with a predetermined goal, like getting up and dressed, but not a general instruction, like 'get things organised!' I find that expression hilariously funny, because I am always organised inside myself, but most things happen spasmodically, so my interface with that sequence is a little blurred. It is the rest of the world that teeters on the edge of chaos.

***

At the beginning of the new term a white mini-bus took over, coming to our front door. The first day Jay had taken time off work to come with me in the bus, but after that I was loaded aboard and the seat-belt was done up. I felt a bit like a parcel being put in the post.

I do not mean that I was treated like a parcel, and I can still remember the warmth of the drivers, teachers and volunteer helpers towards the oddly acting children who flittered and stomped and span through the corridors there.

Some were almost physically handicapped in their clumsiness, and some seemed almost out of place in their comparative normality.

In some ways the Centre was a haven. It was so welcoming in its quiet because the walls and concrete floors were absorbent of noise, and we were so close to the staff at all times that I felt safe and confident in the way that they were able to control me and my activities.

***

For the first time since I started catching the bus to Special School, we had a baby-sitting problem. Theoretically the mini-bus arrived to pick me up a few minutes before Jay left for work, and dropped me off a few minutes after she got home. However, there were meetings she could not avoid, and there were flat tyres, traffic jams and a host of other things that seemed to flock around her like flies at a barbecue.

For two years we simply muddled through. The girls provided emergency backup, rushing out of the school yard so that they could catch the bus as it swung into our drive.

Later Jay arranged to meet the bus at various points, much like she had done with the big blue Special School buses. This was a pretty hit and miss affair because there were different pickup points and Jay's haphazard timing almost drove the bus driver crazy, but it did let my sisters get to school on time.

Each child attended for a maximum of four days a week, and never on Tuesday afternoons. The Municipal Council service for relief for Mums at home with disabled children was not available for working parents. However, there was a wonderful solution close at hand.

Over our back fence lived Barbara, a little lady with long flowing hair whom I had known all my life, and who accepted me with no qualms about the way that I behaved, including the way that I stroked her head at every opportunity. Her daughter, Maria, was in Kay's class at school.

Barbara was able to look after me on Tuesdays, which was my rostered day not to go to the Centre. I was blissfully content with this arrangement, though probably I would have giggled and smiled the same had I been off-loaded onto anyone else. The other days I went to the Centre.

***

When I first went to the Centre, on a typical morning the bus would turn into our drive and hoot. Jay, or if she had left, Hayley, Val or Kay, would push me up the steps.

'Hello, Jo,' she would say to the bus driver, and strap me into my seat. The first section of the message book which provided the daily lifeline between school and home was dominated by Jay's scrawl and the teacher's response about my behaviour in the mini-bus:

Jay: *Jo says ... problems with Lucy in the bus ... my suggestions (1) if good she could tell the girls so we can make a fuss of her at home, (2) if Lucy does play up, Jo could make it clear to Lucy that she is babyish and stupid, and to laugh at her out loud. She sometimes responds to this at home. The words 'naughty', 'bad', etc. seem to make her behaviour worse.*

AUTISM AND OTHER ADVENTURES: LUCY'S STORY

Bob (Teacher): *Rewarding Lucy if she doesn't scream on the bus is the sort of think that needs to be done, and we will do the same this end.*

Jay: *Lucy was extremely complacent when Kay passed on the message that Jo had said they 'had left the Little Lucy at school and brought the Big Lucy home'.*

But a few days later:

Bob: *Lucy is getting up and down all the time, so could you get her off the bus personally. Your approval/disapproval may help.*

Jay: (Pathetically): *Car trouble ... public transport ...*

The message books not only discussed practicalities, but all the activities in which I had taken part at the Centre and at home. Because of this interchange, for five years I never felt as lost as I had in my previous schools because writing in the message book was part of the teachers' daily routine.

***

On the fifth page of the first message book is a thunderbolt:

Jay: *As a result of an accident on Saturday, the close family friend who has been baby-sitting for us on Tuesdays was killed. I don't think that Lucy has any real comprehension of our explanation, or, for that matter, a great ability at this stage of missing people ...*

(July 1979).

However, I did miss Barbara terribly. Years later I assumed that I had been kept in the dark intentionally because I was not 'normal'. Like most children, adolescents, and many adults, I firmly blamed anyone but myself. I could not understand that my family really was sure that I did not understand a lot of what they said. So, they often did not tell me things, and when they did my patchy processing only led to misinformation.

***

Suddenly my life was invaded by strangers again; nice strangers but new factors with whom I had to come to an accommodation. The Council service eventually came to our rescue for a while with dear Mrs. Ryan, grey haired and gentle, but in the meantime first Christine, and then Debbie, sisters who were university students, came to keep me company every Tuesday.

This was all happening in the wind-up period of my parents' marriage. They were sorting out a number of different priorities of which I was only one. I think that they might even have split up earlier had their energies not been so diluted by the sheer complications of everyday life. By its very nature, my need to be supervised did nothing to contribute to an already tense situation. It was essential that Jay have a job, so we simply had to make it possible.

***

Another fact of life was that Jay easily is the most disorganised person that I have ever known, so that my anxious quietness was permeated with her constant searches for keys, garments, books, and just about any item small enough to be picked up and misplaced.

Her searching somehow got embedded in my speech processing, so that later I was to express anxiety in what small amount of speech that I had by demanding keys, hankies and the like. Sounds innocuous?

Imagine an eighty-kilogram young woman running in circles or lying down and screaming because her mother has misplaced her car keys. Not only weird, but horribly frightening to me and other people.

***

AUTISM AND OTHER ADVENTURES: LUCY'S STORY

Each morning at the Centre we would have a 'good morning' session, which was meant to teach greetings and things like turn-taking. The latter I already understood in theory, courtesy of my bossy siblings, but I never saw the point of it in the circle in the classroom, though I learnt to read the cues for going through the motions while we sat there.

We also had songs, most of which combined with actions, though it was only near the end of my time there that I started to be spontaneous in the singing sessions, and I never worked out how to sing at the same time as the other children.

This singing made me very happy and excited, and over the years some kind of crossover happened. The anger urge was confused with excitement. Where another child would yell, I would burst into song.

By the time I was a teenager this general musical response to excitement became a specialised expression of anxious rage. So *Happy Birthday to You* and *Pop goes the Weasel* over the years became cries of fury. My feelings are still expressed in what was almost a spasm of sensation.

***

I was nearly seven when I first went to the Autistic Centre, and by and large I did not express rage towards others, except when I was held still in one place. I did attack a couple of people when I was in my teens, but as a small child I had a habit of tugging rhythmically on the little fringe above my eyes when I was anxious.

'Danger,' it said. 'Lucy, let's retreat together.' And I relaxed into something close to self-hypnosis.

***

In spite of unpleasant consequences to me, I was beginning to be interested in Dad's anger when he discovered I had taken his favourite possessions, and had abandoned them wherever I happened to be when I lost interest, so that some would turn up under my bed, some eventually emerged from the dusty depths of the living room chairs, and some presumably are still trapped in the sludge of the Melbourne sewage system which they reached via the fascinating and terrifying roar of the toilet flush.

Dad only provided one-sixth of the oddments and knick-knacks with which I absconded, but he was responsible for ninety-nine percent of the drama — most informative from my point of view in working out what was anger and what was not.

***

Just after I moved to the Centre, my own anger found an outlet in biting down on my own hand just above the thumb joint, a wonderfully comforting kind of pain, and made me feel in control.

Later I told Jay that I was imitating the other students in biting my hand, but even when I made that statement, I knew it was a load of rubbish, and part of a long running campaign to blame everyone that I could think of for my predicament. Learning by imitation was not really my thing.

Here I was in this programme with its strong emphasis on interaction and speech, with very structured sessions in which I could clearly gauge whether I was successful.

This Centre was a little more health-oriented than the Social Adjustment Unit, so they used sultanas as a reward, which was something of a let-down in my opinion, but did the job as far as giving reinforcement was concerned, so my whole speech instinct was probably stirred up.

I have decided that my hand-biting was an unrecognised sign that I was developing an urge to use more spoken words, because when I was an adult, I discovered that biting my hand nearly always occurs when I would have wanted to make a forceful comment (usually of the four-letter word variety), or a casual observation, such as, 'That was not a bad idea!' or 'Luv ya!'

If only I had had the input from the Centre much earlier, and had also made sense of the speech sounds around me much younger than I did, perhaps my spoken language would have blossomed and my hands would not have fresh half-moon scars at the base of the thumb.

***

Also discussed in the message book during my first weeks there was my reading ability:

Bob: *Lucy seems to have quite a vocabulary in receptive labelling and seems to recognise some written words.*

Jay: *When she was at Special School, her teacher there was sure she could read the names of the other class members on their drawings because of her eye direction, but could not get Lucy to provide any proof.*

I was shown a video of Lucy learning to read from cards at the Social Adjustment Unit, but I can only remember the names of colours, 'Lucy', 'Lucy is a girl', 'Good', and 'This is Lucy'

(Late July 1979).

The school sent home little sets of reading cards, and for homework I continued the kind of activity that I had started at school. Somehow my speech memory could not contain the decoding messages for more than six or eight written words. If I learned more, some of the ones I had learnt previously went into limbo.

***

As the years went by, reading instruction at the Centre was not exactly infuriating, but in some way seemed irrational. I began to realise that the teacher expected me to speak aloud words that I had been able to read for the whole of my remembered life.

The words on *Sesame Street* had been one of my first memories. Without realising it, the girls had been my instructors in the primary school curriculum, especially Kay and Jenny who had been in the lower grades of primary school when I was beginning to absorb all this wonderful magic world of flat soundless shapes.

They had sat at the kitchen table making heavy weather of the reading books set home from school, while I flapped and cooed with delight that I could do what they were trying to learn.

For indirect learning, there had been stacks of magazines and newspapers all over our chaotic home. I could link shapes such as words to things and actions, without realising that these symbols are a representation of the same concept expressed in speech.

The whole spread of language became available to me in this way. Speech from outside my body remained a loving but non-urgent intrusion.

***

Because it barely existed, my own speech for me was not a precursor to reading. I had no idea that sounds were consistently developed, and that most people know that when they moved their mouth a certain way, they would hear themselves make a certain sound.

Secondly, when I used a word like 'nose', I did not think of it as a representation of the thing that others saw, but as a symbol of my own sensation of being the possessor of the feature.

Thirdly, the sounds that I was expected to make, even the simplest ones, only flashed up in my mouth in response to immediate urges.

AUTISM AND OTHER ADVENTURES: LUCY'S STORY

***

As I slowly began to think in the way that Bob and Samantha imposed on me, I was able to attempt the task of repeating the word I saw in front of me. However, the other person had to know exactly what I had worked on at previous sessions, because of my erratic speech memory and its infuriating time-tunnel inability to store what I had learnt.

In spite of all this, I did start to forge some mental links between the words and phrases I had encountered and the kind of books that my sisters and Jay would read to me. These had a very similar vocabulary.

But I did not really wake up to the fact that the little games and cards with names like 'Cat' and 'Dog' were the same process when applied to the fur-balls who over-ran our house. It was some years before I realised that these were simply different applications of one thing, and that that thing was language.

***

That was odd, because I recognised the connection between the television and newspaper headlines, and in years to come when asked the names of the holders of different political offices, readily answered with the people who had done that job in the late seventies, much to everyone's confusion.

I learned to enjoy sport on television, though the reason behind all this activity remained a mystery. I was also aware of various news stories, and clearly remembered what was a big media occasion in Melbourne when, through her introduction to an alphabet board, Annie McDonald, a young woman with cerebral palsy, was found not to have been severely retarded, but indeed very intelligent.

I was only about six or eight at the time, so did not understand what this implied about the connection between speech and reading, though her friend, Rosie Crossley, remained in my visual memory, along with Ernie, Jimmy Carter and Humphrey B. Bear, a human dressed in a bear costume, who had his own show on television each morning and whom I particularly loved because he did not speak and his face never changed, so I found him easy to understand.

***

At that school the fence was high and activities structured. Outside school I was fine at home, and I could be taken to other places like a doctor's surgery or on a very quick shopping trip, so long as I had the undivided attention of someone who could keep me more or less in one place. This was me at nine years old.

About the time of my ninth birthday my parents got their act together and separated. Dad got a lift to an apartment a few suburbs away for his share of our household effects on a covered truck half loaded with rock-concert gear.

***

At the last minute the proceedings were almost reversed. By this time, we had a German Shepherd, Sheila. While the rock band, Jay and my sisters squeezed the upright piano through the front door, they were also keeping me in sight to ensure that I did not make a break for it.

Dad's back had a nasty habit of seizing up, and this was probably not the best day for this to happen, so he was supervising. Sheila had shot through a gap. Suddenly into what was a fairly celebratory scene of displacement, burst our irate neighbour.

'That bloody dog should be shot,' he yelled. 'If she gets into my place again, I'll use my gun!' Jay, overcome by the emotion of the moment, burst into tears. Dad came back up the front steps.

'Darling,' he said. 'Do you want me to stay a while? I can wait around till you feel better.' Jay glared at him through puffy eyes.

'For goodness sake, Dave,' she said in alarm. 'Just get moving.'

He walked to his car with a little spring in his step. The rock band looked relieved. They had just finished hoisting the piano on the truck.

Chapter 5
Big Lucy 1982–1986: Age 10–14

The flights of stairs that led to our father's new apartment had not been designed with large musical instruments in mind. The piano was eventually dislodged from the narrow stairwell where it had jammed, and made its reappearance on our doorstep to be exchanged for the small electronic organ.

Jay had already rearranged what was left of the living room furniture. She accommodated this reject with gales of laughter. What was so funny remained a mystery to me. None of us children played the piano and she is tone deaf.

Only the cats really appreciated its tall splendour as a convenient refuge from Sheila's long pink affectionate tongue.

***

A couple of days later I discovered Jay dragging my bed into what was now her bedroom. This was to last for six years.

Hayley was about to start the second-last year of High School. This would lead to final exams and, hopefully, university. She would get precious little study done if I shared her room. The same applied to Val and Kay.

Jenny was nearly twelve and in the new school year would be going into Year 7. We would have four students in the 7–12 High School system, and all would be wearing the compulsory High School uniform.

Only I would continue to wear jeans to school, which was just as well in view of how I sometimes behaved when wearing a dress.

***

AUTISM AND OTHER ADVENTURES: LUCY'S STORY

Just before all the drama of our becoming a single parent family, I had been suspended from the Centre for a few days because Jay's bus-meeting schedules had become so erratic.

I was reinstated when Jay found a young woman who could take care of me in her home before and after school, and see me onto the bus. She had a little baby called Michelle.

I was encouraged to cuddle Michelle, which I found terrifying. I remember that when she whimpered, I would leap to my feet and push her away as I did with a cat.

This arrangement broke down, though I am not sure if the safety of the baby was a factor here. Then came time in the home of a lady called Carol. This also proved temporary, but I do not know why.

Jay was determined to get my school days under control. She advertised again in the local newspaper for someone who was always at home at the beginning and end of the school day. This brought an answer from Margaret, who was the mother of what was to become my other family.

Each morning for six years I would get out of Jay's car and rush up to their screen door.

'Hello, Lucy,' one of Margaret's five long-haired daughters would say, and let me in, grabbing my school bag as I dropped it in the middle of their hall. Their pretty red-haired mother would look around the kitchen door and smile.

'Hello, Lucy,' she would say, moving slowly into the living room to check if Jay wanted to see her before burning off down the road.

Jay would probably have come in if she had time to gossip, because Margaret had rheumatoid arthritis and, even then, found steps difficult. As the years went by, she moved more and more slowly, and seemed to spend most of her time in a chair by the gas heater.

Fortunately, they were a very well organised family, and after the first year or two I was pretty well controlled in my behaviour there. Their girls were not much different in age from my own sisters.

If they were there, they played with me in much the same way as Hayley & Co. would at home, or I sat and watched television while they did their homework at the dining room table.

I began to understand that, rather than being a whole lot of one-off activities, most of these pages of writing and figures had a definite pattern and purpose to them.

***

We settled down into some kind of routine again, though not for long. One morning my eldest sister announced she was not going to school again.

'Leaving?' squawked Val and Jenny in unison. They both enjoyed school, and were duly horrified.

'Leaving …' said Kay with envy. She had asked to try another school, and again had been absent more often than she was present.

'Leaving!' I thought with fury. I could not see how anyone with speech and the ability to make a pen move in the direction their brain spelt out could be anything but continually happy at a 'normal' school.

Kay struggled on till the day after she reached legal school-leaving age, then simply refused to go back. Once again, I was wild with indignation, which was a pale shadow of how Jay felt — though, after the trauma of trying to get Kay as far as the school gate even two days a week, I suppose she was slightly relieved.

***

AUTISM AND OTHER ADVENTURES: LUCY'S STORY

My school life went on much as usual. The environment at the Autistic Centre was so structured that for me problems with cause and effect were minimised, though of course things were not always logical. We went on outings to the local shops, parks, tourist attractions and the Zoo.

Here I had already established a set of priorities to which my family had learnt to adhere when we went there with Granny Joy on her regular visits. These were the amusement park, the seals and a substantial snack, in that order.

Once they had neutralised these bits of static interference, the rest of the family had a chance to stand still very briefly and glance at some non-events, such as the cage with the mountain gorillas or the lions.

The only animals I enjoyed watching were the seals, because they were like a tactile experience for the brain. Unfortunately, Jay did not warn Samantha that I did not visit zoos to look at animals:

Saw most of the animals at the Zoo. Lucy loved the seals and was great, except when we headed away from the amusements after my saying there'd be a ride later.

My sequence of activities was quite overlooked by Lucy, and it wasn't until we headed back to the amusements that I twigged what the problem was!

(Samantha, August 1982).

***

I was starting to mature a little. Till my tenth birthday Jay had cut my hair by chasing me round and round the house, getting in random snips whenever she got me cornered.

According to Jenny I was lucky. Jay cut the whole family's hair for reasons of economy, and was particularly blessed with the kind of eye which hangs pictures crooked and cuts fringes at an angle. One summer Jenny insisted on attending school for nearly a whole term in a knitted cap with a pom-pom. The cap was pulled down to her eyebrows.

This was to hide Jay's contrite attempts to repair the devastation she had wrought, which had resulted in Jenny's fringe being cut back to the hair follicles.

My objection was not on the grounds of appearance, but because I hated having my head touched. This included brushing and combing, the sound of the scissors terrified me, and I was appalled by the thought of part of my person being detached.

The Centre had been working hard to make me less defensive about having my head touched, and simultaneously working on my joint habits of tugging the front of my hair, and stroking the back in the same way that I did with Hayley's.

I had just learned to sit in front of a mirror for a haircut, when Jay talked me into visiting a hair stylist for the first time. She used an appeal I found irresistible:

Jay: *I asked Lucy if she would like short hair if it were cut in a real shop with lots of mirrors! After a well-considered 'think', she spoke 'short' and has confirmed this a couple of times when I asked her again. So, after pay-day, I will brave a hairdresser. I will have a word with them first, and let her have a look around the day before.*

(Message book, October 1982).

I might not have used mirrors conventionally, but I certainly adored them. Fortunately, the young hairdresser on duty had been at school with Hayley at one stage, and remembered me, so two days later,

Jay: *In spite of speaking the words 'cry' and "air' together, Lucy did not really cry at the hairdressers. She did not like having her hair washed backwards, but she loved having it cut.*

***

AUTISM AND OTHER ADVENTURES: LUCY'S STORY

Of course, the Centre used my hair as a basis for work on spoken language, as it did all activities, including simple food preparation, the puzzles and blocks we worked with and the messages that came from home.

Jay tried to keep her end up, though I feel the staff went beyond the call of duty in struggling to decipher the screeds, as even Jay has trouble reading her own writing.

***

At the beginning of 1983 Jay had written:

We had a good two weeks holiday at Warrnambool (on the south-west coast of Victoria). We ate at pubs or cafes at least once a day, and Lucy's behaviour was pretty good. The only snag was the sea. The coastline is so dangerous that scenic walks with Lucy really were not possible. In fact, if you show her a photo of Loch Ard Gorge, she will speak, 'Naughty!' with a big grin on her face.

Those breakers lurch and roar from the Great Southern Ocean to crash against the inconvenient bulk of the south of the Australian continent. There they have chiselled and gnawed at the coast, leaving blow-holes and cracks like the Loch Ard Gorge.

For me the sea here had been a magnet. Giddy with the noise, I saw the swell as some flat, multi-coloured surface which I simply had to touch and chase.

Further along the coast was a greater wonder, an open silver beach. Here the waves tower, higher than a house, bewitching me with their silky-green mysterious porticoes, overshadowed by white crests that then tumbled to the beach.

I followed these retreating, singing waves, and behind me was a hand which grabbed me by the strap of my overalls, and then dragged me, resigned but irritated, up the cliff path.

***

As far as Jay was concerned, plucking me from the turbulence of the Great Southern Ocean was pretty bland as irritants went.

This was our first and last family holiday in the eleven years since arriving in Australia, if one excepts the long weekend trip when Val had composed my Vegemite Song. Jay had done no long-distance driving in that time, and the station wagon was apt to behave uncooperatively at times.

This was really a bit late for an all-girls-together vacation. There were two camp-followers. Hayley's current boyfriend set up camp in a nearby caravan park a few days later. We were escorted on our outward journey by an overworked little Hillman motor car of venerable age. This belonged to Jim.

He was skinny, tall, with a kind soft voice and a tattoo on his arm. This design was the same blue as Kay's eyes. For the next year Kay was to float around looking superior, with his sleeveless leather jacket swathed over her little shoulders, topped by a series of frizzy perms. I liked Jim, but regretted the perm. I had lost one strokeable head.

***

Val, who had remained sunny tempered and placid right into her adolescence, was to become a little quieter as this new wave of strangers overran our home.

Jenny decided to cast herself as the stock-character twelve-year-old *enfant terrible*, asking impertinent personal questions in the best tradition of prepubescent television urchins, and I ran in and out of any room where either Kay or Hayley was trying to have a private *tête à tête*, giggling and jumping on the furniture.

***

AUTISM AND OTHER ADVENTURES: LUCY'S STORY

Our great family vacation started inauspiciously. In the midst of an open expanse of farmland the car suddenly went dead. Fortunately, Jay was able to guide its silent bulk to the gravel edge. I made my usual screaming contribution to this moment of crisis.

The local petrol station partially cleared the fuel blockage, just before closing down for Christmas.

That was just as well, because a couple of days later the Hillman decomposed by the side of the road, and Jay and Jim spent a good part of the Christmas public holiday driving round with this relic tied to the back of our straining station wagon.

I gather they eventually were delighted to pay some chance acquaintance to take it off their hands. While this was going on, I was firmly locked in our holiday-farm cabin.

While Kay sulked, Hayley read to me. In the intervals between international cricket test matches Val took over, and Jenny taught me to say, 'open the door, close the door', while swinging the bathroom door in the appropriate direction from the top of the adjoining bunk.

From then on, I swung, clicked and banged doors enthusiastically on every possible occasion. One could say that our one and only family holiday had been a great learning opportunity.

Shortly after we all struggled home, Hayley changed boyfriends, and Laurie, a short, quiet man who seemed to be permanently attached to a loud electric guitar, started to be something of a fixture around the place.

***

Granny Joy arrived a few months later, grey haired, increasingly stout and delivered off the plane in a wheel chair. She would sit in this contraption, making weak jokes, and looking both dignified and indignant in its vinyl and chrome clasp.

Once safely ashore, she would walk slowly and massively, leaning on a stick which, with its silver handle and slender shaft, seemed as much part of her as her authoritative English voice.

She strolled slowly. I ran. Jay had to entertain us both. That was why we tended to go to the Zoo, which was built on flat ground, or into places which had lots of playground equipment, so long as there were not too many other children there.

***

Jay also took us on long, unplanned sightseeing drives, during which she never stopped to consult a map, because any uncertainty or discussion as to where we were going drove me into a red-faced screaming frenzy.

Jay was beginning to learn that I got anxious when she dropped her face down while she looked at something, even when she checked in her money purse to see whether she had enough to pay for what had just been run through the checkout.

This was partly because purse-fumbling led to things being removed from our neatly packed bag if she had overspent, or map-reading to the car being turned around if we were lost.

This anxiety was compounded by her face foreshortening as her head bent forward, so that all the shadows and curves of her features made a different pattern, and the person who I was relying on decomposed in some way.

This was not confined to Jay. It could occur with teachers and my sisters if they were the key person at that instant.

***

Granny Joy took all this drama in her stride, along with the rather disorganised household in which she temporarily found herself. She was not really a child-lover and had far too much sense to put herself on a collision course with me, but for some reason I did not bug her.

Because I could just enjoy her being there without having to make a social effort, and because her visits were happy occasions full of outings and excitement, I adored her.

I showed this by not looking directly at her so that I could take her in more clearly.

She always gave us some wonderful big gift when she left. On this occasion it was a full-sized trampoline. On the trampoline I was a different person.

As the mat was so big and strong, there was no prohibition on these nearly-adults bouncing at the same time as I did. When I was on the tramp with any of them, I instinctively flicked my eye towards theirs, much as I had in the above-ground swimming pool all those years earlier.

I suppose that it was the effects of my balancing and bouncing forcing my vestibular system to make demands on those parts of my brain which shunt different sensory messages around.

I remember that my unrecognised constant feeling of being slightly giddy retreated, and the repeated changes in gravity meant that I could move through air with very little intentional body movement.

***

Granny Joy left, and life went on in its usual way. Now Val was in Year Eleven, and was given a very small decrepit caravan in the back yard as a buffer between her and our sisters' social life, and also as a haven from my habit of drawing on or tearing up any paper in sight, including text books.

I not only scrawled my own version of human figures on these, but had added to my repertoire denim jeans and telegraph poles with the soaring wires. Before doing this, I would scan and store the shape of the print, to retrieve the contents later and make patterns with the words in my head.

I still saw no connection between formal reading instruction and this kind of scanning, but I was aware that what I was doing had some connection with what Jay, Val, Hayley and the others did when they sat down, bent their relaxed and absorbed faces over a novel, and effectively shut me out of their minds as far as I could see.

In the bathroom, next to the toilet, I found another stack of word-pattern treasures. Jay had left *The Collected Works of Shakespeare*, *The Penguin Book of English Verse* and assorted classic novels there in the hope of snaring Kay into some acquaintance with authors she had left school too early to have read. One day Kay came rushing out of the bathroom, still hobbled by her jeans, waving a book over her head and screaming.

'Hey, look, I've just found this wonderful poem all about daffodils!'

However, Jay would have been astonished to know that over the long term I got far more out of all this than the other girls did.

***

Jay would drive us down to visit Dad, and we would sit and watch television with him, or walk with him to the shops, carrying heavier loads back because by that time his back was beginning to be quite painful.

'Darling,' he said one day to Jay when she picked us up. 'I was watching Lucy walk on the way to the milk bar. I don't like the way she is toeing in. It's much worse than it used to be.'

'Rubbish,' said Jay. 'It's no different from how it was. You have just forgotten,' and she stalked off to the car, sure that he was having a swipe at her parenting. She sulked at the steering wheel all the way home, and then I think her brain started to tick over.

AUTISM AND OTHER ADVENTURES: LUCY'S STORY

The next afternoon we went for a walk. However instead of me being led by one wrist, we marched. She nagged and swung my arm alongside hers. Her description is better than anything I can do:

Thanks to the work done at the Autistic Centre, she was capable of putting her feet down heel-first on command, and had almost stopped stepping on her own in-turned toes when she was walking. However, she still shuffled, held her body like a toddler and held her arms babyishly, not swinging by her sides.

So, we started walking, on Lucy's part disagreeably and irritatingly. For the first year I would drag her by her hand for a street block or two, or follow her closely, snapping, 'Heels down,' 'Throw your feet out,' or 'Big steps.'

At intervals I would nudge the back of her heels with my toes, or give her a good shove between the shoulder blades. Passing children, avid gardeners and the occasional adult pedestrian would glare disapprovingly.

For a little variety I would scream, 'Chewing gum. Naughty!' every time she swooped on someone's discarded goodie on the footpath.

(Mary Jane Blackman, Article prepared for Parent Newsletter, 1984).

***

The following year my heels were coming down of their own accord, and my arms and body had started to move in rhythm with my legs.

I still scampered, but Jay thought she had the answer to that. We would go down a steep slope near our house. She would move behind me and thump and push steadily between my shoulder blades so that I had to break into a run.

Because the weight of my body pulled me forward, I kept my balance by alternating my arms with my legs, so that I really did run, rather than letting my legs splat from side to side, and my hands flap. I was less than impressed with this, partly because it was so successful.

So, I stopped her short in her tracks, or rather I stopped myself just as she was pushing hard, and I ducked to one side. As she tumbled down the sidewalk in front of me, she spat out an expression that no mother should use to her eleven-year-old daughter, and over her head I laughed with genuine amusement.

This initiation period was partly carried out under cover of early morning darkness. The next stage was to make me walk through a section of the suburb. Eventually we would walk many miles at weekends as the strong impulse to stride out grew.

Poor Jenny, she suffered agonies at school on Monday mornings.

'I saw your mother walking Lucy.'

'Oh, yeah? What was she doing?' (A note of anxiety here).

'Swinging her arms, and she was saying, 'heel, toe', and she was trudging down your street, and Lucy was behind doing her lolloping gait, and your mother was swinging down the street, heel-toe, heel-toe.'

Jenny was decidedly under-impressed.

***

About this time Jenny came back from a school camp radiant with happiness.

'It was the best camp ever!'

'Why?' she was asked.

'Well, George was having a go at me, and one of the other boys hit him, and, do you know what, I think the teachers were glad!'

'What did George say?'

'Oh, just going on about how my little sister was a retard.'

***

There were two main outcomes from our hikes. The first was a new ability to practise decision making in a way that was independent of my inaccurate spoken language.

Usually when I spoke, I could not prevent random stray thoughts from sounding like intentional requests. Once I began to enjoy walking, Jay encouraged me to lead the way or to indicate the direction that I chose with the strange flat-hand movement that I felt as a pointed finger.

As I had better understanding of my own natural movement than the speech-sounds that I manufactured, choice by body movement was completely different from the way that I just threw an acquired spoken word into space.

Though I had been taught to point conventionally, I never did spontaneously, and the nearest that I came to it of my own initiative was to use my middle finger, while creating a circle with my index finger and thumb.

I did not point or gesticulate with any reference to whether another person understood.

If I were offered a choice of two foods, I often grabbed the one that I was obsessed with, rather than the one I felt like eating that day.

This kind of perseveration made using communication cards pretty useless unless they were exact photographic replicas of what I was being offered, *and* the other person knew me well enough to check if I were not perseverating on an image rather than touching the picture of what I really wanted.

***

So, the walking did help in decision making but did not modify my difficulties in cause and effect.

I did not understand until I was an adult that I am exceptional in that I do not always anticipate the consequences of even quite simple actions, or that, when I do, I still cannot learn through experience to modify what I did that led to disaster.

***

Unknown to anyone, even me to begin with, these regular route marches did something else.

Because of my auditory peculiarities, I had never used sentences or other verbal arrangements in my speech.

Also, I had somehow never recognised or processed this when other people spoke to me, so that their words kind of splatted over the griddle of my consciousness, sometimes sunny-side-up, sometimes easy-over, and, more often than not, with a broken yolk and very uneven edges.

They arrived in a random order and often overlaid each other, so I had not established any real pathways to process my own verbal thoughts.

I had acquired and processed the written vocabulary that I gleaned from my sisters' books, the homework on Margaret's dining room table and the newspapers on our living room floor in much the same way.

As well as scavenging this uncoordinated intellectual concept of written language, I had learnt words and phrases at the Autistic Centre as part of the reading programme.

As Jay chivvied, chased, nagged and ultimately walked beside me for several miles, I started to re-scan the photographic images in my brain which had accumulated from these and from the adolescent novels which now littered our home.

As I strode out, this mess, together with some of the spoken words around me, began to coalesce into a new understanding.

***

AUTISM AND OTHER ADVENTURES: LUCY'S STORY

My wasted mental processes started to discipline themselves, triggered by the stimulation that came from regular motion.

Words in speech were still fragmented, and language in reading was not really part of real life, but even so in my own head these were amalgamated in some kind of patchy whole by the time I was thirteen.

The difference between my two forms of receptive language remained as if I were bilingual, and that within two separate cultures, but the frightful chasm between them died away.

However, I assumed that written English had far more silent letters than it does have. I missed so many uninflected words in other people's speech that I still did not know that they were really part of the spoken as well as the written language.

As we silently strode, I started to tell stories to myself, and to have rather formal little interior dialogues, but these were all processed in the word patterns which were embossed in my visual memory. My speech processing was completely unaffected.

***

Language and exercise also took priority at the Autistic Centre. Even nonsensical outings, like a fairy-tale play Samantha tried to make me describe, were used to work on expression. Dutifully she reported back to Jay:

The teachers who went to the Clown Show said that Lucy thoroughly enjoyed it, clapping throughout and giggling a lot at the end. I found it hard to get much out of Lucy. However she drew many pictures of the story. Before she did any of this, I had to find out the information from one of the teachers, and then Lucy would say it and draw it.

(Samantha. April 1983).

This illustrates a problem which still bedevils me. I have not developed clear links between what other people expect of my attempts at communication, and how previous events are tagged in my language.

***

The Centre had its own little pool and a small gymnasium with a long rope and climbing frames. It was rich in the same padded shapes we borrowed from the Toy Library. Input from the physical and sensory-integration parts of the programme was playing its part in what happened inside my head.

This structured environment often irritated me, and some years later I stated that I thought it was a bit restrictive. Yet I would have been happier for the next few years if even part of this programme and its strong emphasis on task analysis, sensory stimulation and behaviour management had been available.

However, in the early eighties the policy pendulum in Victoria swung diametrically away from creating more specialist services for children and young people with autism.

So, when I was eleven and that Centre could no longer cater for me, the choice was between highly staffed Special Developmental Schools which provided programmes for severely intellectually disabled students, Special Schools with eight or nine students to a teacher, or mainstream school, which was not an option.

The way schools were organised then, I could not imagine the point of an illiterate, non-speaking, screaming food-stealer in a Grade Six classroom.

Although I had realised that other children had left the Centre, I had thought I was safe. I had not noticed that I was out-growing the furniture and that lots of the other children now only came up to my armpits.

I was taken on several preparatory visits to my old Special School by the Centre teachers, found that I could stand in line and sit in class OK, and accepted that this was where I was going to be the following year.

Jay organised to pay for a taxi back to Margaret's house in the afternoon, as she would now be working too far away to chase the bus. In the morning, she and I would meet it at a stop from which she would then roar off to her new school.

***

I came back from camp two days before the new term, and the next day our family life was changed forever. I was sitting by myself on the living-room floor, drawing patterns, when suddenly the sea-grass sofa in front of me seemed to explode.

To me it seemed that I had done something to cause this. Only years later did I accept that the conflagration was because of a fault in the old speaker box behind the sofa. As always when in a frightening situation, I did not do what most people would. Jenny found half the room ablaze, and me looking quite calmly at this inferno.

'Lucy!' she screamed, grabbed me with one hand and Sheila's collar with the other, and dragged us both out of the house and to the local police station two doors away, where I was already well known as a retrieved escapee.

The rest of the family arrived at the same time as the fire engine, but already most of our home was a column of oily black smoke. Foam furniture certainly makes for dramatic special effects!

We all sought shelter where we could. Eileen and her husband Jeff opened their doors to Jay and me, but Jay could not expect them to cope with a food-stealing, bed-wetting, giggling dervish while she hunted for rented property and worked to make sense of insurance, as well as starting a new job.

For the next week she booked me into a Respite Care house that coped with six residents drawn from a wide range of seriously physically and intellectually disabled children.

This brought home to me my predicament as strongly as anything else. The staff were kind but could not compensate for the fact that I could only make the most rudimentary social approaches.

When I smiled, they thought I was happy and that I did not understand that my home was destroyed and my family dispersed among many friends. This was disorientating and humiliating. I still thought I was responsible for the disaster.

***

After a year in various rented houses, we moved back to the same site. The new house was clad in brick and had a long corridor running its entire length. Jay had insisted on this wasted space so that at last I had a running-up-and-down-space for my more mobile tantrums and rejoicings.

For the next few years, the family moved in and out, sharing houses or bringing boyfriends home.

One evening shortly before the fire, Val's best friend had set up a blind date for her with her own boyfriend's best friend. When Rolf, stocky, good looking, and, fortunately, very polite had come to pick Val up, Jenny (who as I said went through an *enfant terrible* stage) faced him over our table and grilled him as to whether his intentions towards her big sister were honourable.

Ever since that time Val had joined with Hayley and Kay in a burning ambition to torment her in the same way. A month after we moved to our new house, Jenny started to entertain a tall redhead.

For the next three months they sat on the grass strip between the road and the footpath most days after school. As the weather got cooler, I guess Greg got a little puzzled. Eventually they were driven inside by a downpour of chilly rain.

Jenny took one look at the Grand Jury lined up in our living room, and fled. I will draw the traditional veil over the next few minutes. Poor, poor Jenny.

***

My return to Special School was a watershed. My first two years there were not bad. I was in an Intermediate class, and Jay had managed to find a programme which funded a part-time aide for the first year. The curriculum was manageable as long as she was with me.

I did simple maths and copying, together with homecrafts, swimming and the other kinds of programmes one would expect in a school preparing people for as independent a life as possible.

The playground was another matter. Whether it was my imagination or not, I felt that my lack of speech was a cause for ridicule on the part of children who did speak. However, these children often still had abnormal speech rhythms, which further aggravated my problems with interaction.

So, I ran up and down the echoing quadrangle, giggling and swaying, partly aware that I was angry and ashamed.

I think that the Respite Care house and this experience made me realise that I was in a trap that I could not escape, and the future was one that was full of failure and fear.

That made it very difficult to control my autistic behaviours and even when I managed to do so I found it made very little difference from my point of view.

***

Jay started a message book as detailed as the one I had carried to and from the Centre, and the teachers responded with friendly notes, which reassured me that I was not just hanging in some void.

In my third year I was moved into a twenty-person teenage group, the 'Young Adults'. One of the teachers was my old friend, Mrs. Church. However, the guidelines for this level specified that students were to learn to be responsible for their own communication. There was no role for a message book, except when there were real problems.

***

Even with the change of schools, I still was learning. In an assessment a year after I left the Centre, a psychologist who had known me there said:

It would appear that Lucy has benefited from her Special School placement both socially and in gaining skills ... though she still needs individualised teaching for gains to be maintained.

(December 1984).

Without this kind of teaching, I was not able to take on board all the Special School offered. My giggling, hand-biting, angry-singing days seemed to the staff to be more frequent than my interactive co-operative ones.

They could not know that my comprehension was good enough for me to be distressed by television news or even drama, such as the episode in *Holocaust* where intellectually disabled people were loaded into a gas wagon. If my family had known that was going to be included, I certainly would have been in bed, even though they really believed that I could not follow a plot and that more complex concepts went right over my head.

***

AUTISM AND OTHER ADVENTURES: LUCY'S STORY

There were other factors in behaviour. Now I was no longer a child, so at this time my mother and sisters stopped tickling and chasing me, which compounded the effects of my missing the sensory integration from the Centre programme.

I might have eaten a collection of foods which had left me a headachy, giggly wreck.

Or I might simply have PMS, which in my case seemed to start days before, and then literally reach a crescendo on D-minus-3 as my sound-sensitivity rating went through the roof.

As my hormones curdled, I eavesdropped on Jay's discrete conversations aimed at finding some residential placement which still had an open waiting-list. It was becoming dramatically obvious to me that I was on a one-way street.

When we went to picnics with other children with autism, I looked at them and saw only what the rest of the world saw in me.

I truly believed that I was alone among this group in understanding what I could not express.

***

Also, I was beginning not to enjoy the Toy Library camps. Now we were adolescents, campers with more social skills than I, were more interested in dancing, or even a little bashful flirting, but that kind of interaction was impossible for me.

Although I recognised when it happened in our own home between my sisters and their boyfriends, I did not quite see the point of it. When one of the young male campers tried to chat me up, it only made me angry.

From the sex education and defensive social skills programmes at Special School, I had become very aware that my life did not have the same promise as my sisters'. I was with it enough to realise that I would not marry and have children of my own.

On those days when I was particularly fed up, I would sit around the house in view of all, doing the very things we had been discouraged from doing at school, pulling up my skirt, scratching my crotch or pushing my newly protuberant breasts in and out, while my sisters tried to make their visitors comfortable and simultaneously snarled at me.

***

I tended to be very inert at home. Because I had no instinctive urge to co-operate, I could not reach out halfway to take a glass or a garment from someone's hand unless I was told to do so.

My family got into the habit of putting a drink or a pair of jeans just out of easy reach so that my hand would stretch automatically to get what I wanted.

They would lay out the bare bones of a task I really wanted to do, like putting the various bits and pieces on a pizza base, and then retreat.

If they stayed to tell me what to do, I just went dead, because my auditory and visual processing did not coincide so that I did not realise they were talking about what I had already planned.

***

Unfortunately, in the philosophy of the Special School there was more emphasis on teaching a specific task, rather than analysing how I learned. I sat around at home in a state of adolescent inertia, feeling more and more bored and frustrated because my family was not synchronised with the Special School.

Movies and long drives cost money, and I went silly at things like Handicapped Guides and Riding for the Disabled. The most economical way of getting me moving was to continue with long walks. This also gave a Lucyless time, when the other girls could have friends round on a Sunday without my sitting in on all their gossip.

***

All my life I had dreaded falling asleep, because when I closed my eyes, I felt as if I were falling over a chasm. It did not matter if it was pitch dark. I was more comfortable with my eyes open.

From puberty this became worse, and, as I struggled to keep awake, my vision of what my future was to be curdled horribly with my tired desperation, and I screamed, sometimes till two or three in the morning. In desperation Jay looked around for a doctor who knew about the topsy-turvy world of autism.

***

Eventually Jay got a referral to a rarity, someone who was expert in both autism and adolescence. Dr. Weybridge's office was unfortunately a long way away, so every time we went there, Jay had to take time off work, often losing half a day's pay, and then thunder across town with our exhaust pipe rattling and the minimum number of spark plugs firing in the tinny, little yellow car which had succeeded the station wagon.

Jay would talk, the doctor would observe my irritability, flushed face and bitten hands, and how I would eventually sit my fourteen-year-old body in the play corner and draw, or fiddle with blocks.

This doctor was pretty good. I went home with a diagnosis of depression and a prescription for Tofranil. The medication did relieve some of my horrors, but left behind it a dull dread that was always with me.

This was invisible to both Jay and the teachers at Special School because Tofranil put me on a perpetual high, so that I giggled when

I would rather have cried and my existing reactions to certain foods were more disorientating.

At this time the three eldest had all moved out for a bit, leaving Jenny to take the brunt of my fourteen-year-old misery. The Tofranil dilated my pupils, and Jenny was frightened and distressed by what she called my 'seal eyes'. This was when she decided to leave home at the earliest opportunity.

***

Hayley and Laurie had been trundling up and down the east coast of Australia in an old Kombi van. When the northern summer rains started, they fled south again, arriving on our doorstep tanned, relaxed and hungry. Once again, the chords of Laurie's guitar competed with traffic noise and Jay's tuneless happy warblings.

Then they found a flat, so I was rather surprised when they arrived in a state of excitement on Christmas Eve. I sat and watched the television screen while an urgent conversation took place.

I don't think that Hayley or Jay realised that I understood the implication of the dates and symptoms that were being tossed around. This topic though had been spelled out clearly in Sex Education in Special School, and I guessed right first time. I was going to be an aunt.

***

At this time I was continually grappling with another and more subtle anxiety. I believed that I understood language and the world around me, but I lived in terror that this was a delusion and that I truly was a chaotic mute.

AUTISM AND OTHER ADVENTURES: LUCY'S STORY

The truth was not far away. My terror was suddenly to be scattered like so many dragon's teeth, to sprout and multiply into wonders and difficulties of which I had not dreamed.

Chapter 6
Language Without Speech: Age 14

I was fourteen years, four months and nineteen days old. The hot early-February summer sun saturated the main arterial road outside the converted old single-storey shop. I sat sweating on a sagging green vinyl sofa.

Through the old-fashioned deep-silled timber-framed window I endured the roar of trucks, some laden with containers coded to be loaded at or dispersed through the Port of Melbourne.

Scattered among the larger vehicles were cars, many with children as passengers being taken on end-of-holiday treats or to pick up text books for the new year. It was the last week of the summer school holidays.

The window itself was shaded by a bright yellow awning which curved outwards over the footpath, and which was economically emblazoned DEAL.

The frontage was the same striking yellow. This splash of colour clearly distinguished it from the panel-beating shop which occupied the other half of the building.

I had no idea why I was there. Jay sat stiffly beside me, rather embarrassed and vague as to what she expected from the appointment. I had heard her phone to make it straight after she had been speaking to the mother of one of the younger children whom I remembered from the Autistic Centre.

From Jay's politely controlled responses, I had gathered that the enthusiasm that had wafted down the wire had done nothing to convince her that this lady was not a crank. Afterwards I thought that she had simply phoned the Deal Communication Centre as being less embarrassing than having to admit later to this friend that she had ignored her recommendation.

AUTISM AND OTHER ADVENTURES: LUCY'S STORY

Now she was trying to keep me in one place by glaring at me, and occasionally snapped at me to sit quietly, as she tried to control my continual noises and to stop my leaping to my feet to run around and finger everything that was not fastened down on the temporarily unoccupied desk which dominated the room.

***

From what would have once been the living quarters behind the shop plunged a stocky plump person who took one look at us and swept us through the door from which she had emerged.

'Hi, you must be Lucy. Good afternoon Mrs. Blackman. Sorry to keep you waiting. I'm Rosie Crossley ...'

I puzzled briefly at the expression of enthusiastic determination framed by straight shoulder-length black hair. Then my memory reached back, positioning me on the carpet in the living room of my now totally destroyed childhood home, my father's cigarette smoke in my nostrils and on the television screen before me the same face.

Eight or ten years had not made her any less striking, and, even though she was not enclosed and diluted by a square glass bubble, I had no difficulty in understanding who this person was.

***

The next two hours were extraordinary. The preliminaries were similar to the multitude of language-based activities that I had been given over the years as far as the materials used were concerned.

However, there was an important difference. Such tests usually depend for their outcome on the child carrying out the nominated activity or speaking the word which represents the answer that most people would give, or on the onlooker observing the child pointing to or picking up the symbol or object required.

This woman had developed another approach. She watched my hand very closely to see if I were initiating the correct movement, or she touched my hand or wrist to feel from the action of my finger whether I was attempting to touch the correct symbol. She then prevented my losing the sometimes fleeting, impulse to reach in that direction.

***

Symbols were spread out in front of me. To my right a voice called out names, and under her touch I pointed with what felt to me like practised ease. But at some later point in this sequence, I knew that I was achieving a slightly different goal from previously and that this was completely different from having my hand moved to train me to touch some sign.

Here the action was initiated by me, much as I had once taken my sisters' wrists in my own toddler hands and placed their hands on the snack I could not unwrap.

***

For example, early in the session I was asked to indicate which was the symbol for the word 'triangle'. Paradoxically this was a shape whose name I could speak, whose shape I could indicate by the outline of my steepled forefingers and thumbs, and which I could even draw.

So, in most teaching situations, if I used any of these when I was shown a diagram of a three-sided figure, the person with whom I was working would think my answer meant, 'That is a triangle.'

That was not quite true, as I was making an answer that I had incorporated into my repertoire of automatic responses. Even if I had originally been taught to produce this response to approximate the expression, 'That is a triangle,' it had entered my non-language activities, and was something I simply understood as the thing to do if I were shown a triangle.

However, I did understand a lot about triangles. I had four sisters who had scattered maths exercises around the house, and for six years I had watched Margaret's girls work through the same material.

On this occasion it was the language stream which was self-taught through reading that I was processing, and it was in this convention that I was reaching for that symbol, to show that I understood what I heard, not as a knee-jerk reaction to completing some exercise.

It was a communication rather than performing a skill.

***

I was conscious of Jay on the other side of the table, at first wary, assuming testing would follow the usual pattern, that I would have progressively less and less success with word-based activities, and become passive and discouraged. Then, at about the same moment that I became aware that my own response was different, I had the feeling that she was slightly excited and a little more relaxed.

The adult hand on my immature adolescent wrist steadied it, and stopped when I stopped, following as smoothly as an oiled pulley when I tentatively tried to reach forward. So, I was not frightened by my own lack of control.

***

More importantly, I was aware that my message was processed instantaneously. It was five years later that I suddenly even suspected that this was part of normal spoken language and gesture, and that if one says something it is not communication unless one also has an innate understanding that the person on the receiving end is (and also should be) coded into the same convention.

I did not have any idea of this, just as I lacked the automatic responses that should flash around the body, bringing one's breath and gesture and eye direction together into that uniquely human characteristic — speech.

I learnt a little about this when I grew older and watched my nieces and nephews make their own first explorations of the spoken environment.

Also, I can now understand in a formal sense that questions and answers are linked, giving depth and meaning to each in turn. However, I cannot instinctively make a conversational answer by gesture, typing or vocalisation in many normal environments, unless I am with someone who monitors me as closely as the teacher who now was so responsive to my merest impulse.

***

The sense of reciprocity my new partner managed to impart was captured while the communicative movement which I was making was still flowing.

After all, in normal conversation you do not wait for the other person to complete the word, then analyse it, and give your permission to go on with the next. So, the answer to the question, 'Which is the triangle?' was mine, and my own signals were uncorrupted by uncertainty because her response was so natural and instantaneous that in turn it cut off the urge to change my wavering hand-direction into a stabbing movement towards shapes at random or to perseverate on any symbol occupying a certain position in each layout.

***

AUTISM AND OTHER ADVENTURES: LUCY'S STORY

The session continued — cards and books of pictures, numbers and letters in different colours and sizes. I was still reaching, touching and registering in my own consciousness that I was doing what I intended, and this in spite of my trying to break away and squealing.

The voice next to me called me pet names, and laughed at her own inability to make me comfortable, so I was not embarrassed when this happened.

For the way this large, kind, noisy person touched my shrinking hand and anticipated in her own where my finger wanted to go, as if she could feel the muscles and tendons start to contract, was itself a code breaker.

Physical touch and affection had always made me freeze slightly, but this whirlwind made me respond in the same way that a ride in a dodgem car leaves one so relaxed and stressed at the same time.

[This was also like] the way that the deep water of the swimming pool had released me from the thrall of gravity as a small child, so that I had been able to make eye contact with my sisters, and had been happy to be caressed.

The same lack of stress was present now when my arm was held, not to restrain me, but to give me control of my own hand in a partnership of body and will that most people take for granted.

***

So, part of my new ability was triggered by the reaction of someone with whom I was in close physical contact. In some way it seemed to compensate for my complete loss of spontaneous social interaction.

That I now know is not likely to develop in someone with autism who has not acquired useful speech while still a child. For social spontaneity to develop one needs reciprocity.

Even now I cannot give and receive cues that do not demand an enormous effort from a person who is standing or sitting in front of me. My answers to someone watching me anxiously are either an echo or a word which reflects my previous experience of that question.

But in that little room, sitting on a hard wooden chair, with visual language compensating for missing speech, and real physical interaction substituted for the impossible 'human' characteristic of social interaction, I was about to find real language.

***

On some cards were words at which I pointed. Some of these I had even learned to mouth in reading instruction when I was younger, but here I did not have to struggle with the incomprehensible mystery of why people wanted me to make noises in response to clear written words.

Then there was a pause. Early in the session I had been shown how to work a toy, a structure on which plastic penguins could move up and down in an endless clattering queue.

Rosie had now moved to shelves surrounding us, and, with her back turned to me, was sorting out bits and pieces of equipment.

The opportunity was not to be missed, so, like an iron filing to a magnet, I arrived at the opposite shelf so that I could again lay hands on this piece of enchantment. Jay started to look a little stressed but she exercised reasonable tact and remained a spectator.

My new teacher sat down again, glared, growled me back to the table and propped up in front of me a much less exciting device, a little box with a paper tape dangling from one side and letters in alphabetical order recessed on its surface.

This was a Canon Communicator, a very small simple typing machine that worked by printing on heat sensitive tape. This was completely new to me, and, because it was not identical to a typewriter in layout, and because I had never used an alphabet board to spell out my own language, I had no idea what was about to happen.

***

My partner placed her hand on mine again. This time I was not taken through as many steps. I pressed single keys through the little holes, and suddenly my finger felt again as if it were a willing agent of my mind.

In stabilising my hand Rosie had given me another gift. My hand and my mind were connected.

The eyes are in some ways a periscope between the mind and the outside world. As with a periscope, their effectiveness depends on compensating for wave movement and also the judder of on-ship activity.

However, my body, my mind and my senses had never interacted in quite the same way as my sisters' so I had some difficulty in knowing exactly what I could expect of all my bits and pieces, especially if I were trying to focus on, and also use, my hand in conjunction with abstract thought.

The steady touch on my own hand and forearm somehow made me bring it into focus, and at the same time feeling the point of contact gave me an accurate measurement as to the distance between my fingertip and my sensation of that touch.

***

So, I could disregard the rest of my body and concentrate on my hand and also on the obvious pleasure the teacher was experiencing.

The purpose of this strange little box was now becoming clear. The wavering end of my forefinger moved, prodding at the keys. My own first name, which I could already write accurately, came slowly through the slot as the tape jerked letter by letter as I pressed each.

In my ear a voice asked me to tell her my surname. The voice was not confusing because she did not want a spoken response.

Also, we were sitting so close together that I could register slight vibrations as she spoke — a deep, clear voice with reinforcement in my own skin. I was confident that what my ears heard was reaching me as she said it.

Helpful at the best of times, but added to my new confidence and the enveloping excitement at what I suddenly realised was a gap in my language barrier, it was clear. I typed the eight letters of my surname, a sequence I usually had to copy.

***

I worked through some questions fumblingly, with no spaces and many wrong letters but in words that were mine. Then in response to what I think Rosie would describe as 'hassling', my first real sentence.

The words arrived at my finger slowly — *'IWANTSMOOTHLIFE'* — a form which surprised me as much as my mother, tousled and flushed, facing us across the table with an air of combined excitement and scepticism.

The edge of Rosie's face filled the corner of my eye. She now was insisting that I answer a personal question which I really cannot remember.

Whatever it was, it resulted in the second sentence of my life. I, who could not speak my own thoughts, use pronouns or make comments except with concrete naming words, blurted out, letter by letter, an observation that I now see is as accurate as it is typical of autism: *'IRUNTIMEMYWAYNOT YOURS!'*

***

AUTISM AND OTHER ADVENTURES: LUCY'S STORY

I went back to school two days later. The remnants of my feeling of well-being evaporated at once. I stood in the enclosed quadrangle with the speech-sounds of the other students bouncing off the concrete walls around us.

The instructions of the teacher flowed towards me, and I felt that I simply had to take control of the situation in such a way that authority would be sabotaged, or at least delayed.

As usual I did not act to a plan, but rather allowed my acquired self-control to filter away. The quadrangle was hot. I was sweating in my shorts, and so I simply took them off, and then the panties I had under them, uninhibited by the amused comments of the larger boys and girls.

I would no doubt have gone a lot further if the staff had not intervened. And I was almost fifteen years old! Well, I certainly delayed my attendance at the next class, but I did not escape the consequences.

That afternoon Jay, scarlet in the heat, waltzed into Margaret's house which was dark behind the blinds lowered to keep out the boiling sun, to pick me up. Her voice babbled.

'Hello, Lu — Had a nice day at school? — Isn't it lovely and sunny — Yes, of course I remembered — We are going to have a swim in the municipal pool, as long as ... — Oh, perhaps I had better check for any notes in your message book ...'

No swim.

***

I was in the car, driven home and aware that I had done something that was completely beyond the pale. At least her response was reassuringly prompt and effective.

Back came a pair of dungarees from retirement, a double-pronged attack because, not only did I obviously dislike them (though they were not completely unfashionable), but the arrangement of the buttons on the shoulders was such that anyone supervising me had a little margin before I was completely naked.

***

For a fortnight life had a strange quality of unreality. Jay tells me now that she tried not to remember the impression of my wavering finger prodding at a keyboard and producing intelligent language.

The third day after my fall from grace I was allowed to select my own clothes for school. I thought that the meeting with Rosie was not to be repeated because no one said anything about what I had achieved in the way of self-expression on that one afternoon.

However, two weeks later we were back in that same room, with me sitting at that same table. I faced the keyboard and to my distress my hand typed the frustrating brand names I spilled out at home on the typewriter: '*SAFEWAY, SAFEWAY, WOOLWORTHS*'.

The atmosphere became more businesslike. To my relief I was offered something to keep in my mind's eye as a reward for co-operation. I typed: '*IWANTTOPLAYWITHTHEPENGUINSPLEASE*'. I was promised an opportunity to play with the penguin game later in the session. The teacher worked me as firmly as before and asked me to talk about my favourite television programmes. I typed: '*ISTARTEDWITHSESAMESTREETANDNOWI LIKENEIGHBOURS*'. Jay agreed that both were on in the house, but did not mention that I never seemed to pay any attention to *Neighbours*.

I did not make that statement to try and appear normal, but in the belief that by saying I liked the programme, I would become capable of liking it. I thought *Neighbours* was stupid, but the more able kids at Special School, and all the kids I heard talking outside school, loved it. I desperately wanted to be able to enjoy it because I thought this was another skill that I could acquire.

***

I had some kind of illusion that language shaped events. That of course is true for a child, because if an adult says something is going to happen it does, but, if one is a non-verbal child, the children who speak have the same magic power.

So, to lie about, or to predict, or to describe an event, whether I knew it was real or not, was in itself a cause of its becoming real.

***

My close contact with my teacher did not prevent my hand occasionally swooping down on the wrong key.

If that letter was a pathway to one of the words branded into my mind's eye, such as 'jeans', my finger would stand out from the surround, and the tip would hit the 'J' as swiftly and surely as a professional typist.

My jabbing finger could not change path in mid-flight on its own, but the totally different tempo and the slight rigidity of my hand must have sent out its own signal, so my partner would slow me down.

The sudden brilliant clarity of my hand would disappear, and I could rescue the word which I was struggling to express before it drowned in my mechanical fastening onto another meaningless symbol.

***

Halfway through this session another kid arrived who was a little younger than I. His hand was as uncoordinated as mine, or even more so, but like me he also typed real language when his wrist was supported. As he did, I heard Rosie's voice say to him as she had to me, 'Look at your hand, look at the keys!'

I had the first clue that the way I used my visual surround was different from other people, because here were two of us having to be asked continuously to do something our teacher thought was normal, but that we found so difficult.

Now I can understand that, even with my newly coherent touch, I saw the air as a barrier between my fingertip and the key, as I still do today to some extent — a barrier which could be slipped through when it was viewed obliquely.

It is only when I copy meaninglessly that I see with crystal clarity the path my finger is to travel.

***

I was becoming slowly aware that I was not drawing on the speech and written language work to which so much of my ten years of schooling had been devoted.

In fact, by bypassing these learned responses, I was tapping into my internal, spontaneously acquired visual language, as if I were an exile speaking her mother-tongue after a lifetime of struggling with alien words.

The bursts of sensible syllables among the erasures and errors on the tape which coiled from the side of the Canon were unmistakably not what I had been taught, but what I had learned.

There was another shock to come. The reading tests I had previously been given had relied on speaking words or small groups of words, or on card matching. Now I had the opportunity to glance quickly at a paragraph.

Then, still tracking my hand against the light grip of my teacher, I would point at one of several sentences randomly listed below to indicate which of them most accurately reflected what I understood to be the gist of the whole passage.

AUTISM AND OTHER ADVENTURES: LUCY'S STORY

Whereas slowly working word-by-word confused me and robbed me of the meaning, in this method I could not only show the other people in the room that I could read, but I could also prove it to myself for the first time.

Because I had learnt by observation with no feedback, I was not sure until now that I was really literate in the sense of continuous reading of texts.

***

After this appointment we were both pretty stirred up. Through Jay's spoken suggestion and my excited echo, we agreed to fill our faces at my second-favourite fast-food outlet. (McDonalds was being rationed to one in every four fast food meals as my Big Mac obsession was becoming completely out of hand at that time).

The little yellow rust bucket of a car rattled down the streets over protruding tram lines until we found an inflated illuminated red chicken sign.

The car windows were open, and, in deference to the occasion, what Jay thought was my favourite rock music throbbed around us to the disapprobation of people who stopped next to us at traffic lights.

***

We arrived home. Jenny took one look at me giggling, laughing and barrelling up and down the long narrow passage, and wilted. She was just starting Year 12.

That day she went out and bought a lockable chain for the door of her room, and, in spite of the chain, tried to think of as many hiding places as possible for library books and her work folders. Jay began to look tense in an excited kind of way.

***

We fronted up for another session at Deal. Jay made some rather lacklustre attempts to help me say something, and I worked through more reading and communication exercises.

My records describe my output as 'enormous quantities of tape', a bit of an exaggeration, but I did make a lot of words, and embedded among the repetitions and erasures were sentences which certainly originated with me:

'IAMTIREDOFCOMINGHEREWHENYOUBOSSME AROUND',
'IDONTWANTTOENDUPLIKEYOUJAY OLD' and
'IONLYGETBOREDWHENIAMWORKING'.

I was either trying to escape from an activity which I suddenly realised was going to call for a lot of effort on my part, or to goad the pair of them into making more effort themselves.

***

The whole of that year my behaviour and communication was erratic whenever I used a keyboard because I was in a state of shock that was almost physical in its intensity.

The conversation started to drag. Then I was asked what I thought about in my long hours of self-containment. I admitted to stories and poems, and eventually was induced to type out this rather gloomy little set of lines:

Even I'm not alone -
Not anyone can open my door
Till I want to be gone,
Leaving the prison for more
Ugly worlds walled with stone.

AUTISM AND OTHER ADVENTURES: LUCY'S STORY

That evening Jay and I arrived home with a borrowed Canon, a battery and a supply of thin white tape: a passport to language and to more problems than I ever dreamed.

***

The next day was Saturday, so we sat on two wooden chairs in the back bedroom facing a card table, in rough imitation of the set-up at Deal. There was a pause while Jay looked warily at me. My hand was in hers.

'What shall we talk about?' she chirped.

Irritated I began to wriggle. Her breathing got a bit more grating and her hand tightened to stop me pulling free. Suddenly I had that same sensation of mind and hand being compatible as the pressure on my hand gave it coherence in my lost personal view.

'What is your father's name?' Her opening gambit certainly lacked imagination. My forefinger reached in turn for the letters, first 'D' at the top of the bank moving my whole hand against my mother's clasp, then a slow reach to the left towards 'A'. Jay began to respond in a faint version of Rosie's reciprocity. Her hand easily accommodated to my forward movement, so she had no doubt where the move originated. Then the moment of truth. I had never independently written 'Dad' or 'David', but could speak 'Dad'. My finger swung waveringly down to the 'V' in the bottom left hand corner. I had the impression that she was surprised. I was typing '*DAVID*', a word I had never spoken.

The letters started to stumble, so the tape resembled an obscure code, now and then held together by fleeting recognisable syllables. The disappointment to my right was tangible.

***

Two hours later after a quick trip to the shop, she summoned me again. This time next to the Canon was a carefully laid out tally of Smarties as if I were again in my seven-year-old reading programme.

At that moment I was not particularly concerned that my adolescent dignity was being devalued. Rather I was reassured by my memory of the coherence of immediate reward following small success.

I jabbed at the second row of the alphabetical key board: '*FGHIJ*'. Jay glanced meaningfully at the chocolate beans, and pushed them out of my reach.

'*FAAFFAB WES AE # #*' The sheer effort of bringing my whole, intact visual language into the discipline of letter-by-letter expression was making me giddy, and focusing my eyes was not making things any easier.

My personality was being dismembered and reassembled, and I did not like it. There was a pause while I indulged in a mini-tantrum. Then, as often happened after I had pressed my open jaws hard against my hand, my perception briefly passed over the divide into coherent understanding. The language in my mind rearranged itself, and I had something that had to be said:

'*I#BITEMYHANDBECAUSEIAMCROSS*'

My finger moved on the keyboard and the tape printed the letters that I hit, with only one blob left by the erase button.

Of course, for my mother, who saw my finger linger on and depress the key, the symbol was instantly apparent, and I was aware each time meaning was starting to be formed from each group of letters.

True to her word my partner pushed eight gleaming delights across the table, one for each word.

Then, exhausted by my verbosity I kind of lost track, or rather my slight impulses became too fleeting for Jay to be sure where I was reaching:

'*HUEYDRODSTXHELPINSIDE*'

We both settled down to real effort. The next sentence was a series of little stabs interspersed with mis-strokes, and I can remember my feeling of triumph.

I was getting a reaction, explaining myself, and trying to make the point that I had been aware of my surroundings for a very long time, all at one hit:

'*LUCY###DIDNT BITEHERHAND#### BEFORESHEWENTTOTHE AUTISTICCENTRE*'.

The handful of chocolate beans dissolving deliciously in my bulging cheeks, I scampered from the room, leaving my partner contemplating the near and distant future — an adolescent daughter with a chip on her shoulder as inconvenient as a log of rainforest timber at a Greenpeace barbecue and with the means to express some equally inconvenient views.

***

Then back to the table. Resolutely we negotiated an alternative payment system.

'Obviously you are too old to be paid in chocolate beans,' said Jay. 'I think a cent a word is fair, and you say right at the beginning when we start talking what you are working for tonight.'

'*DONUT*'

'How much will that cost?' she asked.

'*FIFTYCENTS*'

So, we entered the cash economy. Jay had a pile of one cent pieces in front of her and a coin slid to my side of the table each time I completed a coherent word.

Basic questions — my teachers' names, then my sisters' full names: not their usual first names which I could mouth, but the longer names on their birth certificates and on enrolment forms for school which had littered our kitchen table at the beginning of each school term.

With glee I spelt them out. My address — no problems. That was on every letter collected from our mailbox. Our phone number? I humped and spun with the speed of a startled crocodile.

Rallying from the sudden metamorphosis Jay had a sudden thought.

'Oh, of course if you learned the words you type from things that were written down, you probably haven't seen it much. One doesn't often write down one's own phone number at home.'

So, she learnt that my sudden agitation had been caused by my own ignorance. Over the years she came to connect some episodes of sudden distress while typing with my not being able to answer a question, but wrongly she thought this was vanity.

In terms of everyday life, I continue to confuse two basic problems in passing information. This had been the very first time that I had had exact means of expression and yet not been able to give the answer to a question.

My conversation in my imaginary world till now had always involved realities of my own making. So, I roared and thrashed around. This behaviour is actually often interpreted as 'non-compliance' but now I can see that it is often triggered by problems generated by my odd way of learning.

***

In that first week Jay made a very understandable mistake. She tried dictating a few simple words to make me practise hitting certain keys.

'CAT MAT SAT FAT RAT BA ABAT CAT PAT ...' I protested noisily.

She tried another tack, and held up a richly illustrated collection of bound pages with a picture of some animals on the front.

'What is this?'

'*BOOK*' — Something was going right.

She flipped it open at random and we scanned a short paragraph.

'What is rhino horn made of?'

'*HAIR*'

'Good girl!'

'*FENAOP*', and then in explanation of my biting my hand, '*BECAUSEIDONTWANTTOBEGOODGIRL*'

'So, what *do* you want?'

'*LUCYISBRAINY*'

***

The next few weeks for me were a series of minor and major miracles.

I was in the kitchen and, as my hand reached towards the fruit bowl, I was aware of a presence behind me. I turned and spoke.

'Bea.'

A word so clear to me, but the first sound of so many things as heard by anyone else. Before me appeared that little box from which I could grind out words, while an uninvited hand held mine over the keys.

The word was in my mind, and the thought had passed my lips. I saw no reason to go through the discomfort of printing out five letters when we both knew what I wanted. Jay was implacable — no typing, no peach. I typed, but once again not without protest.

Having endured this scene while *Neighbours* was on, Val, who had been sitting in the family room next to the kitchen, abandoned the television for a more pleasant environment and we heard her bedroom door close.

She would probably be sitting on her bed with a glossy romantic paperback on her knees, while her new engineering texts lay open on the desk. Who cared? I certainly did not.

My teeth quickly stripped the flesh from the clingstone peach so I could have the bonus of splitting and splintering the rock-hard pip.

Such fun, because I knew that the kernel was supposed not to be good for me, though the hundreds I had swallowed over the years did not seem to have harmed me.

Instead of putting out her hand as a cue for me to pass the peach stone over, or telling me to put it in the bin, Jay spoke rather offhandedly.

'I guess you know that is supposed to be poisonous. Well, if you are so bright, make your own decision.'

The tone of her voice was so like that which she used when Jenny, now seventeen, did not eat breakfast that I was both disconcerted and proud.

I gnawed a bit more on the intact woody lump before turning from the kitchen bench. As I started to move, the stone left my hand, its chewed yellowed shape resting damply beside the fruit bowl, more as a token of appreciation than anything else.

I was getting more satisfaction out of occasionally behaving 'properly', but I only felt that way if someone was watching and showing some sign of approval, even if that sign was unconscious.

Looking, grabbing and fomenting chaos were still much easier, more fun, and often an automatic response to what in another person would have been an urge to speak.

AUTISM AND OTHER ADVENTURES: LUCY'S STORY

***

The evening typing sessions by now were routine, and I was slowly learning they were worth the effort. The rather waffly comments that I made about other people like, '*SHE IS SILLY*' or '*I LOOK ODD TO OTHER PEOPLE*' made my partner understand that to some extent I was aware of things that happened in everyday life, even if my reactions were a bit weird.

Then I began to understand that typing could be very profitable from my point of view. I did not realise that Jay had decided that I had to learn that typed language *worked*. It was she who paid the price for the first large-scale demonstration.

The Easter school holidays were looming, and so were five days for me in respite care to give Jay a break. More than anything I wanted not to be in a group with a whole lot of people who were even more incomprehensible than my school-mates, and with staff who were kind but thought my understanding was mirrored by echolalia.

When I suddenly typed: '*IDONTWANTTOGOTOTHATHOUSEAT EASTER*', the hand on my wrist went very still for a moment.

Then without a word she got up from the table, picked up the phone and cancelled the holiday booking. I was more than pleased. I was suffused with achievement. I had discovered that the word, as spread by my finger on that Canon, was mightier than my most unpleasant behaviour had been to date.

***

We went to Deal about a dozen times in all. As Jay could not leave work early, Hayley, by now beige-green with continual morning sickness, would drive over from the flat they had just rented, pick me up from Special School and then take me on to a four o'clock appointment.

When Val did not have an afternoon class, hers would be the face over the table while I answered questions, worked on expression, and got used to putting spaces between words.

There were times when Jenny in her blue check summer school uniform came too.

Kay had gone off on a long jaunt with a friend and was currently in Kings Canyon in the Northern Territory, so she was excused.

The three who did come to the sessions felt my hand move to form language, and at home I then was able to make occasional phrases with them.

However, with little idea of what was hurtful and what was not, I managed to upset each in various ways as I typed what I thought were loving attempts at personal humour ('*YOU SILLY BITCH*') or tried to fumble my way through explanations of how I had felt ('*HATE YOU*') when they had assumed my understanding was limited to baby-talk. I was relearning my world with my own, but Kay was missing. Somehow it was a little less satisfying that way.

***

Those sessions at Deal made for some wonderful discoveries. The figure games I had been playing in my mind were real mathematical calculations. The speculations I had made when I glimpsed temperature scales and descriptions of how experiments were set up in my sisters' science books were quite valid. I wrote poetry with my new teacher and luxuriated in the sheer pleasure of being the centre of attention — none of which made me any easier to live with.

At about five o'clock the old glass-paned wooden street door would sound its opening and closing. Sometimes I could hear a familiar voice saying, 'Hi, Jean. How are you?' to the lady who sat at the front desk, followed by a blurred exchange of conversation.

Then Jay would come into the inner room. When this happened, I was less anxious in one sense because all was going according to plan, and, if I were working, was content to continue.

However, when she and Rosie put their heads together and started discussing the next step, I occasionally got confused by the two voices talking speculatively about me and the future. The future as a certainty was bad enough, but when the words 'perhaps' and 'what if?' were thrown about, I was basically panic-struck.

Even when they talked about what I had been doing in everyday life, I was bewildered, and I had to move and even stand at a distance, or run up and down the passage which led to the kitchen at the rear of the shop building.

I was now a participant in the world of language, but I had not progressed far enough to make the distinction between what had happened and what was being said, almost as if the episode was being relived in another dimension.

When my two new language partners, Jay and Rosie, sat down together, I felt much the same discomfort as when the former picked me up from child-minders and my two worlds briefly touched.

***

The next months at home I found I was being taken more seriously in some ways. Having run out of conversation, and having also found I did not appreciate exercises designed to teach communication, Jay brought home selections of Years 7 and 8 text books from her school library.

There was now a pile of English grammar and comprehension books stacked by the Canon each evening. I knew what they were as I had seen them in various school bags and spread open in homework sessions.

Automatically I answered the questions in full sentences or as single words prefaced by the letter or number of the question, as if I were presenting them for homework in the same way I had seen them answered by the others.

I knew no other way. This is how one coped with such material. At last, I could enter the realm of 'real' schoolwork, and in most instances I was prodding the correct answers out of the Canon.

This is not to say that I rushed joyfully to the keyboard each evening. The sessions were still basically initiated and run by my partner, Jay.

I always spoke 'No!' when I was asked to type, but I was blissful beneath my protests when she marched me down the corridor and opened the book. The Canon lay on the table before us, and she gripped my right wrist in a hand like a bolted manacle made of the most responsive Lycra elastic.

The muscles of my previously random index finger ached, but after a few days we managed without the word-by-word rewards, and I simply received pocket money which I could ask to be spent as I wished.

***

There remained one extraordinary mystery. This miracle had unfolded, but I had no idea why it was so impossible to make any sensible words except at Deal or with my immediate family.

What I did not realise then was that, when I tried to plan its movement, I was unaware of the exact position of my fingertip in time and space, much as I was uncomfortable walking on slopes because my foot and my sight were sufficiently out of sync to make me uncertain as to the exact moment my sole could start to bear my weight.

AUTISM AND OTHER ADVENTURES: LUCY'S STORY

Rosie was experienced in working with people with similar difficulties and my family were learning to anticipate my less obvious mini-impulses and stabilise my hand.

I was not learning to type. I was learning to help other people to enable me to stumble around the keyboard so that I could use my underdeveloped internal language in the way I thought speech and writing were used by everyone else.

Chapter 7
Life With Typed Language, 1987: Age 14

The Special School may not have considered the Communication Book an important part of the Young Adults programme but Jay often churned out chatty little missives in answer to prosaic notices about excursions and fees. To make them more legible she used an old mechanical typewriter.

I had been playing with this for the past couple of years. I simply copied anything which caught my eye, or reproduced the names of shops and the brand names of jeans, much as I had not been allowed to on that second occasion that I had used a Canon Communicator, which was when I had met the boy who also did not look at the keyboard.

While Jay was still reeling from her first tentative experience of feeling me form phrases on a keyboard, in the Communication Book there was a notice from the Special School which required an answer. Mrs. Church had written:

Every Monday Lucy has Home Crafts - no lunch required. This is covered by the Home Craft levy you have paid. Every Wednesday we are cooking lunch in our room. If she doesn't want to cook lunch on Wednesday, she can bring her own lunch.

(17 February 1987).

My flippant parent answered, tongue in cheek as usual:

Which of us Kamikaze volunteers is going to tell Lucy she doesn't 'want' to cook lunch on Wednesdays?

She added a postscript that went on for a couple of pages:

AUTISM AND OTHER ADVENTURES: LUCY'S STORY

Not to do with day-to-day routine ... Deal Communication Centre ... appointments late in the holidays and last Monday ... my scepticism ... expressing herself relatively fluently ... not a smooth session ... Keyboard ... Just doesn't use spoken language this way ...

This was the first clumsy step in what was to be a convoluted marathon of correspondence.

***

What I was producing might be fluent language relative to my spoken bumbling about, but Jay was yet to learn that practice would not make perfect in this respect, and that my comments about other people and their actions were as much the product of my own intellectual construction as a record of what had really happened.

So, in blissful ignorance of the quicksands ahead, in the last sentence of the note she stuck out her neck:

By the way, what did they make in Home Crafts on Monday this week?

The answer was terse, having been scrawled while Mrs. Church was trying to pay attention to several disorganised teenagers. It also was a crashing disappointment:

Pancakes and fruit salad.

Jay stopped in her tracks and redeployed her enthusiasm:

When we asked her at Deal on Monday, 'What did you make in Home Crafts today?', Lucy keyed in

'Just sandwiches.' Obviously not the right answer, but I have never heard her respond like that or use that kind of phrase, and 'sandwiches' was spelled right.

***

It is not surprising that I could not make my answers fit the facts. My fourteen years without useful interactive conversation had meant that I had grown up with overlapping craters in what I did with statements, questions, suggestions, speculations and negatives.

Home Crafts was fun. However, I often did not like the food. I had fixated on my own plastic-wrapped sandwiches. I made these myself every day, and always carried them to school, even on cooking days. This avoided the terror I felt when something was missing.

So, when Rosie and Jay had posed this question, my answer was fine, but it did not occupy the same area in my processing as what had really occurred in my day. After all, I had never acquired a language key to remembering how things had been, except in the most chaotic and unformed sense.

On top of all this, Jay had also to explain that I had only tapped out these earthshaking scraps of language with my hand held in someone else's larger paw. My sensation of someone's physical response was equivalent to the reinforcement I had needed from Samantha to unlock my stirred-up memories of the Clown Show.

***

I see now that people who worked with me successfully were those who developed a real skill in monitoring and controlling their own interactions. This allowed me to get excited enough by their interest to create some kind of language, without giving me any cues to act as I thought the other person expected me to.

At that time, though, my own successes and failures all seemed to me to be rather hit-and-miss, and I was very confused as to what I was expected to achieve.

***

AUTISM AND OTHER ADVENTURES: LUCY'S STORY

Jay's sharing the information about my experiences with the keyboard was not my idea. I disapproved for a number of reasons. All these questions about my daily activities arrived in my language centres uninvited. In logging my achievements and errors, I felt that Jay had betrayed a mother-daughter pact.

Also, I could really not offer any reason why my answers did not come up to her expectations. This was partly because I had not learned that questions were asked so that someone else could reconstruct a real-life scenario from words that I formed.

Conversation among other people, stories read aloud while I was shown the pictures, television serials and movies often overlapped in the same imaginary world, and when I had started to construct stories in my own head during our long walks, it was simply opening another door into that world.

I had little discrimination as to what was my invention, what was the fiction of others, what was my understanding of the real world as I knew it, and what was the factual information so valued by my new communication partners.

***

My own mental processing of words and their relation to meaning was sadly awry. When I fumbled for the lettered keys after someone asked a question, I foregrounded what I immediately thought of, and it landed in whatever spot it was inside my skull that my typing urge was starting to develop.

That snagged image promptly became my answer. I confused the word which I saw in my mind's eye and what I wanted to express.

If the hand on my wrist did not interfere with my autistic perseveration just enough to force my thoughts to sort themselves out, the sequence of letters that I formed when I felt strongly enough about this rejected choice might even be the direct opposite of the correct answer. Mistaken inhibition by the hand on mine could be as effective a prompt as a spoken suggestion would be.

However, intentional pushing on my hand only served to confuse me, because I could not understand that other people thought that I would learn to communicate by being shown what to do.

This had not worked in practical things, and speech had not developed when others modelled words, which is why conventional speech therapy had created communication problems of its own. This skill was no different. Special education myths seem to have a high casualty rate when confronted with autism.

***

However, Jay was learning extraordinarily fast for someone who was forty-five, which in my opinion was almost prehistoric.

She had gone on to write to Mrs. Church:

I am sure this is not a complete key to opening a different door for Lucy, but it may make her a less frustrated person over the years. Certainly, I think that it is something which will have to happen only because Lucy wants it to.

That last sentence was ambiguous. She meant that I would not co-operate if I did not think that the enormous effort she saw me making was worthwhile.

She also realised that my inability to finger letters spontaneously in a way which was genuinely meaningful was not due to reluctance or some problem in my subconscious.

She had guessed that the tension and focus generated by the other person in the partnership was a factor in my creating the language-based movement which genuinely expressed my thoughts.

AUTISM AND OTHER ADVENTURES: LUCY'S STORY

***

After the weekend that the Smarties-for-typed-words bribery had worked so brilliantly, Jay made a decision which changed my life, mainly because it did not produce the results that she planned.

On Monday morning she stuffed the borrowed Canon in my school bag, and placed another note in my Communication Book:

Please could you phone me ASAP, today if possible, re Lucy & Communicator. Better you to phone me than my interrupting your only cup of tea or coffee - Jay

(4 March 1987).

I am not sure what exactly was said over the phone. However, it seemed to bring results:

Dear Jay,
We are going to DEAL on Thurs 12th at 9.30

(5 March 1987).

***

So, I went down to Deal with Mrs. Church, and sat and typed with Rosie. After that they talked across me and discussed how wonderful it would be if I could explain what was upsetting me when I felt so distressed that I had to scream or giggle. Mrs. Church did not have the knack:

Dear Jay,
I have tried working with Lucy but got nowhere. She turned off completely. Not unusual. We will keep at it. – Mrs. Church

(13 March 1987).

***

I was terribly disappointed by my failure to type with my class teacher. Because I heard people talk about a special rapport that

I seemed to have with Rosie and Jay when I typed, I had begun to make the same mistake that they did, which was a kind of emotional thing, shored up by my own faith in them and their confidence in my competency.

Of course, if this confidence and faith had not been partially evident at that stage, I could not have communicated, much as an inept speaker of a foreign tongue cannot keep their train of thought going without feedback that they are making sense to their audience. However, that was only one part of an equation which had a number of complex components:

Dear Mrs. Church,

When I started, I operated a system of short-term rewards. We really only used these for a couple of days. In terms of attitude and effort, as a long-term incentive I have promised her a denim jacket if I receive reasonable reports of a co-operative attitude in communication sessions over the next three weeks.

Jay
(15 March 1987).

***

Jay had more understanding of the process than I had, though it was unconscious at this time. She knew that people working with me had been aware that I was intelligent and had been frustrated by their own inability to make me achieve.

Therefore, my success at Deal must be due to some specific skill on the part of Rosie as teacher. So, Jay had deliberately started off by mimicking Rosie's speech patterns, behaviour management and timing to see how best to replicate the conditions under which I produced language.

I think that Mrs. Church believed that she was teaching me, so she did not allow herself to be used as a crutch and a reflection of my movement. She was so much a teacher that I was never in control.

Again, she asked for guidance:

Dear Jay,

Do you direct her hand, or let her go? I have supported her wrist or forearm, but little direction

***

Dear Mrs. Church,

I asked Lucy about where she liked her arm held, and in effect she 'said' with the supporting hand flat under her forearm or elbow.

When she really has steam up, or when I want to be sure I am not 'leading', I put my hand under her elbow, rather like helping a frail person who needs balancing.

However, she cannot go on for long like this. In the beginning I held her wrist firmly, so it might pay to try this. Don't let her continue with 'rubbish' if possible.

***

Over the next few weeks Jay continued to explain what she thought she was doing, though I suspect that she was as confused as the rest of us:

Here is part of last night's conversation. When she started getting in a tangle, I would stop her and growl. She would then pick up again. Sometimes it gets three or four goes to get something out.

The Canon is a communication device, and it is not a matter of presentation. Sometimes, to indicate when we understand the word that is being typed as soon as the sense of it is clear, so the whole process is rewarding.

She then goes on to the next. Other times I try to get her to complete each word for practice.

Jay enclosed some tape from the previous evening to illustrate what she had written:

This is Lucy's part in a two-way conversation about what she wanted most:

ONEDOLLAR GRENTSHIRT YES HAMBURGERS ICECREAM MO JELLY

Then what was my long-term goal?

MEANTOSOUNDINTELLIGENTONCOM[MUNICTOR]

That might be a long way off. Justifiably Jay and Mrs. Church both guessed that my stomach was to be my chief motivation for some time to come.

***

My appointment with Dr. Weybridge was due. Jay and I sat side by side on the sofa in his office.

'Something rather odd has come up.' Her voice was diffident.

She gave a potted account of my adventures and misadventures with the Canon. Somehow the word 'voracious' came up. I think I must have grinned because they would have been talking about one of my less socially acceptable activities.

'Lucy,' said the doctor suddenly. 'What is the difference between 'veracious' and 'voracious'?'

I smirked inside. That was what I thought typing was for — showing how smart I was, not answering stupid questions about real life.

'*TRUE GREEDY*,' I keyed in, to Jay's amusement. The doctor looked at me consideringly.

'What does the school think?'

Jay explained the problem.

Dr. Weybridge nodded and later contacted my teacher. The Communication Book started to be as full as the one which had travelled to the Autistic Centre.

AUTISM AND OTHER ADVENTURES: LUCY'S STORY

***

At home I was getting much more fluent and accurate on the Canon, as long as the questions only dealt with knowledge I had picked up, and not with real life. We had just read through a passage which mentioned Athens. Out of the blue Jay threw a question in my direction.

'Who was Homer?' she asked.

'*HE WAS A BLIND POET.*' That was easy. My disorganised mother had not remembered that a couple of years earlier she had strewn a lot of picture books containing the stories of the Iliad and the Odyssey around the house in preparation for torturing some young twentieth-century persons by standing at a chalk board and interpreting this great classic in her illegible scrawl.

'What did he write about?'

'*TROY.*'

'What happened to Troy?'

'*IT WAS ATTACKED BY THE GREEKS.*'

'Why?'

'*HELEN RAN AWAY FROM HER HUSBAND?*'

'Who was Cassandra?' Jay had obviously decided to show me that I was not all that smart.

'*A PRIEST WHOM NOONE BELIEVED.*'

She almost said something. Then she changed her mind. I think that, in that instant, she had decided that I had to be treated with the respect due to someone who could understand the concept of intellectual effort.

'Do you want to add anything?'

'*PRIESTESS.*'

By this time, she had remembered where I might have gleaned this stuff. She started to throw up questions which were designed to test the kind of general knowledge which one learned in the community.

'Who was Joseph?' I think she was expecting an answer that I would have picked up from nativity plays.

'*A MAN WHO WAS SOLD BY HIS BROTHERS.*'

Oh, that Joseph!

'To whom?'

'*THE EGYPTIANS.*'

'What happened to him.'

'*HE BECAME VERY RICH.*'

I was well away, and smirking at her amazement.

'What happened after that?'

'*MOSES LED THEM TO CANAAN.*'

'What happened to Moses?'

'*HE DIED BEFORE THEY GOT THERE.*'

'Where did you learn about the story of Joseph and Moses?'

I had known that story for ages, probably from the *Good News Bible*, which my sisters had been given and which I had partially digested and then mutilated in my accustomed manner, or even from a picture book.

However, I was beginning to cast myself into scenarios which I thought other people would accept. I threw up an answer which I felt fitted the occasion.

'*AT SPECIAL SCHOOL.*'

'When?'

'*LAST YEAR.*'

That seemed to be an acceptable answer, because I felt a slight relaxation in Jay's anxious tension, and I chalked up a mental note that she was worried about my apparently unbelievable general knowledge.

***

Overall, I remained frustrated, upset and confused. I had assumed that if I were ever able to express myself in real language, my life would immediately be transformed. Fat hope! At Special School I was stuck in the same mire. However, I thought I knew how to escape.

I remembered a conversation about a school where parents had removed their children because one of the men running the programme had done certain things.

I had not quite grasped that this kind of professional misconduct had actually had to have taken place, and, of course, that it had to be proved that it had happened. It was not enough that somebody else had said the words that indicated that a person had committed a crime.

I simply had no idea that speech and other language did not create a fact. Also, I did not comprehend that there could be appalling consequences from these types of accusations, though I had caught enough adult soaps on television to realise that harassment, and its more serious cousins, caused major dramas.

Fortunately, this brain-child was still-born. Jay looked at the tape I had just typed and asked for details.

'When did this happen?'

An unanswerable question. Her stony approach threw me into confusion. I bit my hand.

She was far too experienced in working and living with fourteen-year-olds to ask leading questions, and, in the absence of cues and clues, I was thrown into a panic.

Initially she assumed that this was because the topic distressed me. Teacher that she was, she took things slowly. Three weeks later she was still probing in a gently off-hand kind of way, and beginning to feel more than a little sceptical.

Then Kay reappeared from the Red Centre. My stored-up resentment had another target. I invented a piece of non-existent sister-to-sister cruelty with which to accuse her.

'What do you think I am! Do you really think I would treat Lucy like that?' she screamed at Jay.

Jay went straight to the keyboard, sat down and held my wrist. There was precious little maternal warmth evident, and I was stiff with anger.

'Well?' she growled.

'*I WAS CROSS WITH KAY FOR DROPPING OUT.*'

A stillness beside me.

'And that business at school?'

'*I HATE SPECIAL SCHOOL.*'

Problem solved, and I was a little wiser, though I really could not see why she was so angry, and why after that Kay would barely look at me for some years to come.

***

Dr. Weybridge suggested a class for less impaired students. I was to go into 'Senior W', a class of more able adolescents taught by a Mrs. Wong. I was enthralled by this, and by the lightweight plastic electric typewriter Jay had bought.

I was totally determined to write a novel, a potentially hard-hitting drama of inner-city life. Jay was less than enthralled by my creative urge. However, she was on her 'Let-Lucy-use-typing-in-as-many-ways-as-possible' trail, so she went along with my ambitions.

No sooner had I sat down and typed the first few words and errors which comprised the first phrase of this great work, than I screamed in terror, and tried to backspace.

The minute LCD screen had filled with the first sixteen letters and spaces I had typed. Now the beginning of that line was shunted into limbo to accommodate the next word. I was aghast. This was just the same as having my hair cut when I was small, or not being able to hear myself sing when other voices drowned me out.

For the next two sessions, in the interest of her own sanity, Jay allowed me to work in tiny lines. She turned the paper-feed knob each line, just before I got anxious, but after thirty or forty words on incoherent monologue, which was my idea of a drug-induced reverie, her patience blew.

As this is a sample of my efforts, I can hardly blame her:
DRUG YUNI IOPT
FHABITS HAVE DONE
THEIR HAVOC AND
GIVEN ME THE JITTERS
FUN REALLY USES YO
U UP FIRST YOU HAV
EURGENT NEED TO ...

***

'This is not the time for the Great Australian Novel,' she snarled, her hand tightening on mine. 'And, what is more, you can scream the place down, but you are going to type in full lines.'

Her predictions were equally accurate. We went back to English comprehension exercises. I answered in full sentences. I did scream, but, because she prevented me from manually turning the feed knob, or removing my right hand from where it was suspended over the keys, I went on typing long enough for the automatic carriage-return to work.

The beginning of the lines travelled out of sight, and more screams travelled out of the open window, presumably to the concern of any neighbours within earshot.

In time I was to realise that, as the last space before the end margin was reached, the travelling ribbon-carriage passed across the paper on the platen, and that the whole line really did still exist, and all was well — until the next time!

***

Once I started to see my own sentences as they rose out of the depths of the typewriter, I typed visualising myself as another person talking to the Lucy who I had been for so many years. I had often felt as if there were a second person within my own head when I had imagined using speech. Typing fell naturally into the same pattern.

When Jay saw this conventional written language appear, she thought I was using it like other teenagers do. She did not realise that I typed more fluently if I imagined I was sitting above my own body, watching, as another Lucy would, a new character, also called Lucy, going through the motions that all other literate people did. It was as if I were role playing.

My language use was expanding, and quite suddenly I was producing paragraphs which read as if I had been writing formally for years. I was incredibly proud of myself, and, when my temper was reasonably even, I could be persuaded to make a few comments about the previous week.

The first of these 'diary entries' was to celebrate my promotion to 'Senior W'. This was typed in upper case, but the full stops were all in the right places. Later I used lower case, and sometimes would insert capitals spontaneously, though occasionally I added a few extra as my finger on the shift key went on automatic pilot:

I learnt to make fruit tarts on Tuesday in Trade Kitchen, and this was a good example of making food for lots of people because we made a big batch. We fitted pillows into bags on Friday afternoon at a factory for Work Experience. This is tiring but satisfying. Sunday [I] felt sick, so I stayed home and Hayley and Kay came to see us. This was the best week I have had for a very long time.

AUTISM AND OTHER ADVENTURES: LUCY'S STORY

(Diary, Week ending 9 May 1987).

***

The euphoria did not last. After another fortnight the same old problems had cropped up. I was too bright for the academic work that we were offered, but in class I could not write or type the simplest word, nor add a column of tens and units, though I could whirl them through my head in a happy galaxy of combinations.

My diary persona held forth in the rather stilted language I had absorbed from Val's favourite historical romances:

I spent this week at school reading pretty silly stuff. Vow and declare I am sick of school as you can guess. Dare I hope that one day I can get to go to a real school. Give a thought to being adventurous.

During the week Jenny lost her temper with Val and said some awful things because Mum got mad with Val who lost her temper. No sense in all people. Could books have such characters?

Someone has to work to set us free. Don't you think so? Reaching out is the hardest thing because I feel stupid.

(Diary, Week ending 29 May 1987).

***

'Feeling stupid' in this context meant my body, my mind and my eyes felt completely uncoordinated when anyone made eye contact, or expected me to communicate just for the fun of it. I still had to be compelled to do what I wanted to do most, which was to type to show my brain could make language.

Jenny: *As a child I found Lucy fun to live with. Then in my mid-teens I started to think, 'Oh, shit - this future thing.' Then the Communicator came on the scene.*

I had been so used to perceiving Lucy as this retarded person, and, all of a sudden, I had to change my whole viewpoint of her, and accept that she is more intelligent than I am. I had to come to terms with that, and with the questions that other people asked me, 'How is it that she can be so intelligent, and yet do all these strange things?'

Plus, coping with the fact that every second word I got from Lucy at that time was something like, 'You're a bitch, you're a slut, you're awful!' That started the second time she used a keyboard with me.

Then in the middle of the year, I just said, 'You've got to accept that I knew you in that way. Now I've got to treat you differently. If you don't pull your socks up, I'm just not going to try.'

That explosion was not just with me. Val was there, and there was a God Almighty row between Val, me and Lu who was using the Communicator.

(Tape recording of family meeting, June 1993).

***

That row between Jenny and Val was fuelled by tension which we all suffered that year. In working more intensively with me, Jay had upset the balance she had managed to establish between the competing elements of the family.

Also, Jenny in particular was mourning the loss of her innocent uncomprehending baby sister.

***

In one of my appointments with Dr. Weybridge, I asked him to help me stop biting my hand, because this seemed to make other people upset, and sometimes Jay winced when I did so. Her face would close up, and she would struggle to appear calm and unimpressed.

The doctor suggested attempting to make it less rewarding by applying anaesthetic cream and Band-aid to that spot, so I did not feel the bite.

AUTISM AND OTHER ADVENTURES: LUCY'S STORY

I hated the smell and feel of the ointment, even by itself. The Band-aid was unbearable, because my skin flashed out warning signs at the points where the adhesive took hold. So, after two tries I stripped it off.

However, it left an enduring legacy. If I bit my hand and someone reacted, I had a kind of memory-flash and my mouth would utter.

'Band-aid, Cream! Band-aid, Cream!' I would chant. My family and teachers did not fall into this trap, but a sympathetic person who had not learnt that this was not a request for medical attention to my tattered hand would apply some antiseptic, and back it up with a good dose of Tender Loving Care. What attention I did get increased that wonderful feeling of painful completeness to the point that hand-biting became even more irresistible.

***

Mrs. Wong was liaising with the doctor. She also had trips to Deal to see me working there, and to find out more about the process of dragging language out of my jabbing finger.

Jay continued to pour out typed exhortations. Poor Mrs. Wong replied conscientiously, but after a while we seemed to have reached an impasse.

At home I was using more and more language on the keyboard, or even on home-made letter boards, but was only copying set work at school.

When the teacher held my hand, she expected me to crave to communicate as if I were an ordinary person who had been prevented from talking.

However, I really had no speech structure and conversational impulse. My language was a patchwork of phrases which I sampled, much as a wine-taster does a group of glasses.

When I managed to produce them, I felt instinctively when some of these typed expressions fitted smoothly into the slot in which I had dropped them. It seems to me that it was at the instant that the other person recognised this success that we achieved some kind of reciprocity which was not unrelated to 'normal', non-autistic conversation, an experience that the toddler Lucy had never had.

In those sessions with Mrs. Wong, the hand on my wrist was calm, firm and self-contained. In real terms my social impairment is still so severe that I doubt whether I would ever have responded to this approach.

She did not excite and irritate me to the point that the internal language spots could enter my visual processing and motor movements. Rosie had exhorted and laughed, and Jay now bribed, giggled and growled in a tempo she had deliberately invented.

I could almost borrow their reactions to enhance my own awareness of what my body and mind was doing. This liberated my attention just the right amount for at least some of my typed words to be intentional.

Mrs. Wong used her normal quiet patience, which was great when I wanted to learn by listening, but which left my body unexcited. As it was, I did not particularly want to type with anyone at Special School. All I wanted to do was to shake the dust of the place from my shoes forever.

Mrs. Wong was getting a bit desperate:

Dear Jay,

Dr. Weybridge and I decided the fact that she won't use her communicator for personal 'talks' at school may be 'cos she doesn't trust me as she does you and Rosie. To develop this trust (or to attempt to), I am going to spend forty-five minutes alone with Lucy sometime during each day. I shall report any changes back to Dr. Weybridge.

(Mrs. Wong. 13 May 1987).

AUTISM AND OTHER ADVENTURES: LUCY'S STORY

Jay answered soothingly:

Dear Mrs. Wong,

Don't feel that all my communication with Lucy is meaningful. It usually means something, but isn't necessarily world-shaking, and sometimes is definitely censurable. Some days we barely say anything to each other. But then, how many really significant conversations does one have with the early-mid-teenager ... !

***

Thank goodness my teacher gave Jay the benefit of the doubt. Another bonus was Jay's embarrassment. 'Senior W' headed home most nights with homework, so Jay felt obligated to push ahead and make me do this.

I was not impressed by this material compared with the English comprehension work and simple algebra that Jay provided from her library, but for the first time I had no escape from what I was told to do.

Usually, I could sabotage any task I was given through behaviour or incompetence. For example, the next time we had gone to the pillow factory I was still feeling unwell. The combined scents, sounds and fluorescent lights of the warehouse had sent me right off. I had bounced on the pillows, and otherwise made a nuisance of myself. This had delivered me from pillow-packing.

However homework was inescapable now that Jay had discovered that I understood the words in the questions, and that addition and subtraction were something I could do in my head. What I could not do was fill in the blanks on the sheets spontaneously with a pencil.

I also had to be prompted letter-by-letter to copy my typed answers in writing into the right spots, which I did with great resentment.

Jay made an important decision. She stopped insisting that I do what we both thought was 'busy work', and also stopped urging me to use my clumsy attempts at hand writing to copy out what I had typed.

She believed I must achieve what I saw as important, which was doing age-appropriate school work without being disadvantaged by the side effects of my autism.

She lined up the sheets on the typewriter so I typed into the spaces left for answers, or she transcribed them herself from my typed instructions. As far as the *contents* of my typing was concerned, I was the boss.

My mother made it clear that she did not feel responsible for what had gone before. One day I whined and grizzled on the typewriter, and she said as much.

'I want you to feel guilty!' I typed. Horrid, adolescent Lucy.

'Oh, no!' she said. 'First things first. Let's work for a couple of years at getting this right. I haven't the energy for that and a guilt trip.'

***

Dear Jay,
Lucy was very high today - much hand-biting, singing, giggling - perhaps a reaction to her perfect control over the past two weeks.

(22 May 1987).

Jay checked my dates, and realised that my period was almost due. She drew Mrs. Wong's attention to make the point that there was usually a good reason for sudden changes in my obvious behaviour. She continued:

I had a conversation with Lucy last night. This is her half of it. Because it is not work, and she is rather upset, I told her when I understood the word she was trying to type, and she left that one unfinished, and went on to the next:

AUTISM AND OTHER ADVENTURES: LUCY'S STORY

NO HAVEIBEENBADTODA (No. Have I been bad today?)
YOUHAVENOTBEENTOOGREATYOURSELF NO (You have not been too great yourself. No.)
TOKEEPSTILLISTOOHARD MYSYBESOINQUIS Y (To keep still is too hard. Must you be so inquisitive. Yes.)
ROUNDKMARTISNOT AGOODPLA (Round K-Mart is not a good place)
CE/TOBEQUV KMARTISNOISY Y ONLYWHENI (Ce.. to be quv [quiet]. K-Mart is noisy. yes. Only when I ...)

What Lucy says explains some of the inconsistencies, and why she is sometimes OK and awful in the same day. If she has heightened sensitivity to noise during the PMS time in certain environments, and those kind of environments then trigger off the whole performance, perhaps there is something which can be done in the way of management.

***

A few days later I was back to typing coherently, and was able to say that the noise in the mornings when we lined up in the brick-walled quadrangle at school was far more unbearable just before my period.

From then on I was allowed to miss the morning assembly in my PMS time. At last, I had been able to make a difference in how things were organised.

Years later, Mrs. Wong told me that my own writing cannot do justice to the sheer stress for school staff of working with me, and in trying to plan for a student whose day-to-day performance was so inconsistent.

Only people who had taught me that year could now visualise my flushed anxiety, screaming and potential for distressed giggling which might go on for several days. I had good days too, but until

I actually got off the morning bus at school, no one knew what was going to happen.

However, now that the Special School was trying to make me type and had been following some of the suggestions in the reactivated Communication Book, I was calmer in many ways, so hopefully things would get better all round.

***

Hayley was about five months pregnant. By this time, I had worried myself into a frenzy that the child might not be normal. Jay went along with Hayley to the radiology department in the bowels of the local hospital.

I sat entirely motionless next to her on the bench in the clamouring passage which was a race track for trolleys coming from Outpatients to Casualty. The heavy door in front of us opened and a head stuck out of the gap.

'Hayley wants you to see the scan,' said the head. Jay towed me into the space the other side of the door. We looked at the fan-shaped image on the flickering screen and the wriggling blob within.

'There don't seem to be any problems at all,' we were told. I was rapturous. I did not understand that the information given by a scan is limited. I assumed that we were being told that the baby definitely did not have autism.

Jay was holding the Canon, and for the very first time I had a spontaneous need to reach for the keyboard. I lifted my hand and let it drift towards her. Fortunately, she was looking that way. Her palm moved onto my wrist, and grinning I rested my finger on a succession of keys.

'*THANKS.*' I spelt out.

***

AUTISM AND OTHER ADVENTURES: LUCY'S STORY

That winter I was to feel terrible in myself, in spite of all the wonderful things that were happening. I had come off Tofranil, and was now taking Clomipramine which was less unpleasant than Tofranil. However, it did not seem to have stopped the cycles of nausea nor my general terror either.

I was beginning to realise that I was suffering pain in my joints at the time I was frightened and vomiting. When I was younger I had not identified this disconcerting feeling as pain, possibly because when I indicated the general area below my hip, and spoke, 'Dore leg!', the other person would check it and, when she found now cuts or bruises, would look at me and say, 'No, Lucy, you have not got a sore leg'.

In typing I could express it with much more accuracy because my typed vocabulary included verbs, tenses and prepositions, to say nothing of pronouns.

I have a piece of Canon Communicator tape from about this time which must be my answer to Jay saying, 'How do you feel?'

'*WORSE HAVE A REAL HEADACHE MOR REAL PAIN IN MY THROAT LOTS OF ACHES IN MY JOINTS SORE Y AWFUL.*'

I had placed the unpleasantly painful sensation in context, and my brain had shunted the result through whatever channels create a filing system for subjective expression of a conscious experience.

For the first time I knew that my stiffness and clumsiness at certain times was not simply a result of something that only happened in my lost thought-processes. My language had made discomfort real because I had had an appropriate response from someone else.

***

Granny Joy was coming that winter. Jay and I had established an evening routine by which I did Special School homework or exercises out of the texts she had borrowed each day from her school, though there were nights when I grumbled and fought with her, and others when I just typed nonsense.

Granny Joy fitted happily into this timetable, sitting and watching with her evening tipple, a gin-and-tap-water with a squeeze of fresh lemon. After I had typed, I would then veg out in front of the television, while she sat with Jay, who now had a beer in her hand.

That was when Jay brought her up to date on what had happened within everyone's lives since her last trip.

It was partly these repeated annual recitations of the year's events, and Jay's and my sisters' success in bringing our daily activities alive for our visitor, that brought home to me some sense of the narrative quality of ordering one's own life against that of other people, and that stories differ when they are told by different people, and even when they are told several times by the same person.

**

Hayley and Laurie had stopped dithering, and had decided to get married. Their little apartment had a space for a barbecue, so the ceremony could be combined with a party.

Hayley organised a necessarily shapeless hired bridal gown. We all went shopping for finery. Jenny scored a personal record by trying on forty-nine dresses in almost as many shops, before settling on the first design she had tried.

I had no trouble selecting what I liked because Jay had successfully gone through a necessary preliminary ritual, a fumigation of clothing obsessions.

This shopping trip was the same as any attempt to buy dresses, jackets, school uniforms, underwear, or other frivolous inessentials.

AUTISM AND OTHER ADVENTURES: LUCY'S STORY

We had first gone to a jeans store where I had chosen a new pair of denims. This was essential if I were to choose any other garment at all. Then I was happy to try on a skirt and blouse in a big department store.

If I had not chosen a pair of brand-name jeans a few hours before, the enormous yearning I had for that feel and texture would cut across my trying on what I really wanted to buy.

***

On The Day, the Civil Celebrant stood among the partying guests, wearing a turtle-necked fisherman's jumper in white wool to blend in with the casual tone of the occasion. Over this he had a plain black gown, which I suppose was a concession to his office.

With straight faces, the guests all earnestly assured him the barely eight-months-pregnant bride was well past full-term. In genuine anxiety he barely lifted his eyes above her waist, completed the ceremony in record time and accepted a brimming glass with the air of someone who has just avoided an awkward situation.

Unfortunately, this wedding also coincided with one of the times I felt ill. My elbows, shoulders and legs had the vague sensation that I now realised was pain. The air was full of perfume and after-shave, and the guests' voices rose and rose in my head.

I had lasted just long enough, but I came to the point where I had to go home or scream. One shriek was enough. Jay headed homewards with the bubbles of her second glass of champagne still fuzzing at her lips.

One wedding down, three more to go!

Chapter 8
The New Me, August 1987 – June 1988:
Age 15

The baby arrived a month later, an exquisite little niece which Hayley stunned us all by naming 'Shay'. She had chosen the name from a Mills and Boon novel. I was not invited to comment on the source, which was just as well.

Shay had an enormous fontanel. Everyone commented on the unusual size of this triangle of pulsing membrane in her skull as they passed their stroking finger over her downy little head.

As with any other unusual physical feature, I simply longed to touch and prod. Hayley was naturally terrified, and, although the baby was rested in my arms, there was always someone at each elbow.

I was frightened by the danger I posed to something I so adored. My dream of being some kind of magical aunt had evaporated.

***

The Spring school holidays were with us again. After the fire, we had used some of the contents insurance as a down-payment on a block of land at Dromana, which is a quiet little holiday spot on Port Philip Bay south of Melbourne. Now Jay was talking of borrowing more money and building a little house there.

That was fine by me. I had enjoyed all the discussion and drama of our new house in the construction stage. This enthusiasm was in spite of my being aware that Jay had bought the block as it was near a group residence she sometimes used for respite care, and where she had me on a waiting list for a permanent placement.

The latter was a long way off, and I had extracted from her a solemn promise not to dump me in a respite house, even for a few days.

Jay also told me that, if I liked, she would take me to Sydney for a few days. This suggestion was an indication of how much my behaviour had improved.

Up to the time I started typing, I had made outings pretty impossible, in the same way that I had in the waiting room at Deal.

This was not for lack of effort on the part of the Autistic Centre or Special School. Jay had been working on this too by taking me to movies since I was eleven.

The only selection criteria she had employed were that any movie had to be so visually riveting that I was mesmerised into staying more or less in my seat and that it might have a sound-track which would drown out any noise I might throw up. *Star Wars* and re-releases of *Superman* fitted that bill, but it was not so easy to find something suitable every couple of weeks.

Typing had changed all that. It was obvious I understood the dialogue, in spite of appearing inattentive and restless. I therefore could start to learn to keep myself in control, not only for its own sake as in behaviour modification, but because I wanted to go to interesting movies, plays other than children's pantomimes and to adult places like restaurants, which I could not do if I disturbed everyone else.

***

As a result of the battles of the last six months, I could also now understand that some of my more extraordinary and disturbing activities could be modified if Jay and I worked as a team, though

I have to admit that she did the lioness's share of the work, fine-tuning rewards, humour and the occasional sanction.

The most useful tool she had was my terror of rice which was at least as strong as Val's fear of spiders. A muttered suggestion that we would have fried rice was often enough to keep me fairly attached to a cinema seat during a quiet love scene, and when we were visiting she could encode this by brightly informing our hosts that she was thinking of Chinese take-away for 'tea'.

This was so effective that Jay was in that happy position of hardly ever having to carry out this bizarre threat, and yet we had an effective way of signalling to me when I needed to pull myself up sharply.

Also, I was reacting better because I was trying to live up to these people's perception that I was an intelligent person.

***

However, there was something rather more deep-seated going on. I now realise that the physical and sensory changes were partly due to the feedback that my hand was sending to my brain as I moved to make sensible language for the first time in my life.

The months between my first bringing that Canon home and our trip to Sydney had seen massive changes in how I felt my body move in space. I still rocked, flapped and ran, and would continue to do so for some years.

However, in some strange way my use of language was making me more of a person, with better feedback as to why weird movements did not bring the results that other people achieved in their activities when they moved their heads, hands and feet.

Also, I was getting reinforcement from the changes in the attitude of other people who spent a lot of time with me. I knew that Jay and Jenny spoke differently to me now.

AUTISM AND OTHER ADVENTURES: LUCY'S STORY

Our combined success meant that I went out much more than before, and when we walked together Jay often did not watch me with such a fixed glare.

Jenny was telling me exactly why I made her angry, which was definitely a promotion for me. Her resentment was not tempered by my shredding her hand-written biology assignment.

This was the final day that it could be handed in. These assignments took half the school year for the student to complete, and were responsible for forty percent of the final mark for this subject.

Lucy the Unlucky had struck just five minutes too soon. If I could not get out of the Special Education system, I certainly could spread the misery around.

***

Mrs. Wong set me the task of keeping a holiday diary. It was Jay's job to see that I wrote it. In doing so, she finally jettisoned the idea which I have heard people express, that writing about personal things was something that I should only do when I 'needed to'.

I think she came to the conclusion that having language was a privilege which brought certain obligations. I had started off ungraciously, but after a few days developed a declamatory style that I thought was very appealing:

Yesterday I started the holidays. Hooray. No more school for a fortnight. Nothing is nicer than no school. I went shopping with my mother to Jeans Extra, and bought a pair of new jeans. Jay bullied me into choosing big ones by making me touch my toes.

We ate at McDonalds, and I laughed at the talk of the other people there who were discussing their parents' strictness. They have nothing to grumble about.

This morning, we went to the station where Jay wanted to buy a ticket to Sydney, but the man made it difficult, and Jay said we will drive. This afternoon I saw a silly movie.
Haven't I said enough.
(19 September 1987).

***

As I typed this Jay giggled and sniggered, so I gathered that what I had written was funny, and that humour made a better impression than serious complaints or lies. A few days later I also discovered that subtle understatement and intentional naivety scored high:

Today Jay and I went to look at display houses. She wants to build a very cheap little house on her block at Dromana. I got very bored because none of the houses on display were down-market enough. Really, even cheap houses are very expensive.

The good thing is that I had a say in our choice, which is a pretty house even for a colonial design.
(24 September 1987).

***

We could scarcely take our little yellow car the eight or nine hundred kilometres to Sydney, so Jay twisted Laurie's arm and borrowed the rusty Kombi:

Today I write this from Lakes Entrance [300 Km. east of Melbourne]. *We are on the road to Sydney, and only have got here* [i.e. have got no further than this] *because Laurie phoned this morning to tell Jay that his campervan had a broken fuel pump. There was nothing wrong with it according to the man who was the expert* [the mechanic], *but Laurie wanted Jay to drive to Sydney with the back open, but Jay refused because she did not want to be aphyxiated* [asphyxiated].

AUTISM AND OTHER ADVENTURES: LUCY'S STORY

[Then] Jay helped Laurie fix the brakes. When we finally got going, Jay drove really fast until past Yallourn, when we stopped for a snack and I said I was frightened.

We had dinner at the pub, and Jay made me eat a whole plate of chicken snitchel [schnitzel] *by not letting me drink my Coke until I had finished. She had whisky for her nerves.*

(26 September 1987).

The word 'said' did not exactly mean that I had spoken or typed that I was frightened.

I had sat in stunned, rocking, smiling terror as the bitumen slid beneath the box front of the Kombie, but when we drew to the side for a cup of tea and Jay wrestled with the gas burner in the van, I opened my mouth and warbled my feelings across the picnic ground, so that small children swinging in the distance scurried back to the next barbecue, and then their father's car scrunched back to the highway in very quick time.

It was only when my embarrassed mother pulled the Canon communicator from one of the bags, and stood over me glowering that I managed to use enough language to ensure that the rest of the trip would proceed at a snail-like pace.

***

The next morning, we were on the road by a little after sunrise. We drove through a very beautiful section of the temperate rain forest of East Gippsland. the eucalypts glowed gold and silver, and the air was like spun sunshine but soft enough not to sun me. I was suddenly aware that Jay was talking out of the golden light.

Her voice flooded and fluttered, 'After seeing you type that paragraph, with its clear introduction and ending, with the threat of understated humour running through, and having such fun in writing like that, I don't think we can go on like this. If you like, I'll apply for funding for integration into a High School.'

I felt quite strange, as if someone had pumped air into me and I was floating in the morning sunlight among the soft green new shoots far above the road. Afterwards Jay said I looked as if I myself were golden in some abstract kind of way.

She went on stolidly pointing the blue shoe box towards the horizon with a stunned, worried expression on her face, aghast at what she had just heard herself say.

We eventually came out of the forest, drove between lush pastures, and finally topped a hill to come down into Eden where we looked down over a circular bay which was quite a different blue from the south-facing waters of the Victorian coast. We had breakfast looking at the Pacific Ocean from a grassy seaside mound.

***

The Kombi chugged over the hills and river valleys to the north within the speed limits I had imposed, and eventually hit Sydney, toured the Opera House (oh, those sails), went on many harbour ferries, and finally struggled back to Melbourne:

How rough it is that the holidays are over. Now for wearisome school where no one understands the way my mind works. Just making my point of view known would mean my being treated as a wanted person.

This holidays Jay really took me everywhere and insisted I could cope. She took me to see the bank manager and the builder so that I could understand how the whole business really works, unlike before she knew how capable of understanding I am.

(4 October 1987).

What the bank manager and builder thought of being part of my training programme, I can't imagine. Mrs. Wong read my diary and was more confused than ever:

Lucy,

AUTISM AND OTHER ADVENTURES: LUCY'S STORY

I do not understand whether you mean you want to be treated as 'a wanted person' or not. If you do, now about letting me know how your mind works, so I can understand you. How can I help you if you will not assist me??

(And in reply)

Mrs. Wong,

[Not to be able to] achieve any of the things ['retarded' people] can do, even though I really am of normal intelligence, is very difficult. I don't think you understand about Autism. Many autistic people just will be unable to work without everyone hassling them a lot. You don't push me in that way.

(15 October 1987).

(And from Mrs. Wong)

Lucy,

Just to give me a helping hand, could you suggest a few ways I could hassle you. Should I yell at you, keep you in at recess time??? Should I give you a reward if you work?? I do really want to understand you, so please help me to do it.

However, I had the last word in that exchange:

Mrs. Wong,

How can I tell you how to cope with me when even I don't know what autism is?

(18 October, 1987).

***

The week after our holidays I went on the annual School Camp, and Jay, feeling a bit of an idiot, reluctantly got the wheels moving towards my changing schools, cramming phone calls and other preliminaries into her lunchtimes.

I got back from Camp and delivered another blow to her confidence, and to mine. Reality, narrative and memory still remained a maelstrom in terms of typing information. The account of my Camp that I typed for Jay had no resemblance to what we had really done.

I had described a kind of hodgepodge of camps I had been on over the years. Jay was beginning to realise that by ordinary standards something very odd was going on.

***

On one occasion Mrs. Wong set a piece of homework in which I was supposed to describe a scene in a sketch. I had recognised it as a scene from the song *Waltzing Matilda*.

We had to talk about the scene, not the song that inspired it. I did not spontaneously reel off a list of the items in the picture, but wrote a story of my own.

Even though Jay was holding my arm, I could not describe the picture though I could make the scene part of my imagined world. She sent my effort off to school, but she was not going to give up that easily.

The next night, as there was no homework, she made me do the exercise as it was meant to be done, tagging each item in the picture and describing its relationship to the rest.

That I really found almost painful, in the way that I had found not being able to write my phone number painful. In struggling to adapt to these new demands, my brain sent out signals that made my skin burn and my eyes send even more confusing messages back.

I roared, screamed and bit my hands. This is the conversation as I remember it.

'What is that?' she snapped, pointing to a shape in the foreground.

'A pool of water.'

And what is happening behind it?'

'Soldiers riding over the ridge.'

AUTISM AND OTHER ADVENTURES: LUCY'S STORY

'Troopers [i.e. colonial police], actually,' she murmured. 'And what are those things on each side?'

'Trees and he must be frightened.'

'That is not what you were asked! What is that figure, and what did the picture show. No fancy details.'

'A man in old clothes holding a sheep.'

By this time, we were both exhausted, and my left hand was scarlet with imprinted tooth marks.

***

At some point we saw Dr. Weybridge. If the Education Department were to even consider allocating resources for me to attend a mainstream school, Jay would have to organise letters which spelt out what my support needs would be.

'We have decided to try integrating Lucy into High School,' said Jay, and, before the doctor could say anything, she held out the page of my holiday diary I had written at Lakes Entrance.

'When I watched her typing this, and so clearly writing to a plan and laughing at her own jokes in it, I realised that we had to try something different.'

While the doctor read my masterpiece, there was an expectant hush.

'Fixed the brakes! Good Lord!' said the normally unflappable doctor. I think that after that my ambition to go to High School was pretty tame, though Dr. Weybridge certainly must have been dubious.

We got a few other letters from people who knew me professionally. All of them had one thing in common. If the situation were not to be a complete disaster, I would need a one-on-one aide.

***

Funding!

Would I get it?

Would I be allocated enough hours of aide-time?

My temper got nastier and nastier. Right through October and November Jay went on struggling with me, insisting I type every day, and that I work through sheets of equations and mathematical problems.

I really understood all the concepts of arithmetic, algebra and geometry at that level and protested noisily at this constant repetition, but I think I was delighted that she was so pushy.

I also was getting into the habit of writing paragraphs, poems and occasionally letters when I was set a task, rather than just answering questions or talking about my problems.

In spite of all this achievement, I suddenly cracked it one day. I flew at another girl in the changing rooms after we had finished in the swimming pool, clawing, grabbing and screaming.

In the evening, I explained to Jay that it was because she had a T-shirt identical to mine, and I had a sensation that part of me had been taken over by the other person.

The same week Jay heard over the grapevine that I was being funded for an integration aide. Now it looked certain that I was to be a student in a school with a compulsory uniform policy, so I would spend hours each day with hundreds of duplicates of myself. Was this going to be a problem?

No one knew.

***

My behaviour in the change rooms might have been aggravated by an attempt to reduce my Clomipramine. Obviously my medication had to be checked but Dr. Weybridge had just accepted a new post at a hospital a long way off.

AUTISM AND OTHER ADVENTURES: LUCY'S STORY

One day after school I was inserted into Jay's car, trundled over endless tram tracks and into an informal city office to meet a new doctor.

My visits to Nicky were to last eight years at approximately three weekly intervals. During the sessions I would waffle on tape. Jay would read my words aloud as I typed them, occasionally adding her own observations as Nicky made constructive remarks or confused noises.

This dual-track client talk probably took a bit of getting used to. I wonder if my life would have been quite the same if we had gone to another doctor.

Probably not, because our odd, three-cornered, structured conversations about things I felt to be important, really gave me some idea of social response in a way that I have not experienced anywhere else.

***

Over the years to come, Jay used these appointments for me to practise typing in a way which made it obvious to Nicky that she did not influence the content of what I was expressing.

In December, 1987 I fronted this stranger with my forearm resting in my mother's hand, and no idea why I found it impossible to move the way I wanted to without this contact.

In time I 'talked' with Jay holding the keyboard, and resting her left hand on my right shoulder, rather than supporting my arm.

Then (much later) I found I could manage if she rested her left knee against my right thigh without touching my arm or body.

After five years she did not have to touch any part of my arm or body while my finger chattered on about those topics which occupied my brain at that particular moment.

***

I had to master some of the skills that my classmates would take for granted. One of these was reading a book from beginning to end.

Jay still was not sure whether I could store narrative long enough to read a full-length novel. To date I had yelled every time she had tried to get me to sit still while she turned pages.

When I picked up a book I read what was on the open page in front of me, and then just fanned through the leaves.

My first introduction to reading a book from cover to cover rather than looking at a page and running away, was based on the way I used a communicator.

I was typing on the Canon with no touch on my right wrist, so long as Jay was snuggled so close to my right-hand side that my arm was immobilised from the elbow up.

Unfortunately, this was not really something I found very pleasant. So, if I could, I would simply leap to my feet and disappear. However, because Jay had to squash me into the corner of the sofa to get my arm tight enough to my side, I found myself glued firmly in position.

She held the little keyboard in her own right hand, her left was round my shoulders and I typed without her hand on my arm. This was comfortable for her, and wonderful for me because I always feel so much more competent when I am squashed.

So, when Jay first produced a short book for me to read from end to end, she tried sitting with me in exactly the same position.

Of course, I felt confused, frustrated and angry by being asked to read a continuous text. All my life I had snatched a paragraph from the page, and then moved away.

The idea of reading sentences, paragraphs, pages and chapters in sequence was weird and unnatural. Jay tightened her grip on my left shoulder, and placed the open book in our combined laps. Her right hand gripped my right wrist, and my finger extended as it did when I typed.

AUTISM AND OTHER ADVENTURES: LUCY'S STORY

The first lines read:

Storm Boy lived between the Coorong and the sea. His home was the long, long snout of sand hill and scrub that curves away south-eastwards ...

She rested my finger halfway down the first paragraph. I could not understand why I had to look so long at this group of lines. Now I know that she was reading the paragraph herself in her usual, relatively quick scan.

At length she moved my finger down a notch, and then seemed to wait the same interminable time. We went through the first few pages.

'That is fine,' she said, dropping the book and picking up the Canon. 'What was that about?'

I explained that it described the life of a boy who lived alone with his father on a deserted part of the coast of South Australia.

'OK,' she said. 'Take a break.'

This irritating performance had taken ninety seconds. I ran up and down the passage. She called me back five minutes later. I managed another couple of pages. By the next afternoon I had read my first book, the touching account of a child whose best friend was an enormous pelican. I loved every page of it.

That holiday I discovered narrative in print. The Narnia books, Hinton's *The Outsiders*, Paul Gallico's *Snow Goose* and dozens of other titles jostled with Gerald Durrell's *My Family and Other Animals* as I began to construct clearer pictures from words.

***

At last, I realised that the future was a reality. I definitely was going to High School. I had a book list, uniform strap shoes and a blue and white checked dress. How was I going to get to my new school each day across a morass of roads, shops and people? I was going to try to learn to walk to school by myself!

At daybreak we would leave the house. The High School was about a kilometre, or just over half a mile, from home crow-flight-wise, provided the crow in question was completely deaf.

It would also need a gas mask against the fumes of the nearby major road, which by 7.30 would be packed with cars and trucks, crammed together like a mob of sheep being driven through a chute. Fortunately, very close to the side street to our house was a pedestrian crossing.

Naturally people had tried to teach me road sense, but, because they had believed that my incompetence had been caused by my not understanding what was required, they had not accomplished much.

Now they realised that I understood the theory of road safety just as well as most people, we were all mystified as to why I could not cope with moving from place to place as they would have.

Neither Jay nor I yet understood that my cavalier attitude to pedestrian skills was caused by visual processing, problems with cause and effect, and a very horrible lack of body awareness which left me adrift in the outside world, and without measurable boundaries between my body and the molecules beyond.

***

The crossing signal had buttons, which I pushed whenever I waited with my mother and sisters. I would go on pushing them again and again, embarrassing my companion until the walk-signal appeared.

When that occurred, I expected the other person to move, which triggered a movement in me rather like touch did with typing. Then I lost my paralysis of will and scampered headlong, without checking whether the drivers at the lights had noticed the change of signal. It seemed that it would be a simple matter to teach me the missing parts of the equation now that we all realised that I was intelligent.

The realities of life reasserted themselves. My sensory and reasoning differences still left me moving as an alien in the human urban environment.

No way could Jay get me to leave the footpath without some signal. In spite of all her best efforts, even a slight tensing on her part or a soft exasperated sigh was enough to signal me that she had noticed that the lights had changed.

One morning she started to cross the road at a different point from where I stood, so that initially we paralleled each other and she could roar instructions.

After about a month of this, sometimes she would suddenly disappear as I bent forward to press the button. Initially I really thought she was not there, and that the sound of her voice telling me to move off the kerb was from inside me. Later I realised that she was hiding behind bushes and in driveways.

I gradually lost the appalling illusion that my body could not move unless I had someone to mirror my image of my movement. I could step into the road when the signal turned green, without waiting for a cue.

However, I simply assumed that the oncoming traffic had no option but to stop. Eventually I was able to cross without Jay's distant voice, though I would relapse into inertia if she or anyone else was next to me.

***

Once I got over the barrier of the pedestrian crossing, the real obstacle course began. I was meant to walk up a grassy slope, around the fascinating curves and cubes of the new Library and Civic Centre, and between the shops of our local strip shopping centre, each with its share of mesmerising shapes and colours.

Jay used variations on the crossing technique to get me through this minefield. She darted around shop entrances, lurked in alleys and crawled around the back of dump bins.

Early commuters were likely to find her well-nourished rump appear suddenly in their path when she backed suddenly on all-fours as I appeared anxiously around a corner.

Because she was trying to cut my dependence, she would follow and circle around at a brisk trot to try to catch me as unaware of her as possible, so she could see if I were coping.

Afterwards she would discuss my performance with me, and we would have a good laugh at the expense of our more conventional fellow-suburbanites.

***

Now it began to look as if there were a fifty-fifty chance that on a good day I would drift as far as the school gate. That was where my real problems would begin.

Although I grumbled and emoted about it, I was relieved when Jay flatly refused to allow me to change schools until I had met the classroom Aide and the Integration Teacher, and had made some attempt at typing with them.

So, I started the school year back at Special School. I was bored and furious, so Jay eventually made a suggestion.

'While you are sitting around doing nothing in the Special School classroom, get your mind working,' she said. 'Every evening, I expect you to have planned a part of a story ready to be typed out.'

Silly woman! That is not how I write. I flash up paragraphs, and hook up phrases as I require them. However, in my misery I daydreamed an image of me typing at home, and later that day found some of her assumptions were true. A little planning does make language more effective.

AUTISM AND OTHER ADVENTURES: LUCY'S STORY

***

I started a 'Chapter' set in a non-existent institution. It began with a good dollop of self-pitying resentment about a child I remembered from Riding for the Disabled:

No one could understand very many of the actual words the Cerebal [cerebral] palsied boy tried to say but he was much loved because he was friendly and appreciative. The weird angry roars of the retarded and the autistic ...

By Night Two I had some real characters, who paralleled their movements much as I remembered some children doing at the Autistic Centre, though at the Centre often this was so subtle and so separated in time that it had been invisible to staff:

... The last two cots contained a pair of children who flapped their hands at each other but not incessantly. First Suzie and then Dean would make a movement, while each watched the other's actions out of the corner of a directionless eye ...

By Night Three my little hero had asserted himself:

Taking a running start, he arrived in the main ward and whirled over the depressing green lino wailing in wanton enjoyment as his gyro started to get in time with the near perfect symmetry of the motion.

Carrying a towel the nurse grabbed at the back of his pyjamas and stopped him so that towel and boy tangled into a writhing mass from which Dean's teeth sank hard into her thumb. (February 1988)

***

This confrontation had been lifted from a gossip session between Jay and Grace. Grace's son, Max, is older than I am, and has autism.

Grace also was a volunteer worker at my Autistic Centre, and on her frequent visits to our home had a wealth of stories about the younger children I remembered from the Centre.

So, when I wrote that sentence, I combined my own memory of spinning in the corridor of the Social Adjustment Unit with someone else's narrative. I was beginning to picture myself as a writer in a limited sort of way.

***

One day I was delivered to Deal, where I found Rosie, dark straight hair swinging around her pink cheeks, and a slender, suspiciously golden-blonde young woman seated in the room where I had come for my instruction sessions the year before.

'This young woman was Jaime, the aide who the Education Department had appointed to come to classes with me.'

The atmosphere developed a demanding tinge. I broke ranks, burst through the door to the back passage, flung open the refrigerator inside the kitchen, and felt the wonderful tickle of a full can of Coke cascade down my throat.

A comfortable burp later I was aware I was not alone. A warm, deep, frothy voice spoke.

'Hello!'

I took account of a broad, tall figure in a dress and sensible shoes, topped by untidy blonde-grey hair above a flushed face with large eyes and strong features.

After this flash reconnaissance, I turned and shot back to the accustomed stresses of the room where Jaime and Rosie were sitting. Their heads turned to greet me, and the woman from the kitchen followed me into the room.

'This is Mrs. Lohning, Lucy,' said Rosie.

'Oh,' thought I. 'I wonder what she thought about me and that drink!'

The can of Coke certainly made its mark. Five years later Grania Lohning could describe that meeting down to the last belch.

AUTISM AND OTHER ADVENTURES: LUCY'S STORY

***

Mrs. Lohning was the Integration Teacher who would be responsible for mediating between me and the rest of the school. Her timetable symbol was LO.

LO was to be the constant during my time at High School, bouncing along the corridors looking for me when I went astray, trailing after me in the grounds at lunchtime, or sailing ahead in the crowds between classes. I could follow this landmark with confidence, and rely on it for comfort and love.

She worked with me a little that day. Most of the time I was at High School I would be expected to work with the Aide so, after the introductory session, I sat with Jaime's fair-skinned hand on my arm, and was very relieved to find that I could start to form words with her as my partner. Jaime had some more training sessions with me and Rosie, and all systems were 'go'.

***

Suddenly Special School was a thing of the past. Jaime came to the house to practise her behaviour management skills and get a bit more confident in anticipating and reinforcing my finger strokes. Later I was to realise how helpful it was that she could visualise me in my own environment.

Although Jaime had only taken up her position when the school year began at the end of January, by the time I arrived she was already part of the school, attending the classes that I would go to.

The work was often too hard for her, so she asked questions which distracted the fourteen-year-olds, who saw her as just a rather weird adult. My arrival neutralised this, because then she was following my lead during work sessions, and I was confident with my own grasp of the content of the lessons.

Mr. Ross, who was the mathematics teacher, had no problems realising that I was doing my own work, even though Jaime was holding my arm, because I was getting few wrong answers, and often I had to fight with Jaime to get her to put her hand up to speak my correct solution aloud because she could not see the reason for the method I had used.

I think he realised she was not helping me to type. She was creating a stable environment that co-ordinated my body, mind and surrounding space.

***

Even in my first month there she was finding that she was not able to keep up with me in maths:

Dear Jay,

Today each person in the class was asked the same question. They all gave the same answers except for Lucy. She gave the opposite. Mr. Ross laughed. How could everyone else be wrong and Lucy right. Lucy laughed and 'said' the same answer as before. She was correct. The teacher laughed again, then asked me if I understood why. I had to admit that I didn't.

(Jaime, 29 March 1988).

I was distressed and angry that my classmates should have such problems with this beautiful and simple subject. I complained at home about this:

Lousy dumb classes really seem to give me so much pleasure that it even interests me that the students wreak chaos giving the poor teacher dreadful trouble the ungrateful lousy pigs. Such soul-destroying real boorishness makes me sick when I think how I had to fight to get to school but petty irritations are not important in the overall big too marvellous wonderful lovely picture.

(Evening, 9 April 1988).

AUTISM AND OTHER ADVENTURES: LUCY'S STORY

***

At school I was more direct in how I expressed my irritation and scorn, getting flushed, giggling uncontrollably, running around the room and biting my hand.

From the front of the room lovely Mr. Ross had seen my pleasure in other maths classes when all had gone smoothly. He spoke as if this Lucy-style response to stupidity was the most natural thing.

'Lucy!' His voice spoke to all the class. 'I know you understand this, but the rest of us are struggling.'

In my first euphoria all my classes were as good as mathematics from my point of view, though I think Jaime suffered agonies of embarrassment.

I sang, rocked, and occasionally shrieked. Underneath this I was deliriously happy. I was achieving, and people knew that I was bright. I realised that, because unbelievably they were asking me to answer questions in class.

My arm in Jaime's sometimes unresponsive hand, I typed out answers which mostly were correct.

Working with Jaime put to rest any idea that there was some kind of emotional prerequisite to typing with support. Jaime and I liked each other, and that year we spent a lot of time in each other's company, but for both of us working together was a skill we each had to learn.

It was not an easy partnership and we were both aware of this. One thing that saved us both was that her previous student had been a small child with cerebral palsy, so she was trained to be responsive to abnormal movements.

If she had not been so determined and so brave, I think that my first term at High School would have been my last.

***

I was walking to school, but my arrival was unpredictable, and my behaviour en route was a mystery but everyone suspected the worst.

Partly because of this, Jay sought out another launching point for my progression to school in the mornings.

From then on each day before school she would drop me at Maria's immaculate house, unfortunately just on the wrong side of our main road, but closer to the school.

I was surrounded by polished surfaces, cut glass and china figurines. Jay was panic stricken when she first saw that room, but in all the time that I used it as an alternative home I never broke anything by accident. A little destruction in moments of mild irritation was another matter, though!

My plump, Maltese-born hostess and her Sri Lankan-English husband would point me in the direction of the school, and everyone would hope for the best.

Sometimes I had a clear run with no obsessional hitches, sometimes I would get stuck at a kerb, but could unglue myself eventually, and sometimes I started tearing up leaves on a hedge, and LO would come down in her car and rescue me.

There was one unpleasant occasion when I stood looking at two small children in a front garden, and could not work out how to think my way back into walking mode until they got frightened enough by my staring to throw clods of earth at me.

However, one way or another I got to school, though sometimes I was terribly late.

***

Lunch was another problem. Jay employed a local lady to watch me in the school yard so Jaime herself could get a break. That bombed out, and from then LO rearranged her timetable so that we did things together in the lunch break.

AUTISM AND OTHER ADVENTURES: LUCY'S STORY

But before LO and I began to know each other fairly well, Jaime phoned in sick one day. I went to class with LO. Except for the first time we had met, she had not been a typing partner.

Also, she had no idea of how fast I absorbed print. This was an English lesson. LO was a maths and science teacher, and so was looking rather less confident than usual. Later she taped her memory of that class:

The job in hand was some reading and comprehension questions. Because I hadn't been in these classes with you, I didn't know how fast you read. I was saying, 'Go back and read it properly!'

I felt it was as a sop to me that your finger was going down the page. I said, 'You haven't read it. Try and answer the questions and prove the point.'

After you had answered the questions quite fully and correctly, I had the chance to read the four or five pages of text myself. So, if I had any doubts whether you could read as fast as you do, they went the very first time we tried to work together.

Later in the year the students read through a play called What's Normal, and then had to write a paragraph with the same title. The other kids all struggled to produce one or two sentences.

You talked about Hitler trying to make everyone the same, but that 'Normal' should include a wider variation of differences. I would never have thought of including Hitler; my ideas were very different from yours.

(Grania Lohning. Tape recorded interview, 1991).

***

'Difference' was something that I was well qualified to discuss. I flashed back to one of my strongest memories of human response to difference, the second episode of the series *Holocaust*, which had dramatised the Nazi eugenics and euthanasia policy.

What's Normal

Will you feel that a person is normal if they show no Initiative And if there is nothing special about them which makes them Act differently from others Or do you revel in the differences that make life interesting.

I feel that the thing which makes us human is our differences from another. Perhaps though you belong to that group of people who would have us all be the same. Just remember that this is what Hitler tried to do. He was the cause of great suffering and the death of many because he did not like differences in people. Is this the world we want to live in? Surely our idea of normal should include a wide range of variations in all aspects of life.

(Class work, 18 August 1988).

***

That made another lasting impression on LO, one which mercifully was more favourable than my fridge raiding.

Food stealing, scratching sweets and chewy off the ground, and bin-diving remained a conspicuous part of my repertoire.

School breaks were a problem for the rest of my time at High School. After a while the school realised that this was an integral part of me, and because of this I needed supervision.

So, LO began making time in her schedule to be in the yard when I was. I had constant supervision and then reinforcement from the person who was supervising me in times when there were no structured activities.

Jay's responses to my problems were also consistent. The diary doubled as a message book, so the lines between Jay, LO and Jaime were open and relatively clear.

However, I was still confused that each managed to misunderstand each other several times each week.

When this confusion occurred, either I would keep quiet and follow the wrong instructions that these enthusiastic, bossy women poured in my direction, or I would scream with frustration and bite my hand.

Occasionally I tried to clarify things by typing, usually unsuccessfully. I was pretty good at making my feelings and prejudices clear, but the precision of telling someone what to do or what had occurred outside Lucy's body, was unattainable.

I was becoming frustrated and anxious about this, because my increasingly fluent typed language was bringing me good school marks in academic work, and I found my inconsistencies worrying.

***

Naturally that frustration needed to be taken out on the people in the school whom I loved most, LO and Jaime. For them each day was a new disaster waiting to happen.

Jaime wrote frantic notes to Jay about my lifting my uniform dress up and scrabbling in garbage. LO had to explain to staff about my sitting up a tree with my skirt over my head, which probably was a response to a student hoping to be a friend.

To me the whole social thing seemed weird. I was so happy to be at High School just for the sake of being there at all.

I appreciated the lack of teasing, and was pleased when my classmates said, 'Hello!' without being put out by my lack of response, but I did not have an urge to reach out to them.

However, I loved having this interactive group swarming around, or acting as a backdrop for my swaying happy chanting and noisy chortles.

Weirdly, so many adults seemed to think that I wanted to be just like the other students! In theory I did, but only because that was how I really thought I was meant to feel.

'Labelling' was an in-word at that time, as was the opinion that people often expressed that my difference was only the construction of other people. This seemed to belittle the diagnosis that I was autistic.

I started to think that it was really important to me to work out what autism was for myself.

***

Now I was less anxious as to whether I truly was intelligent, superficially I appeared to conform better to some extent. People confused me when they praised my improved behaviour, because most of the time it was an involuntary response to a different teaching approach.

If someone did not have an effective strategy that helped me to be less disruptive, I felt resentful and angry.

I developed a deep suspicion of people who used the word 'labelled', and was much happier to be identified as having autism than being treated as someone whose problems would just go away or were better ignored.

One day my super-acute hearing picked up a distant grouch-session in the school grounds. One boy was telling another that he did not think I was very disabled, only badly behaved.

All the obvious signals whirled around my system, crossed and exploded. Down came my panties. I bent my knees and my bladder emptied.

Not so disabled?

For goodness sake!

Oh, well! That would show him.

I noticed that LO was a little peeved.

In fact, LO went right off the planet, but I was used to everyone not seeing my point of view, so I expressed contrition in typing and let them draw their own conclusions, whether they were right or wrong.

Chapter 9
More About Me, High School 1988–1989: Age 16–17

In the middle of that year, three things happened.

I got a 'Distinction' in the Year 9 level in the National Mathematics Competition.

That evening Jay answered the phone, and turned down an offer for assessment for a residential placement. She had had me on that waiting list for four years, and knew that there might not be another opportunity for decades for me to leave home.

The third thing was my first real school report. I had done well. There was even a mention of my impressive general knowledge. Silent (or rather non-speaking) television-watching had certainly paid off.

***

In the second half-year there was a series of tests for science for which we had to learn. Suddenly I had a problem. I could absorb facts and somehow spit them out many weeks later, but I had problems with learning on demand.

This is part of how my brain seems to work. I find as an adult that I have to choose university subjects which allow for this quirk.

At that stage I had no idea that I would continue to Year 12. Funding for an aide had to be applied for on an annual basis.

There was no precedent for someone like me going on after Year 10, and there were no procedures for a student working with a communication partner writing the Year 12 examination which would give me access to the university system.

However, I was starting to think about following the same trail as Jenny had, and said as much to Jaime, who paled at the thought of another three years. This pallor was accentuated by her new hair colour, which was a bright green.

This stunned the staff room, but benefited me because beside her I was relatively inconspicuous, though it was a pretty near thing. Jaime's adventure with green hair dye was quite a coincidence, because earlier in the year I had written a short comic piece:

It's Not Easy Being Green

Can you imagine waking up one morning and finding a green hand lying on the sheet. Green is a very nice colour but just at that moment I found it rather frightening. For example it did not look too good with maroon bedding and when one got dressed, a royal blue jumper had not been chosen as school uniform with my new complexion in mind.

Going to a lovely mirror, framed as it was in gold, only heightened the effect and my nice bottle green hair did look a little off with my nice shocking pink combs.

Had the school some warning, they might have coped, but in the event some kids cracked up and the Deputy Principal sent me home to bath.

Given the choice, I reached for the dye and - do you prefer yellow or a nice startling red?

(20 April 1988).

This was featured in a one-page spread in the school magazine, which showed LO and me surrounded by some of my work.

***

AUTISM AND OTHER ADVENTURES: LUCY'S STORY

I had already written to Mrs. Wong, rather impolitely I am afraid, but, being a very nice person, she had written back. Now I updated her on my progress, and paid her what I thought was a compliment:

Dear Mrs. Wong,

Thank you for actually writing to me again when I was so rude really to you. Unlikely though it may seem I learnt a lot from you at Special School, especially how to keep my temper.

Really the other kids have been very tolerant. Really for fifteen- and fourteen-year-old people they have been magnificently supportive. I do know they think me very odd, but they do not actually tease me, and tell off anyone who sends me up.

Someone said in pottery [an elective with students from several forms] *that my aide did my work, and someone* [from my form] *at once yelled down the row that I was bright and did my own work. Wasn't that nice of her?*

Today I wrote a poem for my niece which Jay can photocopy and put in with this.

(13 August 1988).

***

Most nights I grizzled, rhapsodised about school or wrote poetry before my homework.

I was typing up to two hundred words in those diary sessions, and the folder of typewritten sheets from 1988 are a record of the slow process by which my mind and my language became an effective unit, though even today they remain rather cobbled together. I wailed about my lot:

Simple worries like taking off my clothes, or approaching people inappropriately, really bug me and I believe I will never overcome them. Such fear is crippling and I hope to get over it with help, but foolishness is a very strong chain.

(7 May 1988).

Jay was the butt of most of my criticism:

Can the actually indeterminate instructions that you give be useful to anyone. Because you confuse anyone listening and they do what they were going to anyway.

Have you ever seen a really agitated goat with a determination and a perseverance which forces her to have actually distressing and comic mannerisms.

(13 May 1988).

Sometimes I was downright offensive!

Biologically intolerable Irritating parental horrible selfish and autocratic actions are revolting in all senses of the word ... you are really such a lazy and careless, even slobby Person.

(28th May 1988).

***

I spent an awful lot of energy trying to live up to other people's expectations about using shops and walking to and from school by myself:

Dumb dreally [dreadful-really] *silly fears made me just stand next to a gate, but at last a man said it was better to move on, and how glad I am that I did, because for once going home actually was an achievement.*

(13 May 1988).

Did you think how really embarrassed I was when I screamed in Woolworths ... Going to shops brings out the cold shivers.

(3 June 1988).

Also, I was confused about the process which made it possible for me to express myself fairly fluently in formal language when I could feel a person's hand on my arm, but did not really have any spontaneous self-expression when I had to operate as an individual:

I cannot express my wishes [in speech, and often in typing]. [*So, I*] *put Jay into the position of an inquisitor. It is a bit like a multiple-choice paper, and I only have a percentage chance of getting what I want.*

(21 May 1988).

Somehow I realised that I was bedevilled by a language processing problem which was compounded by a real lack of inhibition, though I had only identified the sensation that I experienced when it affected my speech:

My speech really just bulges out of my mouth like a balloon, and the real thoughts in my head just keep on a direct line. The direct line and the balloon are related, but they do not correspond, and the more the balloon bulges, the less sense it makes, until it bursts, leaving nearly all my thoughts scattered, and me wild with anger and shame.

(9 July 1988).

***

I wrote also about the physical aspects of why I needed a partner when I typed:

The assistance you [Jay] give me is a bit like the way that you sally forth and take Shay's hand when she would like to walk, but cannot.

Very weak support is needed so that all her concentration is directed to putting one foot in front of the other, with very little feelings left for balancing, carrying her weight, or going in any direction.

The parallel shows how the effort to get some of my thoughts down without the added distractions of autistic behaviour, and the stupid difficulty I have in hitting the right key, seeing the double image for a few of the beastly things, and even sometimes a triple image.

(6 July 1988).

Later I was shocked to discover that a conventional eye test did not show any abnormality. I had to wait until my mid-twenties to experiment with tinted lenses. Now I also use yoked prisms, which have shown me that there probably were several interconnected processing problems which were responsible for my need for a stabilising supportive hand when first I typed.

***

Behind all this confused reasoning I was in a constant state of stress, pulled this way and that by the person I was, sometimes incontinent at night, often giggling uncontrollably from stress and allergy during the day, bursting with words and churning out curiously formal little thoughts, one letter at a time, with the wobbly forefinger of an undersized right hand:

Can the weird idea of me coping with High School really be true. For the past year so much has happened and so foolish thoughts can be expected, and I am still unfortunately in a state of shock and am almost grieving for the lost Lucy, who was played with like a baby and [who was] given toys for Christmas.

(17 June 1988).

As I had told Mrs. Wong, I had written a poem for Shay's first birthday. My effort seems to reflect some of the lessons that I had been learning and I must have been maturing in some ways:

Even you little baby are just a speck
Floating rhythmically on the foamy surface
Of a sea deep and mysterious
Excitingly inhabited by mermaids and fearful monsters ...
Care for yourself as the centre of your living universe
And those you love will be soothed
By the glow of your sun
And are the beneficiaries of real self-love.
... Such love is a gift and that is given
By those who love you.
Happy Birthday, Shay,
From your Aunt Lucy.

AUTISM AND OTHER ADVENTURES: LUCY'S STORY

***

That winter Granny Joy visited us again, and I was happy to sit and type with Jay then listen to them talk, but after a few weeks I began to find the sound of two women's voices mouthing the platitudes of hostess and guest terribly irritating. I think my short temper was a by-product of my own use of language and a real frustration with my inability to be an informal participant.

Also, I now realise that some voices make my sensory processing go out of sync when I do not feel well, and when that happens I have a real sensation of pain in my head at least as unpleasant as the sensation which I called 'fear', and which was more of a physical than intellectual experiencing of my surround.

Just before I was due to go back to school after the Spring holidays I had bouts of disorientation and screaming. Granny Joy realised I might feel better without her there, so she packed up two days early and flew to friends in Sydney to await the flight she had booked from there, not because she felt unwanted, but because she cared enough to want me to cope with the beginning of this term with the least distress. I was never to see her again.

I was totally ashamed by my lack of control. I found her regular phone calls to Jay were more distracting than before. I heard phone voices as a series of clicks and screeches if I were in the same room as the phone. Normally I could tolerate them if I were a long way away, and I still could catch the gist of the caller's words. Now I felt really angry with myself, with Jay and with Granny Joy when her voice travelled over the airwaves and through the handpiece of the phone near the front door.

***

As the year ended I found that funding was available for 1989, but that I would have to learn to work with someone new. Jaime was leaving to work in the hospitality trade. She gave me a farewell gift more valuable than she knew. She wrote a detailed description of how it had been working with me,

FOR THE INFORMATION OF THOSE WHO WORK WITH LUCY BLACKMAN IN THE FUTURE.

In the beginning I found it very difficult to associate the Lucy I saw coming through her work, and the Lucy I saw doing 'strange' things.

If she sings Happy Birthday, Tie Me Kangaroo Down Sport *or* He's Got the Whole World in His Hands *you will know she is upset about something. She may also bite her hands. Laughing and clapping generally mean she is pleased about something.*

Lucy often doesn't look at you while she's talking to you, or vice versa. She does however try her hardest to maintain eye contact, and succeeds to a certain extent.

Don't be put off. She may appear not to be listening, but she is, even if she gives no indication of having heard you

In class Lucy is listening and absorbing what the teacher says as he or she says it. When the teacher is asking questions of the class, ask Lucy to type out an answer which can be read to the teacher.

In English and History, Lucy reads extremely quickly, and you may be in doubt as to whether she has actually read the page. If she runs her finger quickly down the middle of the page, it means she has already read it.

If clarifying a particular passage, she will run her finger along under the line, but the actual line she is reading is two lines up from her finger.

She likes to play with words, using phrases, expressions and adjectives which are not normally utilised by students of her age group. Her stories are wonderfully imaginative, though you may find her phrasing strange at first.

AUTISM AND OTHER ADVENTURES: LUCY'S STORY

In Mathematics set out the communicator, calculator, a card with hand-written mathematical signs and words such as 'NO', 'YES', 'OVER', 'TO THE POWER OF', etc., together with a note pad for you to take dictation from Lucy's pointing.

Never assume she wants to use a certain sign, make her show you what she is doing. This is where I often got lost, as I did not understand her workings.

Lucy works out most problems in her head, so her answers made no sense to me. It took far too long for her to type out a detailed explanation to each sum and I didn't know the right questions to ask to write down her workings. Mathematics were the bane of my existence. I began to get so uptight about these classes that I would often be in tears, or close to it.

(Jaime, December 1988).

***

Christmas means midsummer, so we would have a barbecue in the garden of the house that Hayley and Laurie had bought so that they would have room for the baby that was coming that year. The house was about half an hour by car — but the car died, unlamented and reviled, on Christmas Eve. For some eccentric reason, Jay refused all offers of a lift, and travelled by rail with me in tow.

This trek involved several fare zones and two main lines. Christmas Day had always had a timetable so skeletal that it was almost non-existent. In honour of our trip and the barbecue at journey's end, the skies opened, and we sat for an hour on the platform at Richmond Station waiting for our second train, gazing down at the stream of bejewelled shiny cars swooshing under the rail viaduct that faced towards the temporarily invisible Melbourne Cricket Ground, that hallowed shrine of Australian Rules Football, immortalised in newsreels around the world as the venue for the 1956 Olympic Games.

In spite of the shooshing slosh of tyres, which always hurts my head, I was perfectly content with this combination of streaming lights and an absorbing sense of being in the centre of my universe.

Dad phoned just after the last of the barbecue had been salvaged from a smoky pan on top of the stove, and apologetically said that he had been delayed because he and his neighbours had been swimming in the flood waters of the main street of their suburb, and he thought it would be a bit late to come to lunch now.

Looking at the pile of washing-up buried under torn Christmas bonbons, I enjoyed his timing, and gobbled up his share of the plum pudding before it could be offered around.

***

Our new car was a six-year-old metallic-brown Toyota Corona station wagon, which Jay swore to love and cherish. This was mainly because I had developed a series of obsessions and fears about cars, only some of which were related to their function of moving one from one place to another.

At one stage I would not allow the driver to leave one hand resting on the gear knob and the other on the steering wheel, because this position was not symmetrical.

At times I thrust and pushed at Jay while she was trying to steer us through traffic because the wind-up knobs for the front windows had about a sixty degree difference in alignment, which meant that when the windows were symmetrical, the knobs were not — and *vice versa*.

Jay kept the situation manageable with a good dose of suggestions about Chinese food and other awful threats, though I often exploded without warning, and this negotiation was often a particularly astringent mopping-up operation that took place at the roadside with our hazard lights blinking and Jay shaking with anger and stress.

AUTISM AND OTHER ADVENTURES: LUCY'S STORY

***

The car radio also annoyed Jay. I thought she was very unreasonable. The treble notes seemed to make me feel ill, and I preferred the radio on a rock station with a strong bass beat which drowned out all other sound when the knob was turned up as far as it would go.

As a corollary, not only did I escape the discomfort of the melody, but also the bass sounds entered my being, and I bounced, swayed and rocked with them.

The same thing happened at school when I followed other kids into the school hall if there was a lunchtime concert or when LO was involved in rehearsing the school play. I really hated that out-of-control feeling, but loud rock in a closed space was like an inbuilt switch.

Jay bore the brunt of my music mania, because the noise made me bounce on long drives. The brown station wagon would hop along the road, while the driver struggled for control and tried to look nonchalant as overtaking motorists stared incredulously.

I wrestled with her on freeways when she tried to turn the radio off, and soon worked out that, if the knob were removed, using my fingers in a pincer grip on the protruding spike behind was as good.

One day the radio simply fell silent, and all my screams did not resurrect it. I was told it was broken, but I have deep suspicions. It was all too convenient, though not for me. These and similar car-related eccentricities continued until I was well into my twenties.

***

Year 10 brought two new aides to work with me, Pauline and Helga, both plump and mature. Helga dressed fairly conservatively. Pauline bounced around in gorgeously cheerful smock-like dresses, and spoke in a deepish voice which I understood as well as I did LO.

With them I matured and made progress. Pauline was more adept at creating partnerships when the fingered language in my head was transferred to tape or typing paper. However the first months of typing with anyone are always difficult. As late as May this was the kind of conversation I was having with her:

Get bit undersand
Get bit upset when we meet people who dont [gap here]
How I dont talk
Englid
Yes tell Them to The talkto me
Have a heart but ma it east ...

LO wrote me a memo to ask why I got so impatient when working with Pauline. I replied:

[Usually] *I have a very structured working envirnment* [environment] *to work in. That does not mean that you tell me how to do the work, but you make it possible for me to achieve ...*

Then suddenly I found that I could work with Pauline really fluently.

I think that it is a good idea that we have this time to talk, because we have such little time, as time is always so scarce ...

(Conversation with Pauline touching my arm. 25 August 1989).

***

My academic progress in Year 10 was more erratic than in the previous year, because I had not learned to compensate for the differences in how I absorbed and regurgitated information, and the subjects often demanded problem-solving practical skills that were beyond me.

AUTISM AND OTHER ADVENTURES: LUCY'S STORY

Science and ceramics were two of my favourites in terms of content. However I had a poor mark in them overall.

We did Asian history, a fascinating conglomeration of names and places which had the mystery of an exotic fairytale, and which really tested my memory. English was fine. We read novels and did book reports.

General Studies was taught by a Mr. Wright. It had elements of philosophy, social history and literature. I waffled happily through the essays, which drew from him a comment that words are for communication, and the more esoteric ones should not be used to 'fluff' through a paper.

I was flattered by his criticism and by a poor mark which indicated to me that he thought me capable of better things. I liked him very much.

***

The previous year a lot of the work in all subjects had been on question sheets, and my type-filled tape was pasted in the gaps left for answers. Now the answers were longer, so I typed them and my partner would copy them onto the sheet.

I typed longer answers and essays on a little typewriter that ran on torch batteries. I had not worked out how to correct myself, so I had to work out what I was going to say well in advance.

The idea that I could dictate corrections had not occurred to me, although I was used to correcting intentional errors in exercises in Year 9 grammar to test our ability to discriminate between the right and wrong form.

I would type out the correct choice, and my partner would insert it if the sentence were more than just a few words. Otherwise I would waste energy just being a copying machine.

***

When I copied, somehow my meaningful language switched off, and my typing became the equivalent of my nonsense speech. My finger movements changed to a frantic swooping that looked to an observer as if I were typing competently.

However the person touching me would note a complete self-absorption, and I did not notice if the original were nonsensical. It became a pattern of shapes in my mind's eye. The letters went from sight to hand, as if I had never learned to read.

The same thing could have happened in Maths had my attention not been kept as directed as possible. LO and Jay worked closely together so that they both learned to take dictation from me in the same way.

That lasted till the middle of that year, when I got sick of Jay struggling to make sense of my clear mathematical vision. Her antediluvian High School Maths knowledge ran aground at that point, and I was delighted to find that she was aware that my distress and hand-biting had a reasonable cause.

'No, Lu!' She giggled and snarled in one, holding a Canon tape at a readable angle. 'I can't imagine 'the wonderful shape of X to the power of ten'. I resign from Maths from this moment. You and LO will just have to put up with each other!'

***

So I dictated graphs and pie charts to LO, and geography diagrams and contour coordinates to Pauline, while driving everyone nuts with my insistence on doing a simple book-keeping course, where I understood exactly what I should be doing, but lacked the co-ordination to draw up the exercises, which had to be done by hand to my instructions.

I explained the layout so vaguely that most people sooner or later teasingly threatened to throttle me. As a result, nowadays whenever I want to say that I am not being deliberately obstructive, my response is automatic.

'No w'ing neck!' I squeak. This is an apology for being so inconvenient, not fear of an irate companion going suddenly berserk. Speech remains a collection of responsive memories, not communication.

***

Helga was practical, steering me firmly through ceramics, and things like a stint of work experience at a university cafeteria, but it was Pauline who took the brunt of my angers and enthusiasm.

The two of them and LO continued to struggle with my autism as I wandered around the school, making noises, giggling and rocking sideways from foot to foot.

Personal hygiene was a continual struggle because I could not bear to close a cubicle door. In the rather rigid if anarchic conventions of a girls' toilet block that would have set me up for some pretty unpleasant bullying.

In the end I simply used the Sick Bay toilet, and the person supervising me had a chat with the School Nurse at the same time. It was like having my own personal peephole into the social life of the staff.

***

In the middle of that year, I started to go to some Saturday morning discussion groups at Deal. I did not like them, because the four or five participants were expected to use typing as if it were general conversation.

I thought of my language on the keyboard as a kind of dialogue between myself and my partner, even though it often involved a third party, such as Nicky or a teacher.

I discovered that the new term for the kind of supported typing that I was using was 'Facilitated Communication', which, like many people, I interpreted as making communication 'easy'.

That seemed nonsensical as it was terribly difficult in every way. I therefore refused to use this expression, and only realised later that it was drawn from the professional vocabulary of those who work with difficulties in motor movement.

***

Later that year I asked Jay to make me try to use a sewing machine. I had done a little machine sewing at Special School, but had not followed a dress pattern. My mother groaned, because she loathes sewing, and took me to choose some black material and a skirt pattern.

She found that if she used the same kind of touch on my arm or shoulder as when I typed, and refused to allow me to stop working when I screamed, or bit my hand and shouted 'No!', I gradually learned to stay still while she muddled through laying out the pieces, and then she indicated exactly where each pin or stitch was to go, while untangling the machine bobbin every few minutes.

I never learned to sew by myself without her standing beside me, but there were some interesting ensembles created which were all my own work, even some little suits for Shay and her new sister Kara, who was born in April.

***

One of the Saturday conversation groups at Deal was to get to know a man called Doug Biklen, who had been an important influence in making mainstream education available to people with disabilities in America.

AUTISM AND OTHER ADVENTURES: LUCY'S STORY

This group included me and another girl who was at a High School, as well as two other people. Doug was very enthusiastic about the way that we used language. The other student and I disagreed fairly strenuously with him about what we could expect in the way of acceptance from the rest of the world.

I was sure that making hands-on typing an integral part of one's life depended on another person being generous to the point that their own personal values took second place, and that an activity which could not at any rate pay for itself in financial terms would be difficult to spread.

I think this shocked Doug, who pointed out that society built roads and airports, and that pathways in communication were also a public service. My fellow student did not think this analogy was very encouraging.

'That falls down, because people can worry about us, but still not have enough money to build airports,' she said. Both of us would have been aware of current arguments about enlarging Melbourne airport, and the continuing saga of the then incomplete South-Eastern Freeway which should have carried much of the traffic which roared past Deal's front window.

A few days later Doug and Rosie visited my High School. LO spilled the beans about my more eccentric activities in the school-yard, and a little later Doug wrote to ask if he could use this material in an article about 'Facilitated Communication' in Melbourne.

I had no problems with the personal bits, though I had a feeling that the subtleties of the rice-driven behaviour management which had avoided worse nasties might have escaped his attention.

***

That winter I was vomiting, sinussy and really uncomfortable for most of the time. I picked and stabbed at my nostrils, and LO and Jay provided copious piles of handkerchiefs, because I ate Kleenexes if they were left in my hand too long after I had used them.

Before long I had managed to transfer this into a series of blazing panics, so that whenever one of them opened her handbag I grumbled the words ''ankie' and 'carkey' with equal terror, cumulating in howls and hand-bites if what I thought was the full complement of little square cotton cloths was not there.

The third quarter of the year I was away from school the whole term. I cowered miserably under Maria's ruffled bed covers between allergy tests, ineffective migraine treatments and attempts at hormone therapy. Those who knew me best conspired to bully me back to school, because I became terrified at the thought of my beloved classroom.

Now I have learned that this whole thing was part of an immune-system and allergy problem, and that part of my terror was due to viral cycles which affected my sensory processing.

***

By and large one could say that 1989 was the best and worst year of my school life, although the most important, bridging as it did my early attempts at using language with the preparatory year for the final school exams.

My diary for 1989 is completely devoted to my disorientation and physical misery. It is in the daily waffle that Jay poured out as a notebook for the school staff and their replies that I can see their struggles to understand my daily inconsistency, problems with learning in the way the other students did, grabbing food from other students in the canteen line, or raiding the canteen shop itself.

LO banned me from the school hall after school, because during the rehearsals for the school play which she produced I spiralled, laughed and rocked to such an extent that the parents who had volunteered to help were terribly put off.

I tried to avoid walking home by myself by hanging around the inside basketball court. On one occasion the Principal and Jay searched for an hour before I was found lying on my back in a corner, and on another Jay actually notified the police that I was missing.

***

After Christmas Rosie had posted me a parcel containing a slim paperback book with the picture of a schoolgirl on the cover, and a seal stating that it had been 'The Children's Book Council of Australia's Book of the Year for Older Readers'. Jay opened the first page, and I glanced at the opening paragraph:

I don't know what I am doing here.

Well, I do really. It's because I was getting nowhere at the hospital. I have been sent here to learn to talk again. Sent here because my mother can't stand my silent presence at home.

I left the room. Jay did not manage to get me to try reading John Marsden's best-selling *So Much To Tell You* for another four months, and then one wet Sunday she literally sat on me while I emoted through the first few pages.

After that I cooed and flapped, entranced by this fictional diary of a girl with a scarred face and no voice, who had just arrived in her new school. A day later in the middle of my evening diary session, I suddenly found the courage to start a letter:

Dear Mr. Marsden,

Last night I read your book. Being speechless and autistic, the character of the girl seemed close to me, though I actually will never speak or make friends ...

(16 May 1989).

LUCY BLACKMAN

***

And he answered! Unbelievable!

Dear Lucy,

Thanks for your letter which came two days ago. I admit it startled me, scared me a bit too. Now I'm a bit stuck to know what to say next. You seem to make momentous statements ('I actually will never speak or make friends') almost casually - though I know these are hardly casual matters for you.

I suppose everyone in the world is like Marina [the girl in *So Much To Tell You*]. *Perhaps we're all on the same spectrum, but you and Marina are further along it than most people. And perhaps the purpose of life is to move as far along the spectrum as we can. Maybe we get credit for the distance we move, rather than the point that we reach ...*

I wrote back. He replied. A few letters later I was able to send him a few of my school exercises. One was a story called *Timewarp*, which I felt was a kind of reflection of my life. I felt obligated to include an anti-parent message. After all, I was trying to be a conventional teenager:

Stealing a catastrophically dilapidated spaceship was a means of showing a very domineering mother and father how much independence I deserved ... The rusty derelict swooped outward on a parabolic course to nowhere ... Fravity [gravity] seemed to grasp my tumbling craft and I lost all awareness of the course or direction of my flight.

At the touch of the sun on my face I stirred, feelings and consciousness at a collision course with intellect. The sun had only been available to the elite for as long as anyone could remember ... My only glimpse had been on my graduation as a capable pilot of mining craft that penetrate the bed rock to bare the molten core ...

AUTISM AND OTHER ADVENTURES: LUCY'S STORY

I opened one eye and found something feathery and yet scratchy sticking into it. From history lessons I recognised the flower of an extinct wild grass seen last before the world city actually spread over the land to meet the fast rising sea.

Dreamily I turned my head and looked at the boy at my side. [His] face and hands had a shine and colour to them, such as the Unburied ones had, and feelings arrived which swept all reasoning away. Yelling like a madman I scrambled to my feet and ran over the soft creamy granular surface that sloped towards unimaginably blue water edged by white gleaming foam.

... The water crept up my heavy direly useless space suit as the ground fell away and the creeping ever circling triangular fin of some mysterious sea creature came nearer. This was the life!

(9A. English Essay. 1988).

***

With it was a copy of another story, a monologue of a girl who met a bag-lady-type person in the bushes by my favourite surf beach at Sorrento. This weird person knew what it was like to feel unwanted and devalued, so she pretended to drown so that the girl could rescue her and so feel needed. It was only about fifteen lines and had no real speech, but I had begun to realise that some of my problems were universal, and was making some attempt to create a character. John did me the compliment to take me seriously enough to criticise my writing:

Now, listen, Luce, I gotta tell you, you're a pretty hot writer. The Timewarp piece is particularly good, and I like the 'oddest Person' very much. But, being a teacher, I can't help making some comments. I think you should ignore your own class teacher's comments about punctuation and bits that 'can't be understood'. You have your own style, and it's fine to experiment with variations from the rules.

I suggest you try writing stories with a more circular structure. In your poems, you might try being less direct. Poems are often more effective when they operate by hints, nudges, comparisons. Instead of writing about the sun, write about its reflection in the water.
Love, John.

I was delighted. So, I was a writer, was I? So much for my mother and my teachers, and their worries about punctuation, truth-telling and being tactful when I wrote letters.

***

One day Jay poked an old Autism Society newsletter in front of me.

'Why don't you try writing to this lady, Sally Borthwick? This news article from Canada might be about the same kind of typing with touch that you are doing.'

I assumed this was a motherly attempt to get me a pen pal. I refused. So Jay wrote a long letter to Canada describing what I was doing, and asking if it were similar to how this student, David Eastham, used his 'Memowriter'.

The reply devastated me. David had drowned in the river in front of his parents' home the previous year, and, yes, we had typed in much the same way. I wrote back, and made another real friend:

Dear Sally,

Stupidly the idea of writing to have contact with David through you was totally repulsive to me. Now I am so sorry I did not write and missed the chance to have contact with him. Thoughts of him dying like that are very sad. The stupid autistic handicap is making me laugh, but really I want to cry. Are your students like that too?

At Special School the retarded children did everything better than I did, autistic behaviours being what they are. Now the kids at High School like me for being bright, because they know my funny way of doing weird things is not the real me.

(28 August 1989).

AUTISM AND OTHER ADVENTURES: LUCY'S STORY

***

Friends came in different categories. The kids at school who spent time in my classes, and stood up to other kids who did not see how bright I was, were one category of friend. They worked across my warblings and screechings in class, and ignored the noise when I felt nauseous and vomited into the plastic container which had become a regular part of my school equipment.

A couple of girls, Jodi and Tracey, even wrote me letters full of the latest 'goss', to which I replied with pompous notes on 'the Meaning of Life'.

I was still bedevilled by my visual processing when it came to faces. Lines had faded, but the contours of flesh were still invisible so that I had no instinctive person-to-person visual signal to compensate for my odd sound processing.

So the image that I visualise when I think the word 'friends' is the written word 'friends', the people with whom I exchanged letters without the hassle of real contact, and who, in many cases, I still write to.

The most special people were beyond the word 'friends'. They are the people who have helped me be a person, some of the family friends, carers, volunteers and teachers to whom I was close when I was young, and especially the people who gave me language — Jay, my sisters, Rosie, LO, Jaime, Pauline, and the others who since that time have sat with me, helped me control myself, and shared my minute by minute responses.

***

Granny Joy had booked a flight for just after Christmas. I was hoping that at least I could be quiet and let her gossip with her daughter, and enjoy the countdown to Val's wedding. I spent the student-free last days of the term in the Library of the school where Jay worked.

Jay laid out rolls of sticky plastic covering and patiently made me move my hands in a mirror image of hers, so that slowly and logically I visualised myself peel and press a shiny skin onto a set of books.

I did not quite see when I was not precise and the edges were crooked, but, taught that way, the result was close enough to hers to satisfy us both. I had added another success to my list. Life was looking good.

Chapter 10
Family Matters, Summer 1989–1990: Age 17

A couple of days before Christmas we were in the kitchen. Jay was watching me try to make reasonably tailored packages out of Christmas paper and tape. Unlike the library covering this was not logical. Each package was different, so my sequence of actions had to be modelled each time if the result were to look more like a sealed parcel than a decomposing bundle.

The phone rang. Jay tumbled from her chair halfway through trying to show me how to mitre a corner on a parcel containing a lumpy toy. I listened from where I was sitting. The sticky tape had been left on the table. I twined strand after strand round my hands, while listening to the clicking voice from the ear piece held against Jay's earlobe about twenty feet down the passage.

This time the voice was unfamiliar. I was surprised because the international call-signal had preceded it. That was usually part of Granny Joy's distant world.

For a moment Jay's grateful mutterings overlaid the strange voice. Then came a lot of discussion about hospitals and doctors. Jay came back down the passage, her face so blank that I knew that she was trying not to upset me. She spoke.

'Lu ... !'

I had not been mistaken. My favourite irritant — my wonderful visitor who had been a stable part of my world all my life — that person who had sat and watched me swing and twirl with sadness and envy, who had observed and believed my first tentative adventures in the written word — had had a stroke.

Now she lay silent and still in hospital. No January visit, no chance to thank her in words and smiles for what she had done for me, and suddenly I realised none of her great-grandchildren would remember her as a person.

And she could not speak.

***

No matter what disaster strikes, Christmas thunders on. Again we were to meet together at Hayley's and Laurie's, because they were the ones with the baby and toddler and no one else really wanted to child-proof their abode.

My nightmare, Shay, was in full two-year-old mode. I was more charmed with her than ever, because when she looked at me she saw nothing odd. With her fontanel closed at last, to my great relief she was in no danger from me.

However this blonde midget flew from place to place, reaching and babbling, so that my adult surrounds went awry whenever people turned to smile at her in the middle of doing something else, or suddenly they would leap unpredictably to rescue her from a fall or from touching a burning cigarette.

Of course Kara was still only eight months old, and her sudden cries, and even her baby breathing, grated on my feeling of well-being.

Hayley had invited Dad again. This time the weather had been kinder, and he had caught the train. What with noise, food and general social overload, my burn-out point came fairly soon after lunch. We gave Dad a lift to the station.

When we drew up at the traffic lights near the station yard, my ever-enthusiastic mother changed gear with what, undoubtedly, she meant to be a flourish.

Just before the holidays she had been complaining the clutch was slipping. (I have vague memories of this phrase featuring frequently in long, tense, oblique conversations about money and car-maintenance in the days before we became a one-parent family.)

Now the car had come back from the mechanic with the clutch presumably right as Jay made happy noises as we drove up and down the hills on the road down the Bay. However I had noticed that the little lever sticking out of the lump in the floor of the car was at a rather different angle from before.

From my back-seat position behind my father, I could see Jay's eye sliding cornerwise, no doubt to see if her high level of car maintenance was making an impression on her ex-spouse. It certainly did.

Her hand, still clutching the knob of the floor-shift lever, flew up like a drum-majorette's to shoulder height. Below it dangled the shaft, with the screw threads clearly visible, and from my vantage point in the back I could see that the ridges looked newly burred. The car stood rock solid.

Gleefully I watched her struggle with the usual dilemma of automotive crisis and the possibility of my impending panic, at the same time as I got the alarm signal of slight buzzing and little chaotic shifts in my view of the world.

***

Here she had another dimension, my father's rickety back. Should she ask him to push, or ask that he steer? Unintentionally he saved her dignity. He shot a horrified glance at the shaft in her hand, hopped with unusual agility from the bucket seat to the roadside, and bent to speak over the half-closed passenger door.

'Sorry, Darling.' I saw Jay's neck tense when that word started to form. 'But I might miss my train. Thanks for the lift.'

The door slammed and he sKaymed over the tarmac, a slowly receding figure in the summer sun.

Grinning internally, and giggling out loud because I was anxious, I realised that I was being hustled out of my back-seat sanctuary. The street was completely deserted as it was the midpoint of Christmas lunch time.

Jay took my hands, placed them on the front of the car, and, standing beside me, modelled how I could bend over so as to put my weight behind the car as she held the steering wheel through the open door.

'Push, Lu,' she said, and pushed backwards herself on the central pillar.

'Walk!' Each time I started to lose motivation, she reminded me firmly that this was a continuous effort.

'Push!' and, as the gears seemed fortunately to be unengaged, we pushed our pride and joy closer to the empty footpath..

We walked back the half mile or so, and rejoined the party. I think that eventually Laurie patched up the thread with some kind of wondrous space-age tape, and Jay lost a hefty slice of her confidence in the motor repair industry.

***

One weekend we joined a bush walking group, scrambling up a long eminence known as Cathedral Peak. I was terrified to find that we were to climb up some boulders, and then to follow the same formation through a chimney.

I was urged to put my hands into niches, to watch the person in front of me and to let my feet find ledges. At no time was the height of the rock more than my own stretched length. However I could not step off the ground without being able to see my own feet.

As the rest of the group were reasonably anxious not to have their Sunday completely ruined, there was a slight movement of impatience, both above and below me.

'Hang on!'

AUTISM AND OTHER ADVENTURES: LUCY'S STORY

No way.
'Don't back down.'
I already had.
'Have another try!'
Ouch.

'Put your hands up, Lucy!' That was Jay's voice. I am sure there were a few disapproving glances at the chainsaw tartness there. Then a strange, large, firm hand on the back of the calf that was already stepped up into a crack. I pushed the other toe against the ground, and another hand was pressed against my buttocks.

Suddenly I knew where each limb was, rather like the way I knew what my hand was doing when it was typing. A most extraordinary sensation!

We got to the top in a hot straggly group. I looked down from the great natural jumbled parapet. Hawks spun and swooped over the plains that spread below us, and I was looking down on those hawks. Wonderful!

We walked down the easy way, about an hour's worth I think. Nearly three hours later we made it. The ancient convulsions that had thrown up this marvellous ridge had left the rocks that it had cracked falling away, almost in a chevron pattern, on each side of what formed a natural walking track.

The height of the mountain was not the issue, and indeed the edge seemed often obscured by bushes and trees that grew among the boulders. To me the shape of the ground itself was completely disconcerting.

I simply saw this strange, bumpy, striped landscape as a collection of shifting shapes. I and my body were adrift in a monochrome world.

I could not understand that this was what I saw, still less explain it to anyone. The people in the group were wonderful. They encouraged me, and told me not to be embarrassed. I disintegrated into a chattering wreck. I might never have walked off that mountain myself had Jay not taken over.

'Put your foot forward!' she snapped. Then, as I stood squeaking in the new position,

'Now the other one!' she shouted.

'Then the next foot,' and so on, until I had edged slowly down this horrifying, distorted landscape. Then suddenly among trees on a steeply sloping earth track, all was well. I had descended from Hell, and my world was whole again.

***

Jay looked for an activity that was one not social, one that I considered important (which ruled out outings with community groups) and preferably one which would be possible for me to carry on with very little input from her.

Because I simply could not perform different tasks and sequences of movement one after another in order, I still needed to be guided step-by-step. However I could think of cause and effect in terms of shape and size.

The previous year Jay had introduced me to the joys of cutting down some of the bushes which were rampant on our still unlandscaped suburban block of land. Sawing through the trunks, she had thought, would increase my eye-hand co-ordination.

Using secateurs had also improved my hand strength, but the whole exercise had not exactly turned out the way that she wanted. I became obsessed with the act of demolition rather than the outcome of making the garden less overgrown.

Unfortunately I also became very proprietorial about my forestry, because it had a charm that was far removed from any idea that I was creating some kind of landscape.

In the end she had turned it into a problem-solving exercise, pointing out the tree that she wished me to fell, starting off three piles, one of large branches, one of small and one of twigs, and giving me the task of reducing the fifteen-foot high monster into a small enough compass to go in the back of the station wagon.

By now the garden was denuded of anything that was not big enough to require a professional tree surgeon. Even the latter category looked rather as if a herd of tree-eating goats had been standing up against them, so scored was the bark.

***

To occupy the rest of the long holidays, Jay decided to let me paint the whole house on the inside. She thought, poor dear, that a constructive rather than destructive task might create a better atmosphere.

Fat hope!

I started with the ceiling, clinging anxiously to a six-foot pair of folding steps. Jay was really delighted that the flat white surface looked so good after being liberally spread with thick, self-smoothing, non-drip paint. She let me loose on the walls. The paint was cream. It sloshed beautifully from the brush and roller, making flow marks and beaded dribbles down the wall.

Lovely!

Jay would pretend that she had come into the room for a chat. Her light blue eyes were stiff in their sockets and her face startlingly tense under the cheerful grin that was the backdrop to twittering approval of my enthusiastic, but definitely self-indulgent, brush work.

'Look, Love,' and her hand would close over my fist on the roller handle. She would drag it through the trough on the tray, and then, with me totally limp in her grasp, roll it vigorously back and forward over the ridges provided for scraping off excess paint.

'That is much better, isn't it?' and I would echo that keyword, 'Better', understanding it only in my received language, but totally unable to transfer it into an intelligent response.

Besides, it was not 'better' for me. Flowing paint felt so wonderful, and as often as my mentor explained why I must scrape the excess off, and moulded my hands to the task, so often did I ignore her as soon as she turned quietly away.

Jay knew that if she tried to work alongside me, I would just degenerate into helpless frustration. So, having become obsessional for my task so long as it was on my own terms, drips and all, I felt my body, taste, touch and vision focused together, as if projected through a lens.

'Reality', which later I called 'normality', was that the paint should spread evenly onto the wall.

For me that was unimportant, because the sweep of my hand, which by now was coated in what looked like melted ice-cream perhaps vaguely butterscotch in colour, was integrated into my vista, and was a consequence in itself.

That the wall was being painted so that it would look smooth and even in colour was, of course, part of my general knowledge. In my personal world view only my moving hand, flailing brush, and the paint dripping from it was real.

The walls were eventually fairly uniform, because my workmate-despite-herself would dash in and frantically make good my most creative contours. Jay was delighted that we had got this far without throttling each other.

***

Assuming that the worst was over, she opened a can of beer for herself in celebration. She told me to get a Coke. We sat down in front of the typewriter, and she gave me the kind of smile which

I assume could be called 'encouraging'. My interior alarm bell tinkled.

'Now, wouldn't this be a good time for letter-writing!' said Jay. So naive, my Mum!

In fact all that I typed that day could have been summarised as a collection of excuses for my painting methods, complaints that people weren't as sough with me as I might need, and a programme initiative of my own:

... very drippy paint has been nice-feeling, but horrible to look at ... learning that feeling and result have to be happily married ... May I do the gutter pipes, keeping carefully to the metal?

(14 January 1990).

Talk about trapping myself! I really wanted to write to John Marsden to say that I had enjoyed his book, *The Journey*, which I had read over Christmas, but what I had expressed was a combination of an obsession and of a suggestion, 'Do you really think that I should move on to the gutters?'

That old problem with words that related to speculation, planning and things that I wanted to do, was coming into play yet again!

In blissful ignorance of this minefield, Jay thought I was still enthusiastic about painting.

I was, but I was beginning to get that over-the-top feeling that comes with my losing control of myself. Resigned to a paint-soaked summer, Jay decided that she ought to encourage me.

She simply made the best of a bad situation, wrapping the adjacent non-paint areas in many dollars' worth of masking tape, and buying twice the required amount of paint. The paint was chocolate-brown in colour, and in the summer warmth dried almost as quickly as the coating on a dipped ice-cream cone, so most of it stayed on the guttering.

Halfway round the house the slope of the ground meant that I had to climb to the third-top step of the ladder. No top-rail at waist-height to clutch Panic, fear, terror!

Jay tried not to reward that she saw as 'behaviours'. She went straight down the street, and came back with a longer and broader pair of step-ladders. I looked at them dubiously, and mounted to what my experience had told me was my maximum safe elevation.

'One more step!' Jay's disembodied voice was level with my thighs. That was not reassuring.

'McDonalds!' muttered the voice. I did not really care what I should have for the next meal. However as usual I was comforted and motivated by this unusual security blanket.

I moved up a step, and found that the top of the ladder formed a shoulder-high railing. If not happy, at least I had overcome my terror. Though the ground was canyonlike, I dipped my paintbrush and made a stroke.

***

The painting saga demonstrated exactly where I was different from my sisters. If they started painting something, they knew right through the time they were working on it what the outcome should be.

However, because I had developed only a very imprecise notion that the immediate future would accommodate my next action, and my memory for the very immediate past through which my hand had travelled was often shrouded, I could not then project a clear trail of future little memories down which I could see that a continuous sequence of these pleasurable brush strokes would eventually cover the wall in a smooth film of cream.

I thought that I had something wrong with the intelligent part of my brain when Jay had said things like, 'Can't you see that the wall is blotchy?' I see now that I was stymied by my fluctuations in sight, sound and balance.

Unbelievably I lived in a world (and still do) where the environment of our Earth, with its consistent gravity, sound waves and refracted light, was but an invention of fiction writers, sociologists and psychologists.

Because I lived in an uncertain world, change of any kind was so incomprehensible that when anyone said, 'I think that I might ...' or 'I wonder if it would be best to ...', my four-dimensional world unfolded like a paper streamer.

***

By this time Jay had received different accounts of how aware my Grandmother was of those around her. I heard her talking to Eileen about this when she thought I was out of earshot. I had seen television news broadcasts of the township violence in South Africa.

Of course I had also realised that for most people of European origin, life on a daily basis was pretty much like how we lived. However I could not get out of my mind a knee-jerk reaction — if Jay went to visit her mother, I might never see her again.

My terror was concrete, expressed in tears and shrieks. She did not realise how mean I felt. Like most people, I had had the illusion that I could put the interests of someone I loved before my own terrified dependence.

I received letters from a friend, full of her own grief at her grandmother's loss of awareness due to Alzheimer's Disease.

I learned from a chance conversation that the mother of the boy whom I had met on my second visit to Deal had died.

Kay had been pretty shocked that Jay had not immediately accepted the offer from the people handling Granny Joy's affairs to purchase an air ticket. None of my sisters could have looked after me that year, what with study, jobs and babies.

Jay had decided not to go to South Africa, because she would not break her promise about leaving me in a respite-care house unless someone could have assured her that it would make a real difference to the course of Granny Joy's illness. Rather than tell me, she chose to discuss this problem with my sister, Kay, in my hearing.

***

Of course Jay could have told me direct, and probably would have if the answer had been an absolute certainty. Because there was an element of 'perhaps' in all this, she knew it was better to allow me to learn of her decision from listening to her talk it over with someone else.

That way I would see the whole scene as an outsider, think about it, and then talk about it later. If she had 'sat me down and had a nice chat' about it, the various fears, emotions and angers that were bubbling around in me would probably have led to an explosion:

Far more really unlovely thoughts came from horrible telling nice, actually caring Kay you are not going to South Africa, but horribly, actually, thoughts, autistic-and-otherwise, began to get happy, because for me the need has got very big for you to be here.

(Typing session, Early 1990).

I was beginning to hate dependence, not for any reason of pride, or even because I feared my mother's death. What scared me more than anything else was that I had no clue why I could not function consistently without the familiar people in my life.

***

AUTISM AND OTHER ADVENTURES: LUCY'S STORY

Australia Day in the last weekend of January was celebrated in Melbourne with a free fireworks display over Albert Park Lake, which is quite near the centre of the City.

I loved the excitement of the train and tram trip in from the suburbs, and relished the music that was provided by a local rock station and spewed forth from a multitude of transistor radios.

Because the many small speakers that surrounded the lake did not bounce their sound off an enclosing wall, I lost the overwhelming urge to spiral and spring from leg to leg, which I found so terrifying and pleasurable in the school hall.

We watched the magic of the fireworks, and streamed back to the station in the midst of a chaotic group of revellers. As the train rattled home that night, in the brightness of my mind's eye words fell about:

Far going rockets
Far blazing stars
Meet for an instant
And the greater dies
To fall in grubby smoke
From momentary immortality ...
(Australia Day, 1990).

***

The last week of the holidays we spent at Dromana. We walked up the hill at Sorrento Back Beach. From a circular gazebo perched on the crest, I stared southwards. Over the horizon the ocean stretched on to Antarctica. Below us great rocks lay in the surf, some the dragons of my childhood dreams. In the evenings I watched the television or typed:

Dear Mr. Marsden,

The dreadful depression and virus that I had all winter has gone, so unlovely awful grumpiness has totally gone, and feelings were helped by reading The Journey. Keeping that thought of life and death, and kindness, and people having differences was so possibly lovely, having had such miserable thoughts.

Caring that you do not think I am happy, I handled this last year as well as lots of nice people could help me to, and I still am hoping that Year 11 will be possibly as good.

(28 January 1990).

***

Dear Lucy,

It was good to get home to a letter from you ... So how was school? Imagine, your first day was today. It's funny how I get such a different view of you in your letters to the view other people must have. It's only from hints in your letters that I realise that your autism must be visible in different ways to different people.

Yet it's not visible in your letters. It's confusing, but I find autism confusing anyway. Presumably it includes various uncontrollable behaviours.

It seems to dominate your thinking. Do you see yourself as 'autistic' before anything else? All the other labels - female, teenager, daughter, sister, student, writer, poet, friend, etc., etc. - do they all fight for second place? Can they never aspire to be first?

It's easy for me to say this, because your autism doesn't show on paper - when I think of you, the labels that spring to mind are more to do with your sensitivity, creativity, eloquence, warmth. I wonder whether you see it that way, though?

Love, John.

***

AUTISM AND OTHER ADVENTURES: LUCY'S STORY

The school year began with mixed news. Helga, whom I liked, was leaving. Val and Rolf had been planning their wedding for some months for the end of the second week of term.

I have clear memories of going to a bridal boutique with our mother so that Val would have the satisfaction of showing her the wedding-dress that she had selected. The whole room was walled with mirrors — multiples-on-multiples of Val-the-Bride, Jay-the-Mother-of-the-Bride, the Saleswoman-smoothly-reassuring, and me, the Married-Never-to-Be, in shadowy, shiny infinity.

To Hell with Val's big day!

I was not only angry, but I really did not see the emotional significance of the whole dress ritual. Jay was stuck in the middle. She tried to admire and croon. In the same minute, she was tracking my progress from display dummy directly to tiara stand. The assistants made tactful noises. I reached for satin trains and dangling pearl beads.

'Oh, Mum!' said Val in exasperation, as the Mother-of-the-Bride act started to come unstuck.

When The Day came, Jenny pretty well deputised for Jay. Jay said resignedly that Jenny was better at 'that sort of thing' (whatever that means), and she, Jay, was probably rather more talented at keeping me company, so it was a better division of labour. Everyone concurred that the Home of the Bride was not the place for me!

***

In due course, the real Mother and I drove through the Dandenong Hills, east of Melbourne, to the beautiful old hotel and wedding centre that they had booked. Jay had expressed the view that the wedding might be smoked out by mid-February bush fires, such as those which had swept up nearby slopes on Ash Wednesday, seven years before.

Instead my sister, now transformed into a radiantly happy fairy-tale heroine, swept up the path to the spun-sugarlike wedding chapel with an enormous, faded beach umbrella held over her against the persistent, unseasonable cool drizzle.

The ceremony went off without a hitch, and we all posed for group photos without incident. The reception was another matter.

Noisy with ventilation, movement, rock music, laughter and breathing, it also involved the smell of alcohol, perfume and cooked food. It might have been bearable if I could have moved around, run back and forward, and swung on the old staircase balustrade, but this was a formal wedding!

Almost relieved, I felt 'sick' whirl around my diaphragm, and knew that my reflexes were not going to let me down. I heaved and gagged onto my newly served main course. The gates of the torture chamber were about to be opened.

'Oh, poor Lucy!' said a guest at the same table.

'Oh, Mum!' said Hayley.

Jay mapped out our escape route so that hopefully Val would not notice that I had made jagged rents in her most important day. The speeches were over by the time she had dumped me at a friend's flat.

When I watch the video of the reception, I notice that she was back in plenty of time to wave the couple farewell.

Chapter 11
School Matters, 1990:
Age 17

The first four months of Year 11 were much more difficult than I had expected. The work was more demanding from the first day, so when my rage and sudden distress at school and in other places where there were lots of people seemed more frantic, it seemed obvious that the pressure of school work was to blame.

I did not realise that my anti-depressant tablets had been making my sensory integration a little more efficient. Also they had caught my panic attacks just before they got out of hand. Because they had not stopped my cycles of illness and the dreadful nausea, I had stopped taking them.

It was not until some years later when I read of benefits that other people with autism had had from similar medication that I realised that my last two years at school could have been much easier.

We had to have interviews for another aide. Indira, who started a few weeks later, was great. A tiny lady who had come to Melbourne from India, she was very responsive to my finger movements — and she was a maths and science graduate.

***

However before this was sorted out, the month of February was torrid. This kind of stress was a direct trigger for terrible behaviour which worried my teachers.

I was no less mobile and excitable than the previous year, and my fuse was a lot shorter. Now it was not because I really wanted them that I grabbed foodstuffs and scratched chewing gum off the ground.

Continual positive comments when I coped well, as well as concrete strategies such as my stamping on especially delectable discarded coloured sweets, and also my growing self-respect, had made scavenging so embarrassing.

Yet these urges still erupted, often at the most inconvenient moment for everyone. However now it was usually an expression of fed-upness or fury. The temptation to shock baited the hook.

Sometimes the homework diary was full of disastrous hints that my behaviour was doing little to convince the school community that my plump, gingham-clad person hid a capacity for creative language and problem solving in maths.

All the people concerned made an even greater effort than the previous term. I was encouraged to collect my lunch from a certain serving-hatch in the canteen where the paid manageress was on duty, rather than from one where there was an occasionally rostered parent, who might be more susceptible to bullying, or more tender hearted.

***

Anyone who knew me well understood that some kind of trigger was needed for self-control, much as 'McDonalds', or similar catchwords, gave me the impulse to do what I really wanted to, but was apparently reluctant to attempt.

Not that 'Fried Rice' had outlived its use-by date, but we were all getting a bit bored. Therefore, in terms of creating a self-monitoring system, an easily provided food that I found totally repulsive was a bright idea.

One day I got a wonderful jolt. I had grabbed a can of drink from a younger student. When Jay picked me up that evening she had been fully briefed by LO:

AUTISM AND OTHER ADVENTURES: LUCY'S STORY

Silly behaviour totally took over at lunch, and the childish grabbing had to be stopped, but Mrs. Lohning has told you about that.
— and then I realised what we were to have for our evening meal!
Fear of egg sandwiches! You have obviated my impulsiveness! Dear Mum, it sounds so silly, but it works! Just Brilliant!

***

She took me at my word. Egg sandwiches were occasionally a portable sanction, as most sandwich shops would make them. Of course hard-boiled eggs, with or without two slices of bread plastered to them, are outside the discipline policy of most modern schools. Mine would have been horrified by any suggestion that this eccentric Lewis Carrol-type tactic was in use.

Jay got immediate feedback as to the 'good' and 'not-so-good' moments at recess and lunchtime. Then the meal that we ate that evening would be a concrete measure in my own wavering memories of how I had controlled the urge to use food both as an amusement for myself, and as an irritant for the people I loved or relied on.

When I was not too obnoxious, we would have chops, sausages, spaghetti, or something else that I enjoyed and often cooked myself. When disaster struck, egg salad or fried rice. When my halo gleamed or sparkled, fish and chips from the take-away.

***

I also worried about how much I disturbed the whole class:
Dear John Marsden,
Lots of people call autism an intellectual disability, but really, for me it is more physical, because I actually want to do things normally but autistic behaviours intervene. So until I was fourteen, my family

thought I was retarded. People still have to help me by helping me control my behaviour. The sight of someone biting her hand and screaming in a Year 11 class is a bit disconcerting for the other people!

(19 March 1990).

When my partner was absent for any length of time, I returned readily to attention-seeking. So the real curb that my distaste for eggs and that old standby, rice, gave me, slowly came to flash through my taste-feeling if my self-control had slipped — though at this stage it was usually after the event!

I think it was this attempt to make me understand and then think through the process of not just doing what my body wanted, which prepared me to think constructively about why I was so impulsive when I began to understand myself better:

***

Dear Sally,

Last year was a bit difficult, but this actually seems better. Really the carrying-on and screaming and hand-biting are easier to control, as mad, lousy, weird Jay has thought out a very good system. I can count on her very soon giving me a hard boiled egg sandwich if I pick unlovely chocolate or chewing gum from the ground. Getting the feeling of confidence is so secure, as I hate eggs more than any [other] food. Weird autism calls for weird management!

(20 March 1990).

Dear Lucy,

My job has me supervising two units for young people with autism. They are 4 years old to 21 years.

I was interested to hear about the dreaded boiled egg sandwiches. You seem to like this bit of help. You say you have a hard time with positives. We have a student who acts terribly after positives as well. I wonder why this is so hard.

Love, Sally.

AUTISM AND OTHER ADVENTURES: LUCY'S STORY

(Ottawa. 6 April 1990).

***

I had not developed any disciplined feedback to myself from babbling and internal language, because I had not developed speech. Nor had I really locked the speech that I heard from others into what my body was experiencing, or what I had experienced internally.

I got feedback in my memory mainly from sound, sight, taste and emotion that related to the experience that I was undergoing in the immediate present.

I did not tell anyone for a long time that my dislike of certain foods affected far more than my taste buds, because I thought everyone was aware of food across their senses.

The previous Christmas, for the first time, I had gained enough experience at self-expression to comment rudely on LO giving me some chocolates:

Getting the mean, dreadful feeling that I do when I see chocolate, basically makes a jarring, very bad, awful cacophony of sound - but kind of noiseless sound. Darling, perfectly silly LO actually should know better, but getting kind thoughts can be so strong that she totally forgets.

(Evening diary, 27 December 1989).

I had realised that I got very excited when I saw chocolate because of sensory crossover, which I described here as a 'sound-feeling'. However Jay thought it was simply an example of picturesque expression. Describing something, and then refining and expanding that description, is how children slowly learn how to tell their mothers what they feel. I had lost how many years of language?

***

About this time I got another link to this fragmented chain of clues about myself. We dropped in on the family of a little boy with autism. I was enchanted. In this beautiful, mobile little Juan, rocketing around the chairs and trying to seize cans from his father's beer fridge, was me so many years younger.

His mother had not lived in Australia very long. I can't remember where she had grown up herself, but I think her home language was Spanish. I thought it was just a cultural difference when she sat at the table with him wriggling and waving on her lap, and fed him occasional pieces of cake and biscuit into his mouth.

I noticed that he seemed to pause before swallowing. At some point in the conversation, she mentioned that it was easier to feed him when she was holding him. I watched Jay's profile, and guessed that she was reminding herself that it was none of her business if the family preferred to use tactics which probably some people would call spoiling.

But it was my business, Lucy-business, though I did not talk about it because I had not worked out why this was so.

Fear of food (other than my favourites) had always given me shuddering discomfort, the same discomfort that now I realise seems to be connected with listening when facing a person speaking directly to me, or with looking at my typing finger.

Holding someone implies touch, and touch which is responsive to the movement one would prefer to make gives one more control over that movement.

A few months later I did begin to recognise this when we dropped in on another family whose son had real problems eating most foods:

Dear LO,

The totally strange experience that we had today was the possible key to offering an explanation for my dependence.

AUTISM AND OTHER ADVENTURES: LUCY'S STORY

We met a lady, and she has a dear little boy who is autistic and so dependent on his mother that he will only eat when she touches him.

Fear stops him eating when she has to be away. That seems like my typing, and may feel a good actual model, which makes sense of the weak links in my abilities. Does that sound strange, because not to me.

The memory of being that age include love of a presence when Jay was there, and that made so much difference at beastly times, because it was really the only autistic symptom that was very precious - the need of someone to cause the fear to go away.

Love, Lucy

(22 May 1990).

***

The mystery was compounded by a misunderstanding as to what each of us, I and my various carers, meant by 'fear'. For me it was a sudden, overwhelming sensory chaos which was painful in some undefined way.

This could be triggered off by the kind of things that other people see as frightening, such as a new school or being asked to jump from a height.

However the identical sensation also came if I were exposed to a chaotic sensory environment, but a lot of the sounds and movements that I found 'frightening' in this sense were soothing or imperceptible to most people.

My fear seemed childish. I was yet to realise that trees moving gently in the breeze were not threatening, and I could only guess that air conditioning vents were not drowning out other sounds by watching those around me.

If I suddenly found that Pauline was standing up and waiting for me to close up the typewriter, so that we could leave the room because the teacher had booked a different room to show a video, I might be quite happy to go along with what was expected.

However, if there were a lot of wind-noise, or if she were chatting intermittently with someone else so that her face changed shape, although her waiting body had taken up a position that signalled her attention was on me, or if I had been looking forward to the class in its usual format and the emotion of disappointment ... — If these, or a lot of other factors were present, I reacted with fear.

***

I had gradually become more and more anxious about walking back home, or to Maria, after school. I developed a meandering progress whenever I walked anywhere if I were not very excited about what was going to happen as soon as I arrived.

Overlaying this was my inability to restart an action which was interrupted. If I stood on the kerb to check for traffic and none came, I might get stuck there.

Now that I was more aware of people, I knew that I was more odd than I had realised when I was fifteen. Embarrassment was simply the icing on the cake. It was about this time that Jay found me walking in circles under the eye of the appalled bird-like lady who made a brief walk on appearance in Chapter 3.

The noise of the container trucks, builders' trucks and cars was not getting any easier to bear. I could not seem to break down Jay's resolve that I should move from one place to another through this booby-trapped mayhem.

I tried a different tactic, walking into a nearby supermarket and grabbing sweets from the checkout. Some of the other students passed the word back to LO.

'Oh!' said Jay. 'If you feel you are ready to shop in that way, I will make sure that there is always some money for when you walk home.'

AUTISM AND OTHER ADVENTURES: LUCY'S STORY

***

The support group meeting was coming up. I indicated to both Jay and LO that I was fed up with being supervised so much. Goodness knows what I thought this was going to do to make me less nervous.

Somehow, like my misconception about one being able to learn to like something because one said one liked it, I thought that I would become motivated to the point of continuing something that I really did not want to do, if I said that I wanted to do more of the same.

I even congratulated myself after the meeting:

I am so glad that the subject of my being allowed to go about on my own is now discussed. Horrible behaviour is the result of bloody mindedness. Actually you said the right thing for a change.

(Evening diary, 26 March 1990).

However that was the final straw. Twenty-four hours later, I was back at the typewriter, writing a letter of apology to the local convenience store, where I had all but attacked an assistant who had tried to stop me helping myself to a frozen drink.

***

Jay obviously had to make some adjustments of her own. She reduced her working hours at the beginning and end of the school day. I was both delighted and apologetic:

The nasty behaviour is a happy way of telling unlovely, desperately dreadful friends that it is foolish and terrifying. Lots, really, of normal people are scared of things to the point of phobia, so why not me. Last night you caringly were actually able to see that, and I am very happy.

(Evening diary, 29 March 1990).

***

At this point the future was drawing closer and closer. Once I left school there was no provision for a full time one-on-one aide. Jay worked out that, if we sold our house and pooled our resources, she would be able to stop working.

If I had been prepared to be in a full-time, in-house programme for people with intellectual disabilities, all these difficulties which stemmed from excitement, fear, sensory discomfort and anger might not have been a major problem for her. However any kind of 'normal' setting would need Jay to be available at short notice.

We decided to move to our minute and bare house by the sea. By moving then, Jay gave me a concrete symbol that reassured me that even if nothing else came up there would be one person available to me who had the experience to integrate behaviour management, my own kind of communication and my own personal ambition to have a university education.

Of course I found a dark lining to this sheltering cloud. I worried intermittently about how sure she was that we could manage financially. In fact Jay was more uncertain than I, which really did not make her elaborate budget predictions, scrawled in columns over sheets of scrap paper, any more convincing.

I was also aware that Jay's income had already reduced by twenty percent. Jenny had deferred that year to take up a job to save up for the next year.

***

I felt vaguely responsible, seeing that already a lot of our mother's earnings went on my being 'minded' while she worked, and on other indefinable costs like double amounts of gutter paint, and a cheap computer she had just bought to supplement my two typewriters.

At the same time I knew that my dependence and my need to be called to order looked babyish.

AUTISM AND OTHER ADVENTURES: LUCY'S STORY

I thought of what I would have said to Jenny if we had been chatting together. As always when I was embarrassed or nervous of someone, I could not sit with her and type. So I did the next best thing. I wrote a letter. My typed words came out in a teasing stream:

Dear madly-and-interestingly-silly, not-actually-as-mindless-as-you-seem Jenny,

('Do remember about hurting people's feelings,' said Jay from next to my right elbow)

Getting a job is very helpful for the rest of us, but please don't vastly overload specially wonderful (but unlikely for me) university years. The time you have there is so special that you must not waste it, and must enjoy yourself.

Remember that I am an adult, and think as an adult. Being yelled at by Jay as if [I were] *a child takes away a nearly insuperable barrier that my odd actions and noises create, so I can be seen more like an adult [by other people]. However I am determined to see myself as an adult, and to become self-monitoring. She has shown me I can do it, but sadly at the moment I still need compulsion.*

***

At school the corridor was a special problem in terms of behaving oddly. I tended to sway and run unless I was closely surrounded by other kids.

If I were excited, I would dash into the emptier foyer-area near the General Office, and dance from foot to foot outside the door of the office of the Principal. I guess this must have made interviews rather difficult with parents who had sat through my highland fling past the waiting area, especially if they had been summoned to discuss the disruptive behaviour of their own child.

On another branch of the main corridor was the Deputy Principal, neatly displayed dealing with day-to-day discipline and staffing matters behind a clear glass window.

I would stand, feet apart, the daylight from the door to the school yard opposite throwing my reflection onto that glass. These reflections mesmerised me.

I saw the thrown images in duplicate, as if separate. If I moved my head through an arc, they moved against each other like cut-out figures on sticks. I swung from foot to foot, laughing and crowing, my hands loosely in the air and my skull swinging from shoulder to shoulder in an arc.

The world on the other side of the window learned to carry on as if I were part of the decor.

***

All was well if I were moving from room to room with someone who was conscious enough of my needs to tune the tempo of her movement to mine, and who was alert enough to anticipate any urge that I might have to lose track of her.

Most of this help with behaviours, noise and odd movement arose naturally in the companionship between me and my communication partner. LO, Jay and Pauline could still my fear by deliberately talking about the thing I had been frightened of, and also by their own confident approach.

They all learned the hard way not to tell me that 'nothing was wrong', or 'not to worry'. By this time, my eccentric social decoder had categorised these as alarm signals.

***

That Easter, Jay and I and the Cats moved down to the house at Dromana, by now resplendent in very second-hand carpet and an old tweed lounge suite that our perpetually moulting pets promptly claimed. In my imagination they sneered at me.

Even now I am a bit vague about what a sneer is, but to me that phrase encompassed the total disinterest these sleek plagues showed towards me. Jay watched them settle in, and seemed to relax as they sniffed, prowled and demanded that she open and close outside doors at their whim. The next morning there was, as usual, a heavy, furry lump on my bed when I woke.

'Nice day for a walk!' Jay muttered over breakfast, and we marched down to the coiling concrete footbridge spanning the freeway, our quickest way to the beach.

Of course, at times I had been frightened by the height of the bridge, the roar of the wind and the distant lapping bay a kilometre away, and the sheer size of the open sky, but Jay had walked me over this arch with such firmness so many times that both of us managed these problems pretty well.

Neither of us was prepared for my scream of terror when we rounded the last curve of the ascent, and the main span stretched before us on that sunny, calm morning.

It was Jay who realised what had made me so frightened. The Canon in her hand, she stood firmly, cutting off the escape route.

'Look, Sweetie!' She must have been scared herself by my violent response to use such an unusually babying term of endearment. 'Look at the shadow of the rails. It's like the angle of those rocks when you were worried on the mountain.'

There across the slightly ribbed concrete ribbon before me was an angled chaos. The shadow thrown by the barred handrail totally broke up my view, so that there was no consistency, no depth, and no definite surface on which I could place my feet.

If the sun had been higher, or at right angles to the bridge, I might not have constructed the shadow in my chaotic vision in quite that way. As it was, I could understand at once what Jay was saying.

I took her hand, poked a couple of times at the keyboard, just enough to let her know that she was on the right track, and allowed myself to be led across the bridge though I pulled back all the way, and clung with my other hand to the rail.

***

This same weird sight problem solved part of another mystery, why I occasionally got frightened in the car for no apparent reason. Because I was settled into my High School I was not going to change schools, so now we had to drive along tree-lined country roads till we got to the freeway.

One morning was particularly beautiful. Once again I was startled by my own fear, though this time I was able to understand that it was caused by a feeling that I was being precipitated into a chasm.

This was in itself something that made the terror less dramatic, because at least I could identify the visual illusion that had triggered it. However it was the voice in the driver's seat that proposed a solution.

'Let's try going slower.'

So for a few weeks, on sunny days we went at twenty-five kilometres an hour, dropping down bit by bit till I just shook and went red, instead of going through the whole tantrum bit. I seem to remember a few blasting horns from behind but Jay survived, and even managed to find a certain obscure amusement in the situation.

She did make me realise that she chose not to use an alternative route just because of sensory problems, and gradually speeded up as I slowly began to become more tolerant of the diabolical enchantment that the sloping shadows of eucalypts had wrought on my landscape.

AUTISM AND OTHER ADVENTURES: LUCY'S STORY

***

Whether walking calmly down the corridor at school in the wake of LO, or allowing myself to be dragged over a bridge striped in terror, I was learning what occurred when my behaviour was controlled at a time when I would have been more comfortable 'doing my own thing'.

This help might not have contributed to creating self-control in the short term. However these episodes gave a continual progression of experience that control was possible, and that when it slipped into place things were not necessarily easier or more pleasant (in spite of the conviction that many non-autistic people have), but were more intellectually demanding, which in itself is pleasant.

***

Tantrums have always been fun. They still are occasionally, when a scream and the snap of my jaw on the heel of my hand gets a reaction from someone that I want to shock.

(I had not realised it then, that lying down and rocking from heel to head, or even clamping my jaw, was partly a counter to a giddiness which came with sensory confusion.)

It was so great to be able to write to Sally about these things, because I did not have to describe them in detail:

Dear Sally,

When good behaviour is so little noticed, and tantrums mean something has to be done, the lesson is easy [for me] to learn.

It is much more difficult to sit still because the pleasure of being happily in motion is so wonderful. The memory starts with the dreadful fear of a stupid, nonsensical, vast daring need to be as far away from where I was as possible, and it was more pervasive if the person with me tried to hold me.

Learning to like being cuddled never came, and I first dreamed of kissing my mother when I was 16, though she taught me to appear to kiss when I was weirdly able to mimic her kissing a Teddy Bear when I was small. The stupid, happy expression she had when I did kiss her of my own will two years ago was so funny, and, [by] getting tearful, she made me feel guilty.

At this point Jay started to rummage through files and folders. We had left our washer and drier with Jenny, so each evening I would go through the motions of hand-washing my socks, undies and school blouse from that day, and they would hang near the small fanless 'Gas-Pot'. Twenty minutes later I wrote:

Having told you that, having startling Mean feelings I wanted to make an impression, so washed my thick woollen school skirt as well as the things Jay told me to wash while she was looking for something she wanted to send you.

She was so self-controlled that it took away all the callous Fun which was sure of feeling.

Happy the day when she learnt it was bad temper, and not lack of understanding, which led to irritating and autistic apparent stupidity.

Learning about me is very relaxing for her, as she is a badly chaotic person, and thought the mad life she was leading was all her fault.

Love, Lucy.
(7 May, 1990).
Dear Lucy,

In our schools in Ottawa, we try to notice the good behaviours all the time. I realise that tantrums are sometimes a way to make a point. We are able to reduce tantrumming by first examining the student's environment, and then by trying to surmise a reason for the tantrum. We try to maintain everyone's dignity, but it's difficult ...

Love, Sally.

AUTISM AND OTHER ADVENTURES: LUCY'S STORY

(Ottawa. 21 May, 1990).

Chapter 12
Curriculum and Communication, 1990:
Age 17

Throughout all these dramas, I was determined to stay in High School, to finish and pass Year 12 so as to establish in my mind that I was bright.

I was delighted when other people said to me that I was doing well. However there were so many other things that they thought were equally important that I had failed to achieve, and which many other disabled people found relatively easy, that I did not place much faith in these people's judgement.

That is why I got so much pleasure out of teachers criticising me, even when I was distressed at my low mark.

However, when people thought that I would enjoy doing normal things as a matter of course, I felt that I was being discriminated against now that I had realised that many of these things were impossible for me, and would not have been possible even had I had fluent speech. This was particularly true in the area of friendship and meeting with other kids in school.

The first two years there I had been something of a novelty, but I now was truly part of the school in the same way as Rachel, and Debbie, and Jodi, and Troy, and the Principal, and the Teachers, and the other nine-hundred-odd souls and bodies who clamoured and jostled through the corridors each morning.

I was accepted, and I was comfortable when it was recognised that I was not the same as the other students.

I know that speaking and non-disabled people can feel alienated in work or school. That is not what I mean. I had no desire to gossip and bitch, and had no real interest in any of the things they thought important.

Sometimes typing with someone who expected me to like the things that the others had hankered after, I would express a longing for dresses, to go to rock concerts or to have a boyfriend. However invariably when that person tried to keep the common interest going, I floundered into non-compliance.

None of this was in any way as desirable as learning how to do school work in a way that would show that I was bright.

***

It was a wonderful year in terms of what we studied. The maths classes were the highlight of any day. As always, numbers, shapes, letters-as-symbols, and values were locked together in an instant, massively satisfactory mindscape. The year was slightly befouled by a new curriculum which placed what I thought was undue emphasis on language in problem solving.

Not only did we have to describe processes that to me were part of the natural order of things as long as they were displayed and worked in symbols, but we had to relate a problem to that wonder of technology, a real bicycle chain and gear.

Fine for some, but when I visited Jenny and Greg, who were the only members of the family to have a bike at that stage, I discovered that every time one turned the pedals to check how many turns would make each spoke do a full revolution, that particular ancient chain snarled on its own rust, and dropped off the toothed wheel.

Not the only thing that snarled that afternoon! What an unforgivable pun — irresistible, though! Writing up the information and relating it to mathematical principles was such fun that I almost forgave the powers-that-be for making real life intrude into such perfection.

***

Economics was new to me. I thought it very amusing that the teacher taught that one could impose patterns on what seemed to me to be arbitrary forces of greed and survival.

He taught from the board, so that speech and writing were together in some kind of shaped communication. These classes were pretty good, because for me men's voices are always clearer and less nerve-wracking than women's.

***

Twentieth Century World History was fun, though I was frustrated that neither of the people who sat with me in class, Pauline and Indira, seemed as fascinated as I by such things as the horrors of China's war with Japan in the 1930s or the earlier competition between England and Imperial Germany to build enormous battle fleets.

Of course there is no fun in being frustrated by oneself. The essay on the naval race was due. I churned it out with Pauline sitting next to me, her hand feather-light on my elbow. As I happily described the events that were news in my great-grandfather's youth, she monitored the tempo of my finger movements, knowing from experience that I was producing strokes that originated in the words that I wished to finger out, rather than involuntary movements which were heralded by a sharper jab, and which had their origins in memorised nonsense words.

In my imagination I designed Dreadnoughts, invented submarines, and then saw the British navy pursuing German raiders back and forth across the oceans of the World.

I suddenly realised that, though my partner was making sure that my words made sense, she was not really paying attention. I ran a little test to prove this to myself. In triumph I felt Pauline stiffen.

AUTISM AND OTHER ADVENTURES: LUCY'S STORY

She checked the last four lines on the paper scrolling out of the typewriter. Even she realised that if my metal, four-stacked, coal-burning fleets had suddenly changed into rotting, wooden caravels with crews petrified of falling off the edge of the Earth, something was wrong. The most fun I had had all day! Then, 'Lucy! What do you think you are doing?'

I rewrote the essay in an atmosphere of disapproval. Year 11 might be fun, but everyone's sense of humour seemed to have atrophied.

***

There was another subject new to me, Literature as distinct from English Expression, a year in which we looked at novels, short stories, poems and drama for what they were, as much as for what they said.

For the first time I realised that writing was not just a matter of telling a story so as to make a point, as I had done in my story about the old lady by the sea.

One did not just write down a poem to show that one was clever enough to have worked it out in one's head.

Literature was a craft, with a history as long as the history of people, turning experiences into a spoken or written form which outlives its creator, and even the culture in which it was spawned.

***

I read Du Maurier's *The Old Man*, her short story of a family of swans who abandon the young male who did not grow up normally.

The other students probably found it sad and felt for the parents. To me it seemed obvious, and far more of a universal dilemma than 'boy meets girl, and are they right for each other?'

I read *Wuthering Heights,* Jay sitting next to me, turning pages one-by-one so that I did not miss out by flipping them back and forward.

The story enchanted and grieved me, not as some great sexual romance but for the waste in Heathcliffe's life. I shouted and smiled, giggling with distress and swaying with pleasure. Beside me Jay was bored stiff.

I managed to sit still through *Cat on a Hot Tin Roof,* though I could not myself then manipulate even the simplest characters, except in first person narrative.

***

The teacher found my essay-writing style a little bewildering. It apparently is a good idea at least to mention the work that has inspired you before starting out to solve the mystery of what it is saying. The Interim Reports came out in April: *Take care to stay close to the question (Relevance!).*

Mr. Wells.

I had not improved much in the next month, judging by the notes that passed between my teacher and myself:

The warring totally expected freely horrible fury at the essay comments were far out of proportion with the good, happy feeling of the really great satisfaction of being taken seriously.

(30 May 1990).

To which he replied:

Don't take too much notice of the marks for an individual piece.

The mid-year report contained a hint which I have devoutly followed ever since:

Lucy's ... main danger is that she may be too *responsive to the question, and either leaves it rapidly behind or relates to it without actually mentioning that she is doing so. Make statements that are explicitly relevant to the question at least once per paragraph.*

AUTISM AND OTHER ADVENTURES: LUCY'S STORY

(Mid-Year Report, 6 July 1990).

***

One interesting thing about that class was that Mr. Wells had to change his teaching style completely, not because of me, but because of Marnie who was deaf. Instead of bounding from his desk and striding around, he had to try to face the class so that Marnie could lip read.

Anchored firmly to a chair behind the stockade-fence of the desk, his roaming behaviour was under control. So familiar to me that I found it my private joke of the year.

Also if I, by chance, sat to one side, I processed his mouth movements in profile, which did not mean that I showed more understanding, but it was less effort to sequence his words than if he were facing me.

Of course, I might have been even happier if the teacher and I had both had our backs to each other, though perhaps that might have caused a few problems for everyone else.

***

The kind of student-teacher interaction that is usual in a class from this level on was particularly difficult for me because, by the time I had typed out even the shortest comment, the discussion was several topics further on from the point I was trying to make.

Unless the class was fairly formal and easy to call to order, the tape that I had laboriously churned out was so much obsolete garbage. As a rule I was able to be included in most discussions, but I never can make off-the-cuff remarks which are the polite version of,

'That is so much——!'

To my embarrassment sometimes a few minutes later, or even in a later class, this uncensored bit of Anglo-Saxon would float to the top, and my hand and my teeth once again would fuse.

Of course, often people thought that what had upset me had just then occurred, and I would come out of my mini-fury to find a head wagging next to me, a 'comforting' smile, and the words, 'Don't worry' still trailing on the air.

***

Just because I was being taught that writing was a skill that should be cultivated by rewriting and yet more rewriting, did not mean that I saw this as applicable to me.

Early in the year I had asked John's opinion of a poem I had written straight after seeing a car-accident scene on a dark night two years before:

Doing the mad gear change
Slamming angry soles foot first
On sinking pedals.
So vortex of screaming steel and tyre
Touches immortality briefly but too long,

*

Calling the heraldic glory
  Of Ambulance and pig in red and blue flashing lights.
  Reality is the tired driver
  Grumbling at a blocked carriageway

*

And the dumb worry of each foreseeing
  Doubtful chances of no claim bonus actuarial risks
  And the real chance of overwhelming pain and sorrow ...

AUTISM AND OTHER ADVENTURES: LUCY'S STORY

(February 1988).

He had said:

Dear Lucy,

The printout that I got was in verses - is that intentional?

(Those weren't verses. They were caused when my pattern-making urge had got the better of me, and I hit the return key. There was no way I could think of explaining this, even if I had understood it myself.)

... The fourth verse - the three lines beginning 'and the dumb worry ...' - doesn't seem to work too well. I think you need to clarify who the 'each' is/are, cut down on the number of words in 'no claim bonus actuarial risks', and delete 'overwhelming' from the next line.

Words are strong. Words like 'overwhelming' and 'pain' and 'sorrow' are very strong. Few lines of poetry (or sentences of prose) can support more than one strong word ... Lucy, if you're mad at me for doing this, then tell me and I won't do it again.

(I was not hurt by his criticism, but mystified. He seemed to think that one wrote poems so that they had a certain effect on the reader.

Eliot, Marsden and Shakespeare, maybe — Blackman, definitely not, because as a rule writing came in response to visual stimuli which had stirred up my internal language enough to link words spontaneously with what I had seen, rather than typing obliquely about what I had felt.

Really, it never occurred to me, in spite of what I heard from teachers and friends, that the prime purpose of poetry was not to make word-pictures of my linked vocabulary, but to rework this so as to let someone else have the illusion they were sharing whatever it was I composed.)

***

Remember, I said, 'Instead of writing about the sun, write about its reflection in the water'? I guess you could try that with your fears. Instead of writing about your own fears, try writing about a fictional character who has fears ... and who will to some extent at least, reflect yours.

(In retrospect, I see that I should have found this funny. How on earth was I to find one of those? At the time I did not even realise that I was expected to distinguish between fear and an unpleasant taste!)

Seems like the best writing often comes by imposing tough conditions. This forces the writing to be disciplined and controlled, instead of indulgent.

How much reading (of books) do you actually do?

Love, John.

*

Dear totally wonderful, basically very reasonable, willing to be friends,

happily not having met me, John,

Really that is a silly start as the word I wanted was 'readable'.

Last reading that I did was the Gospels, because, you see, I had to read parables for Literature. When I read the Narnia books I cried about C.S. Lewis describing the boy losing his dragon skin, and I typed that I saw it was redemption, or at least conversion.

The beastly caring [i.e. being looked after] *that I need is happier when I am conscious of the bestial, maddening nature that the outside world sees* [in me], *because the totally, basically wonderful excitement of what we are doing gets to me.*

Love, Lucy.

(24 May 1990).

AUTISM AND OTHER ADVENTURES: LUCY'S STORY

Translated this means that the whole school experience for me was an experimental adventure with an (as yet) unimaginable end, but I knew that I had changed who I was forever.

***

Four days a week we had English Expression. One of the first sections was 'Clear Thinking'. Not surprisingly, my 'slop the thought to the surface and luxuriate in the vocabulary' was not quite what the curriculum designers had in mind:

Lucy's essay response was a little disappointing, as it drifted from the focus of the task.

(Interim report, late March 1990).

Then there were set texts, which presumably we read to look at how we would relate these personal or fictional experiences to how we saw life. There were several optional reading lists.

Quite logically when one thinks of my comments to John, one of the ones that I chose was 'Man and his Gods'. I knew the *King James Bible* pretty well, because it had been one of the volumes which Jay had placed in the bathroom to entice Kay to continue to read something other than Jackie Collins and Sweet Dreams.

So I had a love and understanding of that type of language. I could then match up these novels and poems against the verses that resounded in my visual imagination, counterpointed against things like television church services, and movies about religious experiences.

My teacher seemed an interested observer, if her comments are to be believed:

The Journey of the Magi - *a cold poem about something most writers talk about with joy ...*

('A very interesting way to describe it, Lucy')

I identify with the poem, because the most satisfying thing is to be looking for answers rather than to be sure that you are safe either in soul or body. Not that one does not always want to be safe, but really safety in faith is an illusion ...

('A very interesting answer')

The Spire (William Golding) - *a continual feeling of light, and the feeling of chaos and distress and doom, at the same time as glory was present ...*

('Intriguing')

I enjoyed Asher Lev *best because that was more about values than faith ...*

('Interesting selection Lucy - perceptive - original')

***

English Expression also launched me on a personal quest. I found out that we were to do a project in Communication, using any medium other than a formal essay. Students would be marked on their own assessment of how the project was received.

I graciously conveyed to Jay that I had appointed her as Organiser, Camera Person and Editor of a video which would show me interviewing people about autism. I would show the result to my English class, 11D. She was less entranced than I with this brainwave, but was compliant.

***

The first target of my video-journalism was May, a lady with a son with autism. We sat at her kitchen table, with my laptop in front of me.

I typed questions, and the nine-year-old wailed and crowed in the background, his eyes moving to their corners as he appeared to examine the opaque video lens.

I wanted to bring home to 11D that it was hard to express love towards a child who screamed and ran away. I jumped in the deep end.

'YOU ARE THE MOTHER OF AN AUTISTIC SON. AS YOU FOUND OUT HIS DIFFERENCES, GETTING A NICE FEELING MUST HAVE BEEN HARD.'

'*Mmmm — that's a very complex question, but it's true!*' said May. '*Because autistic children don't come and love you like a normal child will, I invented a little game. Because Tommy can't speak, every time I gave him something, or he had his dinner, I would make him say, 'Thank you'. And that 'Thank you' was a kiss!*'

'Kissing-Teddy's' furry little face floated through my memory. I departed from the line of questioning that I had thought out.

'THE SAME THING HAPPENED WITH ME, SO THE TOTAL IDEA IS FAMILIAR - ACTUALLY THE FEELING THAT AUTISTIC SENSATION GETS IS OF UNREAL, BEASTLY STRESS AT SAYING 'THANK YOU''.

I meant that saying, 'Thank you' involved approaching and facing someone while speaking, which not only was visually painful, but involved working in two sensory dimensions, which turned me inside-out.

'*So, it's become a habit,*' continued May. '*And he enjoys it too. Now I can say, 'Come and give Mummy a love', and he will do that too, but I always have to say it; he doesn't just come up and give me a cuddle.*'

I can see now that in some ways she needed to make him be hugged, because parents need reinforcement too if they are to stay motivated.

'THE AWFUL TANTRUMS ARE SO WORRYING AND THE STUPID ANGER SO BAD, THAT YOU MUST FEEL VERY SAD SOMETIMES.' That was my next question.

'Yes, I can see that's hard for the autistic person that Lucy is describing. However it is so very hard for the families as well, because we don't understand that either.' May sighed through the words, a breathy sound that was recorded on the tape.

'So in a way we don't understand each other. When we see that behaviour, we think it is for a different reason. We might think they are being naughty.'

As she said that, there was an ear-splitting shriek from Tommy, and his mother flinched.

She stunned me to the core. I had heard teachers talk about not understanding people like us, but had not quite understood that families went through the same frustrations.

The interview was punctuated by Tommy playing obsessively with a plastic chain. This clatter became a continual sound effect, until I heard him change tempo in his vocal noise. Suddenly he sounded frantic.

That was when I first realised how incapacitating my drawing, tearing things up, and copying rote words on the typewriter are. When I have gone on too long, I drown in my own patterns.

***

I found another victim — Chris who worked with grown-up people with autism — just what I wanted! Chris happened to have a heavy cold, had just finished a long meeting, and was facing a traffic-ridden drive back to the office.

The video also was not enhanced by the camera being left on the wrong setting, so that interviewer and interviewee sat staring straight ahead with no eye-contact, stained a deep green, as were the pastel walls, grey laminex table and foam cups.

In this Wizard of Oz-like atmosphere, I look like a specimen under the microscope myself, but I was learning that if one set of human beings does not understand another set of human beings, they are reduced to using science.

That is, my own species has to research people with autism, and the impression that I was beginning to get was that this is not as simple as it sounded.

'In terms of feelings to do with affection, love, bonding and all those sorts of things,' said Chris, *'it was only about ten years ago when people were saying that autistic people didn't have any feelings like that, that they wanted to be away from people.*

What research over the past few years has shown is that autistic people don't really want to do that ... You do find that they certainly get on with parents and with other people that are close to them ... there are always a few people that are very important to autistic people.'

Well, it was reassuring that they were moving in the right direction. I asked about other people's attitudes. Things had got much better since the International Year of the Disabled, said Chris, coughing and almost voiceless.

Of course, in the tradition of the best investigative journalism, I had to have the last word. I don't often get such a golden opportunity.

'*EASY TO DENY DISCRIMINATION - MORE DIFFICULT NOT TO PITY!*' Off-the-cuff smart remarks seemed to be in the same category as historical practical jokes.

The faces around me either went very blank, or uttered understanding twitters. Being taken seriously when one is cracking a funny is the pits.

***

Dr. Tony Attwood, a clinical psychologist, was visiting Melbourne. Would I like to ask him some questions for my video? Why not?

Unless I got more people, the project looked like being short, boring and uninformative.

I met Tony in the back room at Deal. We sat in a row, me in the middle, Jay being careful not to touch me but holding the Canon in front of me.

That was an odd special effect, because as she had set up the equipment, she had not realised that she had left herself out of the picture, so a disembodied hand supports the keyboard throughout the conversation.

Tony turned out to be a slender man with an English accent, and a better-than-average listener, though he had the usual problems combining conversation and one-fingered lettering.

'HAVE YOU SEEN SOME WEIRD PEOPLE ACTUALLY TYPE?' I asked.

After finding that this was the first time that he had seen people with autism and no speech use typed language, I continued.

'LEARNING THAT YOU HAVE NOT SEEN ACTUALLY MANY PEOPLE [TYPE], TELL ME IF YOU SEE US AS INTELLIGENT?'

Tony went into a long spiel on autism, and how professional people used conversation and other tests as a guide to someone's intelligence, and ended up,

'It may be that some people with autism have a problem with communication, not that they are not intelligent. Did that answer your question?'

'NO.' I tried to explain that I could not speak, rather than not having language. 'BEING UNABLE TO SAY SOMETHING, ACTUALLY IS THE SAME AS NOT BEING ABLE TO MOVE IN RESPONSE TO AN INSTRUCTION!'

At this point, Tony lost track. He gathered up the paper tape, which by now had about a metre of words printed on it, and stretched out his hands to read, as though winding skeined wool.

AUTISM AND OTHER ADVENTURES: LUCY'S STORY

There was a little fan-heater going. In blatant disregard for the comfort of our visitor, who had just jetted in from Brisbane, 1600 kilometres nearer the equator, I indicated I would like it turned off as I was pretty uncomfortable with the sound.

However when Tony started to talk about his meetings with autism, both my hands went to my ears again because I was sitting next to him, and would have lost the sense of what he was saying in the rush of syllables and pauses had I not filtered them.

'My thoughts are that people with autism have difficulty understanding the feelings of other people, and expressing their own feelings in ways that other people understand,' he said.

That seemed to me to be letting people without autism avoid responsibility both ways, but I let that go.

Instead, because people in general seemed to have social problems relating to people like me, and as Tony had said that he knew hundreds of people with autism, I thought I would try the other track.

'HAVE THE LESS SEVERELY DISABLED PEOPLE TOLD OF FEELINGS THEY SEE IN OTHERS?'

I was talking about watching other people socialise among themselves, not others talking directly to me. When I was approached by someone, I often had some confusion because not all parts of their face were consistently in the same perspective.

Sometimes I picked up the underlying sign and I got confused. So, if someone was tired but happy, I might see the tiredness and hear the happiness in her voice, but not realise I was missing something.

However I could be in the presence of people who were not interacting with me, and observe them as if I were the researcher. I had the impression then that I understood interactions pretty normally in that sense.

When I questioned him about feelings, I meant the latter situation, but he replied in relation to face-to-face encounters.

'*Some of the able people with autism who can speak have said, 'People give messages with their eyes, and I don't understand them',*' he said.

I tried to explain the difference, but I was stymied because I had not then learned that my visual processing was a mystery to everyone else.

'FEELINGS ARE OBVIOUS FOR ME, BUT I HAVE STRANGE ACTIONS TO KILL A FRIENDLY CONVERSATION.' I changed tack. 'THE GIGGLING LIKE A BABY CAN'T BE BEATEN.'

I ran around the room and up and down the adjoining passage for a bit, while Jay explained that this plus giggling made the other kids quite tongue-tied.

'*Sometimes I get the impression that for some people with autism, there are certain feelings that they find very difficult. Do you find it difficult to express embarrassment?*' asked Tony.

By this time I had realised that we were talking about two different things.

'YOU ARE NOT LETTING YOURSELF HEAR WHAT I AM SAYING. LEARNING THAT FEELINGS ARE NOT YET EXPRESSED NORMALLY IS NOT THE SAME AS NOT UNDERSTANDING.'

'*So, you are saying that a person will feel embarrassment, but not have a means of expressing that embarrassment,*' said Tony. I gave up.

'YES.'

I realised though, from what he was asking, that he knew a lot about the kind of experiences I had in everyday life.

I learnt more from my attempts to answer him in the hour and a half we spent together than from all the years of eavesdropping or from occasional articles on autism I had glimpsed.

Chapter 13
Typing and Talking, 1990:
Age 17–18

The mid-year exams were over, and the staff were to have a student-free day for report-writing. I was to spend the day with Maria.

This still worked fine, as long as I was fairly passive or we just did the kind of things which had an established routine, like getting meals, or making simple versions of the lace-decorated baskets she finished, and sold to local shops. However things came unstuck in situations where two women would normally have chatted together.

I still echoed food words when I agreed to eat something that was offered. If I disliked something, I would speak the word, 'No!' However that did not always apply to things which were not as important in my world view, such as my personal experience. If she said,

'Is Jay picking you up?' and I knew it would be someone else, I probably would say, 'Jay' or 'Yes', because my sense of what was important had not made a connection with the word 'No.'

That was a pretty subtle distinction, and was not always constant. Also I could not express 'perhaps' or other qualifying words in speech.

On her part, Maria had not realised that the complex language that she occasionally saw me typing with Jay or LO was a matter of the other person making sure that they never took what I said as if it were speech.

With them, as soon as I completed any response to a practical question, the other person almost automatically would wait for me to explain or to confirm that what I typed was what I meant.

I think that was because they were used to working every day with large groups of children and adolescents from whom they had to extract some indication that they understood concepts and instructions, and also were in a working environment which gave priority to the written word.

***

Whatever the reason, when with Maria my words were spoken, and had about the same level of conversation as a child under two. That meant my body had not only to cope with its own turbulence, but with my metaphorphosis from student to baby whenever I walked through her front door.

On this occasion, when Jay had arranged that I was to come for the day, Maria had asked would I like her to take me for a hair-cut.

At home, Jay and I had discussed it the evening before, and I had typed that it was a good idea. However during the night I had changed my mind, but there had not been another opportunity to sit down and type.

'Ready for a hair-cut, Lucy?' she said, and I had nodded and spoken.

'Air-cu,' but inside I had been torn into shreds of confusion. Changing the thought to the speech-stream was completely beyond me.

***

I cannot remember if it was before we left or if it was after we got back to the house, by which time what I had on my head no-way resembled how I usually had my hair cut, but at some stage where another seventeen-year-old would have said, 'Why can't the lot of you butt out of my life,' I had stood in front of dear, plump, motherly Maria, and, as her face changed to a frightened mask, grasped her flowing, dark curls, and shaken, and shaken, and shaken her head. In that moment I wept inside. She would never really be relaxed with me again, and I loved her so much.

***

The winter school holidays were going to be a wonderful break from stress. And then — shock, horror!

Jay broke the news that a few weeks before she had purchased a package holiday. Nothing I could say or do would change that. She had prepaid the flight and accommodation was booked on the Gold Coast.

That, I knew from brochures and Val's lyric description of a riotous week she had spent there to celebrate finishing her exams, was a flashy and popular resort south of Brisbane. All Jay cared was that it was warm and cheap.

Flying — Wow — Ouch!

Dear John,

… I have two weeks of being scared because we are flying to Queensland. Queerly the nasty, dreadful fury when I wrote that has another side, because I am so happy that she totally dares to make me so frightened. As unlovely, stupid behaviour comes from fear in autistic people, on Saturday she told me she would make me totally cope, so I would be able to go on really long flights one day.

(July 1990).

***

In the event, I survived the trip and even enjoyed parts of it. It was not too bad on the flight up, because I was excited.

We ate take-away at Surfers Paradise for five blissful days. I rode water-slides and saw dolphins at Seaworld. We enjoyed a quiet cruise on the canals behind the beach resort, and travelled happily up hills in the hinterland, where we were promised stupendous views and a memorable rain forest walk.

Memorable, and even stupendous it may have been — for the other bus passengers.

Suddenly, while the bus was driving along a straight and unalarming stretch of road, and with no warning, I got the unpleasant feeling that usually preceded my winter cycles of illness.

However, probably because the warm air had left my sinuses uninflamed, I did not feel nauseous, but had a sensation which I associated with things like being asked to climb high on a stepladder.

Now I can recognise this as giddiness, but all I knew then was that I was overwhelmed with terror, a thousand times worse than usual because I had no idea why it had suddenly struck.

I screamed, blast after blast of high-pitched undulating sound that terrorised the predominantly elderly passengers.

My golden feeling totally evaporated. I endured the stop for cream scones and tea. I huddled in embarrassed misery while the bus swayed down the steep winding road to the coast.

In its own way, the flight back to Melbourne was just as unpleasant, though I glossed over this when I told people about my trip:

Dear John Marsden,

… The holiday in Queensland was fine, because I actually assisted by being fairly daring and being quiet and co-operative, having feelings for my mother who is not as helpless as I make out.

(2 August 1990).

***

AUTISM AND OTHER ADVENTURES: LUCY'S STORY

The first week back at school, and the usual quota of anxiety was waiting. Indira was expecting a baby, and had decided to leave rather earlier than she had planned:

I feel totally abandoned. Just the thought of starting with a new aide is devastating. I hope that you and Jay can help me to cope. I need more assistance than usual.

(To LO. Lunchtime typing session, 30 July 1990).

However, in almost every other way, this half-year was far better than any other winter since I was a child. The classes were still fun. I had managed to escape the stress of moving around by myself and I had not yet had a continuous spell of nausea.

***

School work was an irritating business, but it slowly was giving me practical experience in making my typed language convey to someone else the point that I was making.

It was not enough to simply give a short answer, as I already knew, but I now was beginning to understand that I was using my language to make a link with people who lived on another planet in terms of what their senses told them.

The Communication Project was not yet complete. To my delight, although I was once again headachy and jumpy, one Saturday about a month into the term I found myself in the seat of our (usually) trusty brown Corona.

A couple of hours after we had left home, Jay started to make the muted, surreptitious glances to one side which meant that she was trying to read the road-map without my becoming aware of this.

What optimism!

We swung off the freeway at a large green sign which was the portal for a country town in the rolling farmlands. Avoiding the impressive little Victorian-style town centre, we moved through a new housing development. She eventually drew into a street, and said with relief,

'This must be it!'

We sat around a table, me, two women who were about my own age whom I knew had been diagnosed as having autism, and a slightly younger girl who had rather different problems. However we all used pointing to get our message across. We were outnumbered two to one by Mums and their friends.

I did not risk trying to explain the broader outline of my project to this noisy, chaotic, social group. Instead, on the original tape that we took home, my mother's voice waffles about feelings and understanding other people, in an extraordinary hodge-podge of imprecision.

***

I was particularly pleased that Sue, whom I had met before, was one of the people with autism.

Although she did not have a physical handicap, she had great difficulties in starting and completing actions, and as we settled down I was interested that her mother held a cup up to her face, instead of placing it in her hand so that she could drink by herself.

I suppose it was because she sometimes spilled liquid, which I know is always difficult for parents when the family are guests.

Under the circumstances, I departed from the line of questioning I had planned.

'HAS ANYONE BEEN HAPPY TO BE SEEN AS HELPLESS?'

Then the combination of too many people, the lasting effect of the sound of rain on the long drive out, and my own embarrassment, got too much.

AUTISM AND OTHER ADVENTURES: LUCY'S STORY

I bit my hand, and could feel my face flushed and the corners of my lips turned up in the early stages of a nausea attack. My part in the unedited video was brief.

I sat for most of the time with my back to the camera, turning to ask a question. So I only registered that Sue had fingered,

'NO.'

It was only later when I saw the video that I realised that the younger girl, who had a lot more experience at using typing as she was in high school, had told us,

'NOT REALLY BUT IT DOES MAKE LIFE EASIER.'

Then Sue had rested her fingers on keys that spelt out,

'MY FEELINGS ARE ERE.'

This obviously was not what she wanted to say. On the keyboard that she was using, 'E' was next to 'D'. Was she trying to form 'dreadful'. I could imagine this word might be in context there.

Or was it a mis-spelling of a word she had heard, but never read. Most of her experience with language had been with heard speech and simple word recognition. With hindsight, I wonder did she perhaps mean 'weird'?

Of course it could have been a sudden, unplanned thrust of her finger. I will never know, but whatever it was she was trying to say, she went on,

'MY FEELINGS ARE VERY MINE.'

Her Mum thought she meant 'private'. She was probably right, but there was a chance that Sue was expressing what I had learnt, that what other people expected to be important in her life were interpreted in terms of a world-view that was so different that it was indeed 'very mine'.

Far-fetched, perhaps, but no odder than some of the interpretations that non-autistic people have put on some of my spoken and typed words in the light of their own experience.

***

The hostess brought the meeting back to some kind of order. I remembered that my main question was to deal with the topic of autism and the understanding of facial expression, with special emphasis on whether autistic people themselves thought this was a problem. I typed,

'*CAN YOU LEARN HOW PEOPLE THINK FROM THEIR EXPRESSIONS?*'

Someone repeated the question, rephrasing it to make it simpler and unintentionally misinterpreting what I had been asking.

'Can you learn how people think from watching them?'

On the video I look even more flushed. I bit my hand, chanting 'Band-aid'.

I had lost any control I might have over the thrust of my research. Whether I got any comments on the video on how Sue interpreted other people's feelings was going to be a matter of chance.

Sue's Mum relayed the words which Sue had pointed out.

'*NO CANT TELL BY LOOKING AT PEOPLE WHAT THEY ARE THINKING*'

Then a pause, and she added,

'*SOMETIMES.*'

Jay stepped into the breach.

'How do you feel your Mum is feeling now?'

Sue's Mum looked at her daughter in confusion.

'She says '*WARTY*'. I suppose that could be, 'Wary.''

Sue had more stamina than I that day.

"*HARRED*" — Oh, I think she means, 'Harried.''

On the television screen her mother certainly fitted that description.

AUTISM AND OTHER ADVENTURES: LUCY'S STORY

***

We drove back through torrential rain, and I dived under the bedclothes. However, at least I had Sue's permission to show part of the session to the class, which meant that apart from the conversation, they would also see someone else rather like me, though with different head, hand and body movements.

***

There was one more thing that I wanted to record before I showed parts of all these encounters to my class. I wanted them to picture themselves in my situation.

I had thought about this at intervals over the past few months, and had decided that the only exercise that had any parallels to what they saw when I had problems, was communication breakdown.

As I still had advertising slogans embedded in my speech, and because I could not answer questions that related to 'real life' when I spoke, I thought that it might teach them a little of my own puzzlement with other people's expectations if these two eccentricities were combined in the one activity.

The teacher nominated the 'volunteers'. Each wrote down three slogans advertising foods that were very attractive to them. Then, two by two, they stood in front of the camera.

Comfortable with the discipline and order around me, I watched with pleasure as Mrs. Heriot directed the students from my typed instructions. They each slipped a mask, a blank paper plate with two tiny eye holes and no facial expression, over their own orthodox human visages.

The cast moved restlessly, their bodies looking strangely un-coordinated when one saw them with only a white disk for a face. Following my instructions to the letter, Mrs. Heriot told them to remember what they had had for dinner the previous day.

They moved from foot to foot. Then she told them to describe these meals, using the slogans which they had written down and signed, and which she now had in a tidy pile of paper in front of her. No chance to cheat — a great lady, Mrs. Heriot! After all, if I was permanently in a state of atrophied and twisted expression, why not them?

'You go.'
'You go!'
'Go on!!'
Silence, giggles.
'Um ... '

They protested. It could not be done with the phrases they had chosen.

'Just try!' said Mrs. Heriot. 'Just use your hands.'
'Yes?'
'Yeah?'

'Snap, Crackle, Pop — Rice Bubbles.' Fingers manipulated a pair of pencils in a gesture strangely similar to an autistic finger movement. This was presumably Chinese take-away, but what on Earth was, 'A Mars a Day Helps you Work, Rest and Play,' with a two-handed cutting movement.

If that was the nearest this person had come to a slogan which could describe a knife-and-fork meal, what were her other phrases? Why had she chosen a chocolate-covered caramel bar to use as speech? Was it colour, texture or shape that had kicked in, or simply association of ideas? I now regret that I did not ask her that.

***

AUTISM AND OTHER ADVENTURES: LUCY'S STORY

There was one other thing that I wanted to try. I had thought that some people might have a familiar song or saying that passed through their mind when embarrassed or nervous.

It appeared from the girl who answered the question that I was wrong. She bent over almost double, flexing her knees and letting her long blondish hair swish forward and back, while her voice was heard firmly saying,

'No! I don't have anything that I do that is different when I am embarrassed!'

Around me, 11D roared with laughter.

***

I relapsed again into nausea. I stayed at home, miserable and terrified, except for a trip into Melbourne for counselling. Looking at my streaming nose, Nicky said,

'You know, that looks very like allergy to me.'

'But all those tests were negative,' Jay wailed. Still, she was relieved, I think, that at last someone was muttering something other than 'stress' in her ear.

There was only one way to find out. In the morning, I awoke to find the house stripped of the second-hand carpet she had laid. Our upholstered lounge suite was already outside. In a corner were the cat baskets, full of angry Cat in triplicate.

'I'm going down the street, Lu. Just listen to the radio till I get back.' Stony faced, she slung her friends in the back of the station wagon.

I have to admit that when I visit Hayley, and sit manipulating the shoulder blades of her cats with my finger and thumb, I feel a little wistful — but not so wistful that I ever want to share a house with a cat again.

***

The rest of the year passed quickly. We perched on canvas folding chairs in front of a bar heater. (Jay had also switched off the gas to our folksy little imitation pot-bellied stove). My sinuses began to clear a bit, though I was still giddy and anxious.

Petra, the lady who was taking over from Indira, had started just before I got sick. Then had come the September holidays. So I spent Term Four working towards the end-of-the-year exams, and getting to know Petra. Such a nice lady — but I was surprised to find that I was not comfortable with her for the first few weeks.

One part of the problem was soon solved. LO and Jay exchanged notes, and had a small embarrassed mini-conference on the phone that identified one reason for my distaste. Petra was heavily into handicrafts; not dress-making, but things like making Christmas decorations.

She was determined to be my friend, and showed me the many things she had concocted as table decorations. I had an intense, knee-jerk antipathy to creating decorations, partly because it was an activity which had no purpose in my world-view, and partly because I associated it with my time at Special School.

The baskets and mirrors that Maria had trimmed so lovingly with lace had been different, as I saw them as part of her lifestyle, like her husband and son and her meticulously polished furniture. However handicrafts had no place in my High School life.

At home I confirmed what they had guessed in a short typed tape:

'*I TOTALLY HATE HANDICRAFTS!*'

Embarrassed Jay tried to soften this bluntness with heavy-handed humour scrawled on a piece of typing paper to which the tape was glued.

'*Sorry, probably hereditary on both sides; therefore incurable! (Though these days Hayley makes a nice egg-carton caterpillar with Shay at Playgroup).*'

AUTISM AND OTHER ADVENTURES: LUCY'S STORY

The topic of Christmas decorations died away. Maybe LO suggested Petra stick to the more attractive things of life, such as economic systems. I hope she did it tactfully.

***

The other problem eventually Petra herself identified. Like Jay she had a clear, highish, English voice, which on some frequencies gave the sensation that I think some people get when a finger-nail is dragged over a chalkboard. On other frequencies it would just drop out.

Jay had circumvented this by using body language, cues and writing. Petra started to write memos to me, even when we were sitting side by side. That was what Jay did at home.

I think that I may have suggested it to Petra, but she developed it further. We would have typed conversations, passing the typewriter from side to side of the desk.

***

By the following year, I was comfortable enough to consider her a real friend, for which privilege she had to pay the price of my trying to send her on a guilt-trip every time I was worried about my academic work, or had made a fuss in class:

Petra: *OK? ... try to please look pleasant [to] please me.*

Lucy: *... My look is not in touch with you because you have not been here ...* [typewriter malfunctioned] *... that you really not happy with me?*

Petra: *I am happy with you. I wish we would go straight to the typewriter or the Canon, and, for your sake, we could keep down the noise* [which you are making in class]. *I am happy to see you. I have been quite sick ...* [and explained her children had been very sick too]. *OK? I like you a lot, so don't be insecure.*

Lucy: *That is an understatement. I'm always insecure about my life. I am very insecure in the classroom because you have missed so much ...*

Petra: *When you write your book, put in a recommendation that people using 'facilitated communication' in schools should have an allotted time to talk about all aspects of the day-to-day functions, so that neither person becomes anxious.*

Wonderful! There we were, back discussing communication breakdown again!

***

In the meantime, we went on getting to know each other, and my class of that year saw The Video. They found it long and confusing, but several said it had helped them understand me better.

I was going to pass into Year 12. The school felt it could cope with my working the curriculum, and I wrote to the Board in charge of assessment to support the school's application for special conditions.

Then came Presentation Night, and I was to get a certificate for achievement in some of my subjects. In trepidation, LO rehearsed me to stand in line, take my turn to cross the stage, then grab the piece of paper and walk quietly off the stage to where Jay was waiting to guide me back to the class.

Unfortunately LO had not rehearsed Jay, who, enthralled by all this, popped a camera in her jacket pocket so she could snap me coming off stage holding the certificate. I got to the top of the steps, and saw her right hand drop to her bulging pocket.

Hankies! — How many? — Right ones?

The questions flipped in my head like a desk-calendar. I relapsed into noisy distress, even before the shutter had a chance to click. I doubt if this was quite the family cooperation that LO wanted.

AUTISM AND OTHER ADVENTURES: LUCY'S STORY

***

This saga took place against the activities of a city of three million people. Two of these were my nieces. Shay's speech began to shape her world. She stacked blocks, told us what colours she was choosing, and then gave a name to her creation. To her a pile of coloured cubes was not a pattern, but a 'tower'.

Kara started walking, then talking in a younger and more immature version of Shay's vocabulary, chatting to her sister and describing the little games she was playing in a flowing babble. They asked for snacks and watched their request carried out.

'Tell Daddy what you did today. You were really clever!' Hayley would say to Shay when Laurie came home from work, and would then prompt her to recall a few key words on which to string a one-sentence narrative.

I did not realise it then, but they were not really using speech yet to give or collect information. They were shaping their own understanding of the world, and the interface of past, present and future.

***

Hayley was pregnant.

Val was happily surveying flood plains and catchments.

Kay was working in the finance department of a university nearby.

Jenny was going back to complete her degree at the same university when the academic year started. Locally all was well on the family front.

Granny Joy was in a nursing home, still without speech. Jay withdrew into herself slightly whenever she was mentioned. I knew that Granny Joy had some hand movement and that there were days when she was alert.

I suspected that Jay felt, as I did, that the same skills that worked for me might for her. The subject was never mentioned.

***

In the other part of my life, there was real excitement. Doug's article on his visit to us had been published in *The Harvard Educational Review*, and it certainly had faithfully stuck to the conversation we had had, though I had my doubts still as to whether the world and supported typing were ready for each other.

I knew, better than most, that for me language could never be a code for expressing the world in the same terms that others experienced it. Whatever it was that I was producing, other people were often disappointed. I was still bewildered by this, though I was all too aware of it.

Out of the blue, Rosie phoned. She was going to a conference in the States. Before she left, a group of people using Canons was going to demonstrate their progress to publicise the work that she was doing. Would we go along?

This was not a communication group. So I went. Jay managed to corner Rosie for an instant, and asked had she known of David Eastham, because we had been writing to his teacher, Sally Borthwick.

'No,' said Rosie. 'But I'll ask around at the Conference.'

We sat down with three other families, two with school-age kids, to discuss some of the things we had been doing with typing with a couple of people from one of the local papers. A nice, friendly, relaxed end to what, for me, had been a long year.

Chapter 14
A Question of Touch, 1991:
Age 18

Christmas was heralded by a letter from Tony Attwood:
Dear Lucy and Jay,
I would like to ask Lucy's opinion. I seem to remember you making a comment about making the wrong word or action from the one you intended, such as indicating 'no' when 'yes' was what you meant.

A family I recently saw were concerned that their autistic daughter was lying. She was saying things that were obviously untrue, such as answering 'have you tidied your room?' with, 'Yes!' She may wanted to avoid the chore, but I wondered if sometimes she couldn't help saying the opposite of what she intended. Do you think this could be the case?

(Brisbane. 18 December 1990).

In my reply I was referring to the way that I produced speech, but I might as well have included typed answers:
Dear Tony,
The question that you ask about the saying of 'Yes' is desperately awful, because that kind of thing is something that has made my having autism so difficult.

The expectation [by others] *is that the simple answer will nearly match the way other people would think.*

[This] is really stupid, because the whole basis of my difference is that the processing of my information goes out [of sync].

The question about a 'tidy room' is terribly difficult to work into my speech, and I would possibly do what that girl does, or echo, 'Tidy room' to show that I had received the question.

My mother would feel better if she had made sure actually what I had done before she had opened the subject.

The question ['have you tidied your room'] *is so vague!*

(23 December 1990).

Not only was the question about room-tidying vague, in that it did not relate to something that was important to me (or to any other adolescent that I had met), but it did not refer to a concrete result that impacted on my own body or to something so obsessional that it was a part of me. That is why I had said that I could not work the *question*, rather than the answer, into my speech.

***

I was still dressmaking, Jay closely monitoring each mini-section of each step.

Sometimes I found that in following the diagram that came with the pattern, I now could see the connection between the picture of how the pattern pieces and seam lines fitted together and what I was meant to do with the pieces of fabric, the pins and the treaded sewing machine.

But if I did not have the second dimension of a spoken instruction, I was confused and motionless.

I had chosen to make a sheath dress, with a jacket which had unfitted shoulders over shoulder-pads. Tubby women with sloping shoulders, beware!

This is not for you, especially if you have a horror of altering anything if it is wrong, and refuse to try it on in the construction phase so that it fits in the first place.

AUTISM AND OTHER ADVENTURES: LUCY'S STORY

I insisted on wearing it to the party which Grace was throwing for Max's twenty-first birthday. She had hired a hall, and some of the teachers that I remembered from the Autistic Centre were there.

These familiar faces from my childhood chatted and smiled, so that my response became babyish, because in my temporarily confused memory they were framed quietly working with us in small, quiet groups.

The hall was noisy, and there were lots of ex-students from the Centre. Each ex-student was there as a family member with parents and their friends.

When we were urged to form a circle to dance, I stood on the dance floor, as on dance floors at so many gatherings, unable to sense why the people around me could produce synchronised movement to the blurred sound of the music.

My head was too giddy to allow me to sway and spin in my own world. I realised that I was in the middle of a nausea attack. As the goodies from all our Christmas visits and the food from the party rose in my gorge, Jay dragged me to the car park just in time, and we hid behind the bushes while I threw up.

***

Home at last, and Jay was looking particularly grim.

'That was definitely allergy,' she growled. 'There was as much phlegm as food! There is a teacher at my school who cannot eat yeast. That is one thing we have never tried.' I was resigned to more odd meals, and she continued.

'We will go on leaving out wheat, not just occasionally, but make a proper job of it. You realise, don't you, that there is yeast in beer, some vegetarian protein and' — she grinned here — 'Vegemite!'

I wilted. I consumed vast quantities of this salty black spread, and was also obsessed by it, to the point that my proudest possession was a towel emblazoned with a picture of a large jar of Vegemite.

'Well,' said Jay. 'There's always rice.'

'No rice!'

'So it will have to be puffed rice cakes and rice-bubble breakfast cereal — you eat those!'

***

I had sent a copy of Doug Biklen's article to John. It is not every High School student who is quoted in *The Harvard Educational Review*, even if the article had included some rather dramatic incidents in the school-yard:

Dear Lucy,

Well, I read the article - I'm not sure if I'm glad or sorry. I didn't want to have any images or perceptions of you, other than your own words in your letters, but I guess the article doesn't change that much ... I was startled by descriptions of you eating used chewing gum and pissing in the playground. Nice one Luce! -

(Wonderful! The sarcastic beast was treating me as any other student, and to Hell with being tactful!)

I'm going to Paris in early February for nearly six months. Keep writing to me there.

Love, John.

(January 1991).

***

The Gulf War was in full swing, if that is the right term for miles of desert, oil pipes, tanks, rockets, tired men, frightened civilians, and unknown chemical weapons, stirred together by international tensions, and then filmed, edited, commented on, flash-backed, and delivered to the living rooms of the world.

We sat in Hayley's home, one eye on the television and one on her mounding tummy. She had now been pregnant for nearly nine months.

We had been there for several days. Jay had said we would be available to come to look after Shay and Kara as soon as Hayley went into labour.

Then, one night our phone had gone at two in the morning, not my best time. Jay had fumbled her way to the telephone and picked up the handset. I had stood next to her, jumping up and down, and chanting,

'Bye-bye — OK — No!' etc. between mouthfuls of hand.

We had driven along the deserted tree-lined road. Jay had been meaning to fill the car up that evening, but of course had forgotten.

The little petrol-pump icon on the dashboard glowed about fifteen minutes into our trip.

'What a good thing,' said Jay, brightly and untruthfully, 'That it gives us so many kilometres in hand before it runs out!'

Then, miracle of miracles, the lights on a small service station flared ahead. Neither of us had realised it kept such extended hours.

We had arrived at Hayley's to find all was a false alarm. Once was enough. In the morning we drove back home, picked up two foam mattresses, my computer and some clothes, and moved in for the duration.

***

So here we were, surrounded by small children and Scud missiles. Jay occasionally did grandmotherly things with the kids, like feeding them, or letting them ride on her back while she crawled round the floor.

In front of us, men with something like terror on their faces stood in Tel Aviv, Jerusalem and Baghdad, as they broadcast against the din of war. I do not think I will ever forget the reporter standing against office windows without his gas mask, and, with half the world watching, wondering if the showers of light behind him were carrying some appalling bacterial agent.

I simply had to reach out, so I sent a message across the world:
Dear Sally,

Keeping the vision of the men in Jerusalem trying to broadcast on CNN, and being so frightened, and so brave, made me think about fear and terror and love, and the very great need we just have for each other ...

Did David like that kind of thought? I have a big thing about space and astronomy and clouds. That is a possibly understandable obsession, as I think other people are just as fascinated, but do not carry on about it. ... David's poems ... are nearly unbearable.

(19 January 1991).

***

A day later Hayley staggered off to hospital. Her parting words to three-year-old Shay, who was longing to take over and run the world, were,

'No! You can't wash the dishes. I really don't think that you can get the plates clean enough.'

'Perhaps you can wash-up when Mummy has gone,' purred Jay, as she saw a perfect distraction if Shay were to suddenly wonder where her mother was.

Hayley opened her mouth to re-establish her authority, and was caught by another contraction.

As Laurie, who had been summoned from work, gunned their car out of the drive, Jay slapped together peanut-butter sandwiches for the kids, and rice-cakes *à la* peanut-butter for me, and popped the BBC version of *Hamlet* into the VCR for me to watch in preparation for the forthcoming literature course.

As soon as the last soggy crust had been dropped onto Kara's plate, Shay's voice clearly cut across Renaissance Man.

'But, Jay, you *said* I could wash up when Mummy had gone!'

So, when one of Hayley's friends popped in to check that all was well, Shay, aka Cinderella, was perched on a wobbly chair, swilling water over Hayley's better plates, Jay was paying her the compliment of reading Agatha Christie to herself at the kitchen table, and I was cooing and swaying with delight at the wonders of Shakespeare's playing with double meanings in speeches so crafted that, four hundred years after he wrote them, they were being spoken by these marvellously clear men's voices.

I noticed that, apart from wanting to see her new grandson, Aaron, Jay was bursting a boiler to get to the hospital to get her version in first. I was not the only one of her daughters to inspire a degree of nervousness in our mother.

***

I had to admit that I had stopped feeling nauseous, and that my sinuses were no longer full of gunk:

Stupidly the strange food is getting to be actually a help, so let's go on.

The silly, totally awful giggling has gone, and so, because I am keeping it under control, has looking at people, but the eye business [touching and pushing on my eyes] *is feeling irresistible, as really I don't know what to do with them.*

The whole of my face feels stiff, and that is, actually thinking about it, why I cannot smile at the moment.

(Evening diary, 31 January 1991).

***

There was an increase in sound sensitivity on some frequencies, because my head was less clogged up.

This sound sensitivity was so odd that I did not recognise it because I felt it as vibrations rather than as noise.

My response to this was a deadness, which was all the more obvious because, in contrast, my regular virus attacks did not result in non-stop vomiting.

When they hit, my former excited, headachy, giggly fear was transformed into sudden inarticulate terror, as it had been in Queensland.

I still had that strange feeling occasionally that my body was a thing that was separate from me. However, by and large I felt better.

***

In the first month of the school year I got a letter back from Canada:

Dear Lucy,

The war is indeed a sad perturbing event. The stress of watching it in a safe environment is surreal. I have to remind myself that it is real, and not a TV program.

You asked about David's thoughts of these things. David would be very upset over such inhumanity.

There have been many programmes on about autism recently. The latest is Annabel Stehli's book, Sound of a Miracle.

She tells of her daughter's cure by evening out her audio levels. I really don't know much about that. I have heard only snippets.

Love, Sally.

(Ottawa. 6 February 1991).

***

AUTISM AND OTHER ADVENTURES: LUCY'S STORY

The High School had a compulsory three-day camp for all final students. I joined in most things, though I had a feeling of being a visitor from another planet, seeing all these familiar people in a different environment and in strange roles. There was a letter waiting when I got home, a window into another exotic landscape:

Dear Luce,

I'm having a great time exploring this extraordinary, exotic, elegant city ... I've just been wandering the streets, pop-eyed at it all, like a country kid having his first trip to the city ... This is what cities should be like!

Suburban shopping centres now suddenly seem about as exciting as flat, warm Coca-Cola ...

Thanks for your letter. It seems a kind of miracle that a sheet of paper from the other side of the world can come unerringly to me, can track me down - and so quickly.

Love, John.

(Paris. January 1991).

I replied with my own view of things:

Dear John,

... The partly thought-out worry is that caring for the future only corrupts the present, and so I need to enjoy this [year] as it is something I never dreamed of.

The feeling about my personal writing for English Expression is that the safe, actually wonderful internal world must be shared.

The thought came through that the daring to express oneself can shape one's intellect, and that typing has made my life a new overwhelming experience.

(1 March 1991).

***

I had had a wonderful morning, sKayming down the water slide at Rosebud, and, once dressed, had followed Jay into the news agency opposite to collect the Sunday paper.

I had assumed that the news item about our meeting at Deal had sunk without a trace over the 'silly season', which in Australia is over January and February.

However there must have been some activity. 'Facilitated' typing had hit the headlines, but not quite in the way that I had hoped.

I stood, too astonished to bite my hand, or even move. The paper had neatly, though selectively, put together a brief outline of the different viewpoints on typing with touch.

There was a plentiful sprinkling of words and phrases like *'charade'*, *'academics, not real-world people'*, *'controlled study'*, *'deception'*, *'government funding'* and *'psychological factors'*.

There were two photographs of people who were strangers, though I thought one should mean something to me, and a long account of communication programmes in some disability centres of which I had heard, but to which I had never been.

***

As far as I could make out the difficulty was that in supported typing the communication partner often had to be able to anticipate what the non-speaking person might intend.

If 'Little Lucy' is typical of the other people who need this kind of feedback, perhaps the explanation is simple.

A person who had never used language in an effective way as a child in the way that my nieces were learning to do, has not had this catalyst for the process of becoming an interactive human being, nor for organising how he experienced the world in terms that could be communicated to someone else.

AUTISM AND OTHER ADVENTURES: LUCY'S STORY

On one side of the argument were people connected with Deal Communication Centre, many of whom were used to accommodating these problems in the course of their work, and who thought they would eventually be overcome if an appropriate testing procedure could be developed.

On the other side were theorists, academics and groups of disability professionals, all of whom had been dismayed at the inconsistencies in this fingered language, especially when they found out that the people using it had been influenced by what the hands-on facilitator guessed they were going to 'say'.

If my own early experience of typing was any guide, a person who had such a severe communication disability that she could only make a meaningful pointing movement when in physical contact with someone else, had little experience in making statements.

It had been all too easy for my partners and friends to jump to a mistaken conclusion that some of my stronger hand-movements were in the direction that I intended, miss the more subtle and less frantic controlled impulse that would touch the letter that really was the one that I wanted, and so unconsciously prevent my expressing what I really was thinking.

This was infuriating, but in my opinion a small price for being able to use language. Anyway, after the first year or so, most facilitators got much better at avoiding this.

Also I had found out that working within the discipline of a school curriculum had done wonders for my language, especially when it related to written texts and the kind of exercises that the teachers set from these books.

***

The various people were talking about the same thing from such different points of view! I now know that this kind of argument is usually conducted in deathly-dull prose in a sequence of scholarly articles in skinny journals or fat academic publications that are not often seen by the general public.

Here the opinions were summarised, split up by dramatic headlines, and peppered by photographs. There, in the middle of this first report of many, was a picture of a grown-up man who had sat alongside us at Deal when we had talked to the reporter.

His forefinger projected from the tangle of his father's clasp. Next to the photograph the reporter had written, 'He began looking away from the keyboard in a manner which made one wonder how he was able to continue typing accurately.' It was quite understandable why the experts were sceptical.

The battle raged in that paper for weeks. We had nothing to contribute that had not already been said, though Jay wrote a letter which pointed out that, as a senior high school student who was using a new communication technique, I received a very high level of supervision. This must have been too unexciting for the Letters Editor. It never appeared. Eventually the topic died away.

***

Since that time, I have read things written by people who, like me, have autism, but who have developed speech and fluent writing. I suspect that there are some common features in how we use language and process information.

However, even then I did realise that I had problems in language use that were not obviously 'autistic', but were as crippling as a severe stutter. I could only hope that in the course of time all this would sort itself out.

***

AUTISM AND OTHER ADVENTURES: LUCY'S STORY

I hardly needed John's reminder that all this clutter of words was a bit hard on anyone who read what I typed:

Dear Lucy,
... 'Daring to express oneself can shape one's intellect'. This is a true statement.
To polish each sentence in a book so that each one is separately perfect would be a huge undertaking, and very difficult, because one keeps getting caught up in the flow of the story, so the individual sentences then become part of that flow, and lose their separateness like people in a crowd, or drops of water in a creek.
Which reminds me: I think you should cut words like 'really', 'actually', 'totally', 'very' and 'just' down by 90% when you write. There deletion makes for much stronger writing - 'it was hot' is a much stronger sentence than 'it was really hot'.
Paris continues to be a fascinating, exotic experience - though not for the last four days as I've been sick ... Last week was great though. Went to the catacombs, where 5 million or so bodies are stacked, bones stacked head high, in piles up to 10 metres deep, the world's weirdest tourist attraction.
I'm watching Superman III *in French while I write this - it's also quite a weird experience.*
Love, John.
(Paris. March 1991).

I thought he sounded a little less euphoric than before, and that he might even be finding the cultural gap a little wearing. Then I changed my mind:

I start to think that ... I am having the impertinence to take meanings from someone's thoughts that they do not have.
(26 March 1991).

The newspaper brawl had taught me a lesson in communication breakdown. After all, both sides in this way-out argument cared about the happiness and well-being of people without speech.

It was just that, even with a common tongue, they were separated by their experiences.

***

At Easter the Gulf War was technically over, leaving behind it a massive and dramatic clean-up job. I enthused in verse. It was a bit gooey, but felt right at the time:

Good Friday
The now bleeding sea
Can be more blue than red
Fearfully being a lung and organism of the earth.

*

That awe that the floating pearl
 Showered on the earthbound ape
 Has sadly brought a sadness
 That we should not be asked to feel.

*

Then make us rejoice at Easter
 That we dare renew
 The joy and hope that we share with mother, babe and corpse
 That mines can start the explosion of peace
 And the daring flight of oilless birds.
(29 March 1991).

***

AUTISM AND OTHER ADVENTURES: LUCY'S STORY

The topic of facilitated typing might have been on hold as far as the newspaper-reading public was concerned, but not *Chez* Blackman.

Since I had started typing on a typewriter, Jay had worked hard to encourage my hand to move spontaneously, in the same session swopping from holding my wrist to touching my shoulder, to stroking my arm rhythmically.

But, if I were feeling tired, or were concentrating on the content of what I was saying, this was too distracting for both of us.

She had never allowed me to hold her hand, except when I was very upset and she had to find out the problem in a hurry, or except when we both knew that I was being 'silly'.

As a rule the palm of her hand rested lightly below my right elbow, with her fingers tickling gently about five inches from my wrist.

That tickling sensation had been a wonderful tool for me, because I slowly developed more awareness of how my hand moved against the space through which it passed. The tickle was like the gauge on a pair of dividers.

***

I had no idea that when I used a 'normal' size keyboard, my odd visual processing meant that my hand passed through several overlapping fields of perspective, each slightly different, rather than being a multiple of virtually identical images.

That is why my hand felt out of control. Because I had always lived with this kind of visual image, I was unaware of it, and I thought that my inability to press the exact key that I wished was somehow an intellectual problem.

***

This was a different sensation from how I typed on the little three-inch-square alphabetical keyboard of the 'M' model Canon when it was held in front of me.

Because the Canon was narrower, there were fewer of these booby-traps, but I still had no idea of the exact instant in which my finger should depress the key. The Canon keys were smaller, so that the benefit of the smaller keyboard was discounted to some extent.

***

Nor was the keyboard as clear when the Canon rested on a table, without my knowing why.

Unless it wavered spasmodically, and my partner closed the minuscule gap when my finger did find the key, I was frozen in a small, panicky instant of immobility, or once again was lured by a letter which flashed at me from my internal fantasy.

However, after years of practice, Jay no longer had to move the little keyboard to meet my reaching finger when I ear-bashed people like Nicky and Tony Attwood.

She was still indispensable in this kind of typing, because she would make me concentrate by pulling the Canon back from my reach every four or five key-strokes.

This was not always obvious to the other party in the conversation, which sometimes gave the impression that I could have managed fine on my own.

***

However no one could have missed Jay turning the little machine upside-down every now and again. I suppose I had given some involuntary signal that I was fixating on certain letters and combinations, probably because the stroke of my finger changed.

AUTISM AND OTHER ADVENTURES: LUCY'S STORY

When the Canon was turned over, the keys abruptly vanished, and the sudden tunnel through which I had started to make a swooping, homing motion decomposed.

When the keyboard was turned up again, I was back to the usual slight confusion.

So I needed my companion's help to focus my attention and know what I was saying, but I was no longer in thrall to the wizardry of enchanted letters.

***

We had consciously developed this partnership, so that when I had to speak with our family doctor, or during the long counselling sessions with Nicky, all three of us would be reasonably comfortable that I was typing words that I chose myself, because my own hand was moving unsupported from letter to letter.

However on the standard size QWERTY keyboard I still needed touch, and I did not know why, though I suspected that part of the problem would be solved if Jay could hold it for me, as she did the Canon.

This did work occasionally, if Jay had the strength to balance the light-weight plastic typewriter on her hand. However she had to draw it to my right if I attempted to reach into the uncharted area left of

E

D

C

As that end of the keyboard came towards my hand, I could recognise 'S' and 'W' and the rest of that little cluster for what they were. In the original position they were clear in my vision, but not part of my spelt language.

***

Touch somehow made this divide close over. I cannot say why, but I suppose it was something to do with my body-image.

It was only a long time later that I first heard the term 'midline' in relation to visual processing. I now conceptualise it as a kind of science fiction barrier between two kinds of understanding. Whatever it was, I could not cross it unless a hand resting somewhere on my person told me I was real.

***

Working with Pauline and Petra, and at home with Jay, I usually moved my hand, finger and wrist fluidly from a pivot provided by this light touch on my elbow that tightened (probably unconsciously) when my movement became perseverative, and which lightly signalled me when I should stop typing.

Sitting with LO in maths, I could point freehand at mathematical symbols, because they were part of an on-going exchange:

The idea that the people that see LO and me under classroom conditions have, is that she is taking instructions from me, and so there is totally no issue when my work is assessed.

The very success that weird combination of the aides [Pauline and Petra], *LO, Me and you* [Jay] *have had is a tribute to the way that the others have seen me as an intelligent person, rather than an actually disabled childish person with autism.*

(25 April 1991).

***

I think that, because I worked in the same way with several people, and for a cross section of teachers who learned to recognise my individualistic way of showing interest and pleasure, the issue of my needing a partner was accepted as something that was just an inevitable part of my overall problems.

That was all very well! We had just had a loud, media-driven reminder that there was a big world out there.

***

In Year 10 we had made a video to demonstrate how I typed and did simple tasks at home, and in 1990 in Year 11 had used the same borrowed camera to duplicate this, to record any overall improvements, of which there were few. I still needed a hand on my arm, though it was often just above my elbow, rather than below.

In the intervening twelve months Jay had been drawing her hand further up as a matter of course, regularly making me tolerate her placing her hand on my upper arm, or right against my ribs when I used the typewriter or laptop. As a result the shot taken of me in April, 1991, was rather different.

It shows Jay sitting to one side but behind me, holding my right shoulder while I typed for over an hour about *Hamlet*. She is occasionally pulling back on my shoulder, but otherwise there is no obvious interaction.

I look as if I am completely self-absorbed. Actually I felt as if I were seeing my hand at the end of some kind of bionic lazy-tongs.

'Is this what we should be doing in a communication activity with someone with autism?' said Jay, half-laughing, half-serious, when she viewed it.

***

In the printouts for that same month is what could be called my side of a conversation about what I felt when Jay deliberately moved her hand around on my back and shoulders, while my finger searched for sensible words on the keyboard of my laptop.

She would lift her left hand from its grip just above my right shoulder socket, and, holding her arm in an arc so that it did not touch my back, hold my left shoulder. While she did this, I complained:

This is actually harder [for me] than the [i.e. your] standing behind me. The actual feeling is that I am not really quite there, and that there is actually a sheet of glass between us.

Then she rested her hand on the bone at the base of my neck, and while I typed ran her fingers up and down my spine, or in great firm sweeps round and round the top half of my back.

I was back in my own personal time-machine, my body and my understanding momentarily were back in a Special School classroom, and a teacher's voice was saying, 'How about getting the chalk from the box, Lu. There it is. You're looking straight at it!'

And so I was, but, without her pointing it out to me, telling me to pick up a piece once I had walked over to the box, and then talking me across the floor to put the stick of chalk near the chalkboard, I was completely paralysed.

Now I could summon up sufficient movement to type, but I recognised a similarity:

The feeling is like when the beastly dreadful teacher tried to make me do things that offered the same total challenge, such as the getting of the seen chalk.

However I could not decode the script for Jay. She looked at the printout, and brightly said, 'Oh, that is interesting!' in her best 'let's keep her motivated' voice.

***

I was getting as frightened as when on the mountain with the chevron rocks. My arms and face were quite stiff, and I tried to pull Jay's hand from its place on my back to its usual resting place between my rib-cage and the inside of my typing arm.

AUTISM AND OTHER ADVENTURES: LUCY'S STORY

The stream of information began to dry to a trickle:
The starting of a nasty new skill totally gets me as greatly rigid as the stupid fear does.

***

And then Jay went back to an old trick from my childhood. She turned me towards her, pushed my arms up, and tickled me with gusto.

As I started to giggle, she pushed me round to face the typewriter again, placed her hand in the middle of my back, and, lo and behold, I suddenly felt as confident as I did when someone had laid out the ingredients for a sandwich in the exact order in which I should combine them.

I recognised at once that this was the reason that skills learnt in the Autistic Centre were mastered more easily than when I was asked to do the same thing in someone's kitchen:

... And the very sensible way that the [i.e. my] *hand is changed totally tells me that the typing is the basically safe thing really that the people working with autistic tasks are aiming for.*

The excitement from being tickled had briefly changed my visual processing so that my eyes almost scanned, instead of gazing on a jumble among which I could not aim my finger in any logical sequence.

I lost the slight confusion between the images, and the memory of what my hand was doing was almost as good as when a firm touch on my arm gave me continual awareness of its movement.

***

The classes at school were pretty similar to the previous year, though most of my 'work requirements' had to be carefully supervised and checked, so that if later there were any queries about my typing, there was evidence that I had been responsible for it.

In Literature I had to draft and redraft several poems, which I found almost impossible to do. I had such difficulties drafting anything at the best of times, but for poetry this involved changing something that I had 'sight-felt'.

I could draft essays by making sketches in point form, but I had no ability to type the same thing again and again with minor changes. However the assessment process demanded that I complete several drafts. If I were just to write the poem once and hand it in, I would fail.

***

The poem that I wrote at Easter had been my first attempt. I was not going to change it in any significant way, no matter what the new teacher said, particularly the juxtaposition of Madonna and dead body, which she seemed to think that I had put in the same line by mistake.

However I was expected to fiddle around with the other three that I had produced. In the end, I resorted to the methods of my Year Nine English language exercises, going through the poems line-by-line, and telling my partner which words in each I wanted changed.

This conversation was kept, printed out, and included with the drafts in the completed project when it was handed in.

***

I sketched out a gut-feeling composed of the landscapes through which we drove each morning, the cows chewing stolidly in the pastures en route, and the annual newspaper coverage of the battle between hunters and animal lovers at the beginning of the duck season.

This year there had been a particularly emotive photo of a black swan cradled in death in the arms of a would-be rescuer:

Realism and the gleam of light
Are the easy slopes of hills that curve ...

(This visual conglomerate appealed to me. However I was a little confused that the others in my life, such as my teacher, did not appreciate that sight was reality, and wanted me to insert a more specific verb in the first two lines).

Actually it is a statement that the slopes are an illusion, and that queer use of 'are' means that the actual light and apparent realism are painted to be something. That makes sense to me, though the words 'sketch' or 'paint' might do.

But even I recognised that these lines in the mid-section were prime candidates for a little culling!

... cattle that the land can feed
At the beastly costing
That we count in methane and meat ...

*

The beastly 'costing' is clumsy. What about 'accounted by'? Actually the line could go, and the next line read,
   'Accounted for in methane and meat.'

*

I want to see it in the poem, and then I will know.

***

This was the first time that I had corrected finer details in my own creative writing, as opposed to correcting factual or grammatical errors I had made.

I could now start to see that it was the path to other people getting more pleasure and therefore more impact from my stories. However it was not yet clear to me exactly why this was so.

***

Silver and Black
> *Realism and the gleam of light*
> *Are the easy slopes of hills that curve.*
> *The silver and gold tassling leaves that sway*
> *Old and still new at the drowning of the bay,*
> *Shade cattle that the land can feed*
> *Accounted for in methane and meat.*
> *The abattoirs less public than a shotgun*
> *Dare not the stance of basic heroism*
> *That rises bearing shot and drooping swan.*

Chapter 15
Looking To the Future, 1991:
Age 19

That year we also were to do another Communication Project.

In all the publicity about supported typing, no one had asked what seemed to be an obvious question. Was anyone using typing to help severely disabled people analyse and learn the simple tasks to which so much time was devoted in instructional programmes?

So I thought that perhaps I could ask it myself, and broached the subject in a letter to Rosie:

Dear Rosie,

... The thing that Jay totally thought when I started typing was that these [her] *new thoughts* [about me] *and my feedback could be used as a close partner to a conventional behaviour and skills programme.*

So she asked me what I wanted to do and [then] *made me do it. So that it was not perhaps the slavish following of instructions, or the conditional treat* [i.e. reward] *that I was offered, but being in a situation regardless of my autism ...*

The ideas that she gets from autistic programmes are still valid, but she asks me what the actual method should be when easy communication is possible.

Against that is the 'carrying on' that I can put into place, and that is not just put on. The confusion, and the fear, and the problems in making a nice movement are devastating, and the way something is organised totally makes the difference.

Jay says I am going for a walk, but I think it is part of her plan to desensitise me to carrying a phobia about a certain kind of hill which gives me a dreadful, horrible fear.

LUCY BLACKMAN

(14 April 1991).

***

That premonition was all too true. It was a lovely sunny autumn Sunday, and we went to Cape Schank, where a huge mound of gravely rock topped the far end of a normally windswept promontory.

There was a long boardwalk down the steep slope from the bushy mainland, and it ended at the foot of this little hill. One then scrambled up a four-foot embankment, and could climb to a vantage point where once again I could dream dragon-filled dreams of the ocean that stretched to the polar icecap.

Loose gravel made the descent a little challenging, and that final four-foot drop was always a problem, with Jay having to hand me down.

That day she had different plans. She preceded me, sliding down, tummy inwards, over the lip. She did not look very relaxed about it, but her cheerful grin was more alarming than that. She did not quite have the gall to carol out,

'Isn't this fun, Darling!' but she might as well have. She turned at the bottom, and took three paces back to stand and look up at me.

'Have you worked out how to get down?' was what she did say, and turned her back to walk towards the foot of the boardwalk. Obviously this was a sink-or-swim experience.

I was to stay there, watching her shrink slowly into the distance until my anxiety about losing sight of her outweighed my reluctance to get down that little bank.

Very clever, Jay! but you reckoned without Gallic charm. Where Australians would (and did) walk and clamber past me, politely ignoring my still presence, a delightful, though inconvenient, young French tourist smiled, extended his hand and helped me down.

Jay was just making a turn where the boardwalk went round and outcrop, and witnessed the tableau.

**

The next day the wind was powering in from the Roaring Forties, the rain floating on it like a segmented river. Jay stood again at the foot of the bank, and I, padded parka in place of the T-shirt of the previous day, was again poised at the top.

One thing about the weather, except for a couple of rubber-clad fishermen in the distance, our particular brand of craziness was without witnesses.

I was profoundly relieved that we were trying again, because the object of these antics was as much to train Jay in general ways to cope with my anxieties under controlled conditions, as to teach me how to get down a four foot clifflet.

There on the ground, about a yard in front of where I would land if I slid down, was that chocolate and caramel bliss, a Mars Bar. She had another in her hand, and was slowly unwrapping it.

I knew that then she would gobble it down, pick mine up from the ground, and get stuck into it. I had about thirty seconds. I sat down and slid into space.

**

The research for the booklet that resulted from my Communication Project was at once a disappointment and a revelation.

The various support workers and parents of the six people with whom I was able to make contact had not used typing to break down and structure tasks in the way I had in that first adventurous year, when typing had seemed to me to be the pick with which I would crack open all my oysters.

So I interviewed a couple of the people who worked with me at school, added these to the other transcripts, called the completed booklet *Communication, Competence and Interaction*, and in disgust drew up some rather sloppy questionnaires. This pretentious foolishness got the scant pass it deserved.

However, I had been amazed to find that the different support workers with whom these various people typed, themselves felt empowered and more confident in their day-to-day encounters with people like me.

I was even shocked by the emotion shown by one lady who said, 'I am beginning to understand the people with whom I work. I see millions of reasons for the way they act — total frustration, total boredom, total distress, total pain. How do they survive?'

More than ever I understood that there was no easy answer. Nor, of course, were there any solutions as to why we could not do the simple tasks that were asked of us.

***

At least I had completed the interviews before my winter illness hit, but this had been an unnecessary precaution.

This year, for the first time in six years, I had hardly any vomiting. I was very sound sensitive, my fuse was even shorter than the previous year, and my skin was as flushed and uncomfortable as always in an heated environment, but I had lost the non-stop feeling that I was about to throw up.

The key factor had been yeast. Wheat may also give me problems, but when later I started eating wheat again, cake had nothing like the instant effect of bread and do-nuts. If I have a few days of eating yeast, I feel quite weird.

AUTISM AND OTHER ADVENTURES: LUCY'S STORY

However at that time a diet based on rice bubbles, rice cakes and beans seemed the path to feeling more human, but what a price! Most of the goodies that Jay tried to bake either decomposed on the spot, or had a texture that made me gag.

So it was difficult to find a cake recipe for me to follow. This was to be part of the current video record, and the notion of my baking a cake was good, because it involves a precise sequence of steps but does not lead to an immediate result, as happens in mashing potatoes and spreading butter on a sandwich.

For the first time it would show me trying to work from a written recipe, and, if we wanted to, we could then duplicate the exercise over a number of years for comparison purposes.

***

But I certainly would sabotage any food I disliked!

So when I was videoed making Swiss roll, it was because it was the only cake made with wheat-free flour that I would eat — and what a complicated recipe! (Jay usually confined baking to a 'four ounce' butter cake).

After eggs came spoonfuls and cupfuls of cornflour, arrowroot and a whole host of odds and ends which had to be mixed on different settings of the electric beater.

After the first session, we made the same recipe twice more for the camera, with Jay working parallel to me each time with her own set of bowls, cups and spoons.

The first time we did it, she would model the action, and I would follow suit. We had duplicates of most utensils, but not the electric mixer.

This was unfortunate, because Jay had to speak, and mould my hand to try to make me switch to each different speed, 'beat' for sugar and egg-yolks, 'whip' for fluffy egg-whites, and 'fold' for sifted flour.

Rather than reflecting her action, which then could have been slowly faded over the next few months, I could only hear her instructions and feel her hand over mine, but could not visualise my body going through the motions that were required.

***

The second version, which was on video, we worked parallel, but already I was having problems. This was the usual pattern with anything that I was asked to do more than once.

In spite of this, Jay decided to try to make me follow written instructions at this point, holding my hand up against the sheet of paper, and saying firmly,

'Now, get that out of the cupboard!'

Ha, ha! There was a nice opening. I had no intention of being treated like a baby, so I refused. I was not upset enough to feel a full jumping-tantrum come to the top, so my voice picked up the signal, and after a swift snap on my hand, I could hear myself say,

'Up, down. Up, down.'

The stubby finger pointed again to '*sugar*' on the list of instructions, and the other rather middle-aged hand pulled the door open. I doubled over and bit my hand again.

I had suddenly changed my mind. I really wanted to co-operate, but I could not make the connection between, 'Get the sugar out' in Jay's clear block letters and the printed pack of sugar. The two simply did not mesh.

There was a hand firm on my shoulder. I touched the written word, 'sugar', then looked at Jay.

'Well?' she said.

I rested my hand on the squarish white pack, and felt the hand on my shoulder relax a smidgen. The palm of my own clutching hand slipped of its own accord to grasp the sugar bag, and my

AUTISM AND OTHER ADVENTURES: LUCY'S STORY

moving hand and the packet swung through the air to the work-table.

***

During the third attempt, she tried to make me take the lead. By this time I had picked up some of the sequences, but lost others into my memory so that I could no longer put the beaters into the mixer. This I had been able to do without supervision for five years.

I could oil the paper lining of the Swiss-roll tin, but I could not at that moment see a reason for it though I understood the theory of cake-mix not sticking to oil.

So wiping on an oily sheen was simply a matter of making my hand move a certain way. The smoothness of the oil was unimportant.

***

After the flat cake was baked, the time came to sprinkle caster sugar on another piece of paper in which the cake was to be rolled up to give it texture and shape.

I could see the purpose in theory, but, because I could not control the amount of sugar pattering from the folded lip of the pack onto the paper, I lost the understanding of the aim of the exercise. I poured in heaps rather than trying to control my movements to achieve a slight dusting.

Earlier I had been able to switch on the oven, but only to some figure that I arbitrarily decided. I had been taught the correct settings so many times, but the idea that my following instructions, whether spoken or written, had any effect on the outcome was a black hole in my universe.

Then when the alarm on the oven went, I knew exactly what I should do if the cake were not to be ruined, but my body was in a different dimension.

***

All the teaching in the world was not going to make me a different person. However I did impress someone:

Dear Lucy and Jay,

I was most impressed by your video. What a terrible shame Lucy wasn't on camera before her first Deal visit. I don't think people viewing this video would be too excited unless they had known her then.

No head or trunk waving from side to side, hand-flapping or squealing, and when she did exhibit some 'fury' (the noises, hand-biting, etc.) it is hardly comparable to days before typing. Her concentration came across as being 'normal' for a Year 12 student, once again not comparable to the concentration span of a few seconds that she had in '87.

Regards,
Mrs. Wong.
(5 April 1991).

Her long years working in Special Schools certainly qualified her to recognise improvement, but I was unimpressed because I could not really see that all this effort was making much difference in my life, and there was a pressing reason why I was going to have to change more.

***

When I moved around the shopping centre or in the city, even when I was with people who could help me walk at the same rate as everyone else, I had a habit of swinging my head from side to side.

AUTISM AND OTHER ADVENTURES: LUCY'S STORY

If I were walking fast, I would then stiffen my legs and swing from side to side in a kind of star-shaped trotting movement, or I would surge to an arbitrary point, stop suddenly and stand flapping my fingers.

This was not unconscious. I felt more complete when I went through these motions. I still had no idea that they were an attempt to rid my world of sensory distortion.

At school this looked odd and even ridiculous. If I were accepted into any tertiary educational centre, I simply had to be less conspicuous.

This was not a question of my right to a university education, but of whether I would convince other people that I was there on my merits, not as an act of charity.

With my acute ear for other people's comments, it would only be a matter of time before I got embarrassed and gave everyone in the vicinity a true taste of what 'weird' really meant.

***

Jay knew that learning to walk steadily from point to point, even when she was with me, was a pretty ambitious goal but one I had to achieve. I certainly would not progress to moving inconspicuously on my own unless I first could do it with a companion.

I had improved enormously as far as my gait was concerned since those days when Jay had dragged and pushed me from lamp-post to lamp-post when I was ten years old.

Often I did walk quite normally, but I seemed to have no inbuilt inhibition — so back to pounding the footpaths for one hour every night after school

A stream of growls from beside me.

'Stop wagging your head!'

'Swing your arms!'

'You don't need your hands in your ears!'

'Are you sure you want sausages for tea?'
'Don't you know when you start waving that head?'
'Go back to that fire hydrant. That was where you were when you lost control.'
'Back to the wall!'
'... to the post-box.'
'... to the tree ... Oh!' to a little lady into whom Jay had cannoned as she walked backwards in front of me, barking out this strange litany. One good thing about being at school a long way from home was that none of my fellow students saw our evening route marches.

***

As the weeks went on, and the cool grey winter evenings drew in, I began to be aware of when my gait had changed and, after several months, almost anticipated it.

As long as Jay kept me in her line of sight, I could walk the whole two miles without running or swaying. However I missed the rocking movement, and I got very stressed and sometimes came home feeling rather disoriented.

***

It was becoming more and more likely that, if I applied for university, my score would certainly qualify me for a place in a B.A. course. This did not solve the multitude of problems that my constant need for a trained companion and my communication difficulties posed.

I visited the oldest university in Melbourne. We parked the car in one of the many parallel streets that surrounded this quiet enclave in the inner city. As we walked in a gate and between the buildings, I noticed that they were all different and spanned every architectural style of the past century.

We stopped in front of one nondescript structure to ask the way, and I was delighted to see that the Caff was hidden in its bowels, so visually it was not a focal point in the landscape.

Looking at this ill-planned campus, I realised that it would be much easier to move around here without getting the urge to prance off into the distance. Not the usual reason for preferring a long-established university!

I spoke with two members of the academic staff by typing freehand on a typewriter held by Jay. They were encouraging, and seemed to be more interested in my academic potential than my social integration.

***

Although we all knew that resources for helping me would be a problem, I was so delighted that when we left I went into freewheeling motion. When Jay emerged from the stone gothic cloisters which had so attracted me, I was nowhere to be seen.

In my enthusiasm I had not turned left once I was clear of the building to follow the path to the road from which we had entered.

Instead I shot out of the nearest gate and into the bustle of the most cosmopolitan district of Melbourne — and right through it.

I walked through streets lined with old pubs, run-down shops and little factories. I watched kids on school holiday hang out around fashionably restored historical cottages and bleak-looking Housing Commission tower blocks.

I was hungry, thirsty and terrified. I could not ask for help, and people who asked me 'what the hell I was doing just looking at them' eventually moved away.

Round dusk I walked through a great park. I remembered television news items of people being attacked in parks like this, but I must have been a non-person that night.

Eventually I was in a long street where old men with bottles sat in the gutter. I was approaching an open door, and as a figure ahead of me moved into the lighted space I went through it.

Chatter, clatter, moving glasses in people's hands, the smell of beer. A glass was in my hand and consternation round me. Attempts to make me speak.

Another drink, this time given to me. A dark jacket with the badge of the Victorian police force on the sleeve. Then the quiet of the police station, the sound of phone calls, and, eventually, Jay's voice.

***

We drove home through the after-theatre and end-of-evening-shift traffic.

'Well,' she said, her voice deliberately non-committal, and just about as devoid of relief as she could make it. 'You had better get to sleep ASAP. We have to talk to the Disability Officer at Deakin University in Geelong tomorrow morning.'

The trip to Deakin was most unpleasant. I was irritable, sinussy and very tired, as a result of being frightened, beer and not enough sleep. I giggled intermittently in the first stages of a migraine, and screamed whenever Jay tried to work out our route.

We took a couple of hours to get to Geelong as the station wagon had to be nursed along the freeway, to the fury of the truck drivers who hurtled past us.

Neither of us had been to that university before, and did not realise it was on the far side of the town. While I shook with terror, Jay struggled with the map, eventually found the university site and parked.

AUTISM AND OTHER ADVENTURES: LUCY'S STORY

***

I looked at the campus, and my heart sank. On the side from which we were approaching was an enormous grassed court, enclosed on three sides by fairly symmetrical buildings with horizontal layers clearly marked by continuous windows and balconies.

Across the intervening space was a long, flat pedestrian bridge, which I instinctively knew would lure my scampering feet at the first opportunity.

To one side were flat, rectangular concreted ornamental ponds, one with a fountain. I did not have to be a mind-reader to guess that Jay was estimating how many days I would last before I waded into the collective memory of any students sitting at the outdoor tables.

We walked past the prominent and exciting student cafeteria, not very big as uni caffs go, but full of video games and junk food.

At that moment the fire alarm went, and the whole building was evacuated. The fire-drill was brief, and then I found myself, giggling and flushed, swaying on an old orange swivel chair in a little office. Fortunately I could still type.

There was only one saving feature to the whole debacle. If I were ever to set foot on that campus, there could have been no doubt that I needed very special help.

However that was immaterial. Wild horses would not have dragged me back to Deakin.

***

That week was certainly a full one. We were to hear some strange American on something called 'Auditory Training'. There had been a flier in one of the many newsletters we received:

A SEMINAR FOR PARENTS, CARERS, TEACHERS AND AIDES OF AUTISTIC PEOPLE

LUCY BLACKMAN

Presented by, Mr. Michael McCarthy, Autism Consultant
One of Mr. McCarthy's particular areas of interest
is in the area of auditory training programmes to
reduce sensitivity to sound and modify the speech
of autistic people.

I did not realise that this was the treatment to which Sally had referred in her last letter, and cared less. This bloke was going to speak on autism. For all I cared he could have been a clown or a theologian — the focus of his talk would involve people like me.

Jay had been surprised to find out that, far from resenting being called 'autistic', I was aching to learn more about the differences between people like her and people whom I thought of as having my kind of problems, because I saw myself in them.

Now when there was a speaker on autism to whom it seemed appropriate to take me, we both went.

***

Mike had come to Melbourne after having seen Doug Biklen's account of the DEAL programme in *The Harvard Educational Review*. He was there partly to observe the work at the Centre.

So we met with him there. (I seemed to have had more contact with that old building in the past year than in the previous three rolled into one.)

I was very pleased to find that this person was not an augmentative communication professional, nor a generalist worker in the field of intellectual disability, but a hands-on, full-time teacher of smaller versions of me.

I relaxed and fingered out my thoughts on what I could and could not hear, and what I wanted to do when I finished school (which seemed to startle him a little).

I was so carried away by all this, that I suddenly expressed something that I had never described before. When I looked at an incandescent light globe, and spoke the word 'rainbow', I was saying exactly what I meant.

I could see the whole colour spectrum in certain light conditions. For some strange reason, this silver-haired, low-voiced foreigner seemed almost as enchanted as I by this phenomenon.

***

That night I heard him speak, and his interest made sense. I looked at a diagram of the whorls of the inner ear thrown up on a projection screen, and heard the same voice talk about a speculative new treatment, Auditory Integration Training (AIT), which appeared to reduce sound sensitivity in autism.

We now learned that it was suggested it might help some people with autism to become more fluent speakers. This procedure had been developed by a French doctor, Guy Berard. A recent biography by Mrs. Stehli about her daughter, Georgina, had been featured in *The Readers Digest* in the United States.

I felt a slight stiffening among the predominantly conservative audience, including Jay. To me however the rough outline of the experience which Georgie Stehli had undergone made sense, because Mike spoke of improved eye contact and better initiation following a reduction in sound sensitivity. Jay remained slightly amused, judging from the careful interest on her face.

'There only appears to be one reported side-effect,' said the figure by the overhead projector. 'An increase in irritability, which is believed to come from a resentment at 'being held underwater so long".'

I felt a coo in my throat, and my hands flapped in amusement. For the first time, Jay began to take real interest. She looked at me, and indicated she knew what I was celebrating.

'That sounds very much like you, when you had been typing for some months, and started to get so angry,' she murmured.

***

The voice from the stage continued in an unintelligible collection of references to modulated music, filters, frequencies and cochlea hairs.

Apparently for the treatment to work really well, one should have an accurate and specialised audiogram, a luxury for most non-speaking people with autism. So that was why Mike was interested in facilitated communication!

I guessed, though, that he was going to have a new learning experience. I doubted if he had any idea how impossible I found it to give accurate information about myself to other people. I expected that his prospective clients might be just as inconvenient.

Though Georgie Stehli was relatively more able, I was interested that Mike mentioned one incident that was somewhat like one of my more irritating childhood habits that had carried over into adulthood.

She would fixate on other people's hair, and, when younger, would stroke it. Wow! Definitely my kind of person! At school or in the theatre it was more strategic to seat me behind someone with curly hair.

Sometimes my sisters forgot this now that we did not live together. Val's kitchen tea the previous year had been enlivened by my seating myself behind her blonde, straight-haired bridesmaid, who had not been totally initiated into my family's weirder activities, and, to her astonishment and my embarrassment, my stroking the back of her head as I had done to my sisters as a child.

***

I had not been told that the McCarthys had been on a holiday as a prelude to his leaving teaching and setting up in practice himself.

AUTISM AND OTHER ADVENTURES: LUCY'S STORY

However I did realise that I had a new target for long, self-opinionated letters about what I had to say about how I experienced the world.

The grass under my feet still had not cracked its seed cases when I dashed off my first letter to him, to be hand-delivered before he and his wife left Melbourne:

Dear Michael,

This is partly a thank-you letter for last night, as really the idea makes sense. The noises I make to myself are audible, but not the same noise as if the sound is repeated by someone else. That is, I do hear the noise, but it does not make a big impression on me.

Typing is simply showing the reality [of what goes on inside my head], *and working on hearing, providing regular exercise or managing behaviours is only taking shots at aspects which make the disability more awfully hiding of the person behind the snaky mask.*

The strange 'carrying-on' is, of course, made worse by all the things you talked about, because [for me these] *things are not as the world assumes they are, and one reacts accordingly.*

The idea that the use of [facilitated] *communication could be part of this hearing programme is not the most practical idea for many kids, as the good use of typing is erratic and not easy.*

Good massive luck. This you will need.

(16 July 1991).

***

By this time I was half-way through my final year of school, and miraculously did not miss any classes through nausea, though this earthshaking metamorphosis was not even mentioned in the typed conversation diary at home.

I produced folders of school work, and the homework diary/message book, and even the phonelines between the aides and home, ran hot.

My various 'Options' and 'Common Assessment Tasks' poured off the typewriter and the old Apple IIC at school, but at home on the laptop computer I also was talking more and more about sensation, because I was consciously beginning to suspect that it might be some part of my problem.

I had always thought that my inability to speak all except a few short words had been due to some abnormality in thought processing, and in the same category as the strange way that I seemed to have no control over the words that I did speak.

***

I was in a take-away chicken store, and trying to ask for a 'Hawaiian Pack'.

Because I had been thinking about sound, I saw that the first movement that Jay was modelling was ending in a definite pressure by her tongue on her top gums.

I made a conscious connection between what she was doing, and what sound-symbol ended the word that I was trying to say.

Of course I could make that noise! I did so whenever I asked for a banana. However I had never heard it at the *end* of a word, and had assumed that the 'n' at the end of 'Hawaiian' was silent.

This time I consciously tried to make a sound from the information with which I was presented, rather than simply modelling it because I was told to move my mouth a certain way.

If only I had known what I knew now, I might have acquired real speech at the Autistic Centre. I passed on my theory to Jay:

The fact has just occurred to me that the word 'Hawaiian' is about the first that I have said and [yet] *heard inaccurately. The beastly reality now is that there are words I understand that I am reading and partly hearing. That is a strange thing, and I did not realise it before.*

(23 July 1991).

AUTISM AND OTHER ADVENTURES: LUCY'S STORY

She looked at me as if she were saying, 'For goodness sake, all this from one wacky lecturer'. (In fact, I later was to discover that my whole heard vocabulary was but a travesty of the English language.)

***

The next few weeks, though, she must have been thinking, because she suddenly put a suggestion to me after she picked me up at school one day. I suppose my rollicking progress down the corridor had something to do with it.

'You know!' She swung the station wagon out of the school gate, and past the kids clustered round the bus stop. 'I think there *must* be something funny about your inner ear, because if I swing my head like you do, I feel dizzy and sick. I tried it today in my library, and it was horrible.'

I only hoped none of her students had been lurking behind the bookshelves. I sniggered at the thought, which she took to be a chuckle of appreciation.

The diary entry that night, though, shows that I must have spent some time on this notion:

The thought is, unlikely though it may seem, unlovely differences in hearing are the cause of movement problems, giving me the urge to bounce about. Then, the rolling about feels so good, so that might not be so.

(12 August 1991).

***

I really could not see that there was going to be any opportunity for me to try Auditory Training until it reached Australia, which could be years. Just to keep a foot in the door, though, I went on nagging about the subject:

I actually do see a difference between active and passive comprehension ... I just know what is going on, and then, having absorbed it, I am still frozen into the physical non-comprehension if the affected part or action has not been practised.

This damn well is the most exciting idea I have heard, and so, though it is so experimental and risky, and I am so old, I actually think it is worth trying to get to try it.

(18 August 1991).

***

Just to keep Jay motivated, in general I tried to throw in a few compliments, though this, drawn from another form of political correctness, an anti-fur demonstration, brought a suspicious sideways look.

However I truly was grateful when she made herself look as if she were over-protective, or deliberately acted the fool to relax me to the point that I could move spontaneously to do what I wanted:

There is no better way of getting me to cope than making yourself ridiculous, and that is not the only talent that you have. There are more ways of skinning a cat than the obvious - and, then, you are on average pure fake fur.

Dreadful fear of well-meaning people makes me so grumpy. The way that you are a caring but competent twit is so helpful.

(3 September 1991).

***

I wrote to Mike again:

Dear Michael,

... Being all and every day with someone who understands that the way that I act is not a comprehension problem is so helpful.

AUTISM AND OTHER ADVENTURES: LUCY'S STORY

The fact that I may not type much [during that time] is not important as long as, if I need to, that person can make me [do so] right away.

There is no doubt in my mind that the typing and the use of behaviour management and the adjustment of the environment go together as a way of making life more bearable.

The strange thing is that I now know that I have a lack of distinction between sounds like 'B' and 'D'. Before this I thought that all words I read were more ideograms than phonetic.

This has only come to massive light as my mother has been asking the right questions in the past three weeks. Getting a new view of this has made me more hopeful about other things.

The trip to Australia became a memory some time ago, I expect. This is actually a hope that you had a good time and that you will come back again.

(9 September 1991).

***

Then at the beginning of the holidays I wrote to Kay (who had moved to Adelaide) about my new obsession — here the word 'happy' relates to how I felt about writing to her!

Dear Happy Kay,

There is a wild idea that we have that would confirm your worst fears about the calibre of Jay's sanity, as there is a treatment that I think might help me.

That would be expensive and is only a dream at the moment. I now know that a lot of my problems are sensory, and not intellectual. That explains so much.

The difference that all of you made to my early development must mean that the battering of senses by a crowd of other toddlers is a good thing. I don't mean just an occasional playgroup, but being bullied and carried by the whole litter.

I have passed my trial exams, and Jay is about to leave her job. That should give us something to panic about, but it may be stimulating.

Love, Lucy.

(20 September 1991).

***

The year was drawing to a close. Jay's resignation was to take effect after the two week September–October school break.

She knew what her payout was to be, showed me what she would bank for a rainy day, and took me for a long drive through my favourite rolling hills next to the sea.

As we drove along, she made it clear that such joy-rides would be rationed in the future. That nest egg had to cover any large car bills.

We swung into our driveway, and she collected the single letter from the mailbox, giving it to me to open, something she would never have done had she known what it contained.

I read the two pages of typescript, and felt my skin warm with pleasure:

Dear Lucy,

It was wonderful to receive your letter yesterday. And, no, Australia is not just a memory. If you are interested in going through Auditory Training, I would love to provide it.

I would however like a small favour in return. If you do come here for the Berard program, would you consider keeping a journal of your reactions?

I have found a comfortable bed-and-breakfast at a concessional rate if you come in January. If you decided to take the plunge, that is when my facility will be fully operational.

Lucy, if you want to come here for auditory training, one way or the other, we will make it happen.

AUTISM AND OTHER ADVENTURES: LUCY'S STORY

Love, Mike.
(Vashon Island, WA. U.S.A. Sept. 17. 91).

No way could Jay say that a few car repairs were more important than this. I don't think I was in any doubt as to the outcome.

I was going to America.

Chapter 16
Going to America,
October 1991 – January 1992

At that point I had a sudden inspiration, triggered by a photocopy from the *New York Times Magazine* of 6 October, which I had been given.

Sometime before I had been delighted by an article by Dr. Bernard Rimland, the editor of *The Autism Research Review International* which is published in San Diego. He had described three non-verbal people with autism who had been discovered to have instant reading abilities which I thought were not unlike my kind of page-scanning.

In the *New York Times* article was a brief description of autism and facilitation. Titled 'The Words They Can't Say', it sketched pen portraits of a few people who were typing in programmes which had been started by Doug Biklen after his visits to Melbourne.

It touched on the controversial nature of people diagnosed autistic. (It used my unfavourite term 'labelled'.) As an illustration, it quoted Dr. Rimland:

"*Their experiences seem to be remarkable,*' says Rimland, who over the years has written of many cases of autistic people who revealed through writing more skills than they were previously thought to have.

'*There's no doubt in my mind that there are some people who can communicate far beyond what we would imagine for them. The real issue is what percentage. I'm now inclined to believe that the percentage is considerably greater than what I had previously imagined,*' although he says it is nowhere near the 90 percent that Biklen proposes.'

AUTISM AND OTHER ADVENTURES: LUCY'S STORY

***

So the first frame of a slide show of our Grand Tour would have shown me on a Saturday morning in the centre of the City of Melbourne. I stood in the Bourke Street Mall, with plastic bags full of purchases lying around my ankles. In my hand was the Canon, which I was pushing in Jay's direction.

Trams are still an integral part of the Melbourne public transport system. The Mall is a hybrid, a pedestrian walkway in the middle of the city but, as a concession to sentiment and economics, the original tram lines have remained so it is a sound-pit of buskers, crying children, clanging tram bells, shouting lovers and screeching steel wheels on the rails.

Of course, that is without the constant roar of a myriad of air conditioners, and the tingling presence of traffic on the city roads outside the immediate walls.

I doubt if most people know what that does to initiation. They might if they tried completing a word-based task in a boiler room on a coal-fired ship. (Acknowledgements for that image to an old war movie.)

This unprecedented action was easily explicable if one glanced at the tape dangling from the keyboard:

'DARE I ASK TO GO TO SEE DR RIMLAND'

I had not realised that Jay had no intention of enduring a trans-Pacific flight with me, and then falling off a plane like a zombie straight into the clutches of this enthusiastic psychologist in Seattle, who would expect us to be eager to plunge into the unknown horrors of doing a precise audiogram with her as facilitator.

So she had already decided on a flight that allowed for a stopover in Southern California until we had got over jet lag, however that was going to affect me!

My request neatly solved the problem of how she was going to fill in this time. I had already told her that I did not want to go to Disneyland, which in my eyes was on a par with being treated like a small child.

After this episode, when she booked the tickets she also booked the six-night free stopover which was part of the package, in Los Angeles for one night, and then for five nights in San Diego.

She certainly was not as enthusiastic as I, but, in spite of her reservations, she made contact with Dr. Rimland, and eventually an appointment was arranged.

***

All this took place during the final few weeks of my school career, and nothing could have been less conducive to my working quietly towards my long coveted goal.

Even without the effects of my yeast allergy, once winter had set in I had fought the usual physical discomfort of singing head and stunning vision, which showed itself in giggling, sudden rages and a continually warm feeling in my skin. This year the pressure of doing the final year of High School against the controversy in the media about supported typing had made it worse.

On one occasion in Nicky's room, it developed into something like a tidal wave. That was just after Jay had asked Nicky for a letter to accompany my visa application. This was the first time she had mentioned in my hearing that autism, like criminal insanity and a conviction for drug dealing, required a special waiver on my US visa. I suppose she thought there was safety in numbers.

I was wild that autism was in such notorious company. Jay grabbed my right wrist, and shook my fuzzy hand until I regained enough self-awareness to focus vaguely in the direction of my index finger.

AUTISM AND OTHER ADVENTURES: LUCY'S STORY

So, with one hand restrained over the Canon, I was, thank goodness, still able to type. The rest of my body thrashed with rage that was reminiscent of how I behaved in the agony of my early attempts at expression of strong emotion by typing.

If Nicky had thought that Jay was worrying unnecessarily about how I might impress the staff on the immigration desk at Los Angeles, I had given a text-book illustration of why she had better have all my documentation in order.

***

The idea of myself changing began to occupy my thoughts, and yet I had no clear idea of what would change, if anything.

Daydreaming about myself having the same feelings as I imagined other girls to have, I suddenly tried to think about making overtures to a man. Somehow I got the speculative story-telling signals crossed with the physical response that I suppose was never far from the surface.

That night Pauline sent home an impassioned plea to Jay to turn down my school-uniform dress, which was as short as that of all the other girls — that is, just on the borderline that the school administration could tolerate.

***

As usual it was easier to express my confusion to someone invisible:

Dear John,

Wanting to write to you makes sense at this time, because the essential thing in my life is to reach out, and this is one way to do it. That was actually a very difficult thing to write, and while I was typing it I was speaking the word 'song' (which is a kind of shorthand way of saying I am upset, as when I am really upset I stupidly sing nursery rhymes very loud and fast. That is not as good as having a real tantrum but can help me calm down).

The treatment may make no difference, or it may change my perception of the environment to some extent. That in turn may make me able to change some aspects of my actions. That is a terrifying thought, and that has suddenly hit me in the run-up to the exams.

The problem that I have is that, looking at boys, the thought is that, if I acted normal, they might talk to me, and I have gone back to behaviours that I had when the girls used to bring boyfriends home and I felt so angry. The aides at school are having a traumatic time. This is really the most awful thing and so the atmosphere is awful.

Then there is the awful fury that the aides are not going to be my friends in the same way after this year. The total fact is that real friendship is only possible with someone who can feel me communicate ...

(16 October 1991).

***

This was the end of the school year for the Year 12 students, and, because the final revision time was so unstructured, my behaviour became even more unpredictable.

One day Pauline was sitting with me in an English class. We were meant to be rewriting a piece of work as practice for the exam. What on earth was the point of that? For once the rest of the class seemed to agree with me; at any rate, no one was doing any work except for Lucy, and that only because Pauline felt obligated to see that I did!

There was a sudden flurry. I was aware of handfuls of short, curly hair in my grasp, and Pauline's deep voice, frightened and fierce, saying,

'Lucy! Let go!'

AUTISM AND OTHER ADVENTURES: LUCY'S STORY

The unanimous decision precipitated by this was that I withdraw from classes a couple of weeks before the other students.

Jay had carried out 'The Plan', and was no longer working, at least not in a paid capacity. So I hung around her neck (metaphorically) as she got organised for our trip.

She was also trying to make me less anxious about flying, which was not helped by a kind of folk myth, inspired by some accidents on their superseded fleet, that United was a dangerous airline by which to fly.

Back came the answer from the friendly void, with yet another puzzler attached:

Dear Lucy,

I've been in Perth, so haven't picked up my mail for three weeks. You sound like you were under a lot of stress when you wrote, close to panic even. They say all humans are afraid of change, and you're faced with the possibility of big changes in your life.

These are almost changes in your personality that you're talking about, so it's pretty fearful stuff, like changing the Earth and its relationship to the Universe. (You are your own Earth, I guess).

... Do you write with your hand at all? If not, why not?

***

Dear John,

... I cannot write with sense of thought, and that is something I do not understand.

(13 November 1991).

And, by what seemed like return of post, another bone to gnaw on:

Dear Lucy,

I'm puzzled by the last sentence of your letter, 'I cannot write with sense of thought'. What does that mean? that you can't put into words the thoughts you have? Or your writing lacks an intellectual basis?

How come you don't use a pen? Do you use a knife and fork? Do you play a musical instrument?

What I'm getting at is, is you're not using a pen something to do with co-ordination and manipulation skills, or is it something else?

How are your exams going? How's the stress and tension?

Love, John.

***

The exams came and went, and they were very satisfying as structured activities usually are for me.

I wrote separately from the other students, with a supervisor supplied by the Board responsible for conducting the exams. That, at last, was the approval that I had been waiting for in my own mind. I had been seen to compete on equal terms in the educational system.

Selection for a tertiary institution was in the hands of the examiners and the lap of the gods (depending on how many students with higher marks wanted the same course as I did, which I knew was likely to be a problem as more students were staying on at school each year, and university places were limited).

However that was a long way off in time. The marks, which were due to come out during January when we would be in the States, were to be phoned through by LO.

***

Presentation Night was looming again, and again I was to get an award for excellence. Learning from the debacle of the previous year, Jay, with our new video camera, stood at the back of the hall.

She recorded a bent figure tread nervously onto the stage from the wings. My hands were hard against the side of my head, forefingers in my ears and little fingers pushing against the corners of my eyes.

I just managed to reach out my right hand to grasp the certificate, and then a deluge of sound battered me. In spite of all instructions against applauding individual students, the whole audience was clapping!

***

Now I had time to write again:

Dear John,

There are a lot of questions that your last letter raises about the nature of autism.

There is no known reason why the people [with autism] *who do speak have a strange way of saying things, and where the missing thought goes.*

Then many of us can feel hot but not be able to open the car window. I have stood and watched something burn on the stove, having no urge to turn it down.

That is different to having a frozen reaction. There is a co-ordination problem, but it undoubtedly is more than that.

There are people who, like Jay, can be more fluent in writing on paper than on a blackboard, and she thinks that is a very mild version of the same thing.

There are some [normal] *people who have to be helped by conversation to make their thinking clear, but others can talk to an audience.*

Then Jay handed me something I typed four years ago. What you asked is touched on. I said then that the words were in a straight line in my head, but when I spoke they bulged out like a balloon, and the balloon then burst, covering me with confusion and shame.

So we asked the weirdly difficult thing that the [high] *school did not encourage me to speak.*

The writing that I do is only obsessive words like trademarks. There has been no success [for me] in writing with physical contact, but there was a programme in the States in the seventies that succeeded with some [autistic] kids, using writing with touch.
(24 November 1991).

***

Almost before I had time to come back to earth after the exams, I was being desensitised to the terrors of flying. Now that my Number Three sister was in Adelaide, Jay had an excuse for a short flight.

Up till now Kay had managed to keep her new boyfriend, Dave, away from the more eccentric members of her family, but, lulled by the loneliness of being eight hundred kilometres from home, she warmly invited us to stay.

I was whipped out to the airport, and onto a plane which drove skywards while Jay held my hand and watched to anticipate any shrieks that might lead to complaints from the other passengers.

I realise that my fear was not unlike that of most people but I certainly expressed it rather differently. Unpleasant sensations obviously are to be expected in a roaring creaking cylinder suspended above the earth, and I vocalised accordingly.

Words are probably not very appropriate for most people in that situation, but perversely on that occasion I found one that fitted all my emotions.

'Down,' I exclaimed as I thought we might sink back to earth, as the engines strained up the incline of the air.

As we sailed safely over banks of clouds and through great chasms I could glimpse green fields and grey hills, 'Down,' echoed gruffly from our row of seats.

AUTISM AND OTHER ADVENTURES: LUCY'S STORY

Then as I was forced into the sensory grinder of the plane losing height and decelerating, I broke into a positive barrage of panicky 'Down's.

By the time the wheels thumped on the concrete I was silent, firmly in Jay's embarrassed grasp, with one of her hands positioned to cut off any further comments.

***

Our visit happened to coincide with Kay starting a job running a small snack bar in an older area of Adelaide. One of the inducements was occupancy of a rather tumble-down but very large house behind the shop.

As this meant they needed to find a new tenant for the comfortable apartment they had leased only a few weeks before, there were several prospective sub-tenants wandering in and out during our three day stay, including the family who walked into our room one night as we lay as motionless lumps under the blankets.

Kay pointed out the outstanding features of the little cream cube. She finished off with a flourish in our direction.

'That is my mother and my sister.'

This was definitely a time to suppress any desire for self-assertion.

***

Fortunately Dave and I took each other in our stride. Jay had finally decided that she should tell anyone who was going to spend much time with me what she understood to be the reasons behind some of my disconcerting activities, and I was surprised and delighted to find that it seemed to make things easier.

The shop was nothing if not noisy, and disastrously full of junk food, but fortunately we spent little time there. There was one day trip which brought me full circle. I have a short video of me standing lumpily on a long flat beach. Behind me is a crowd of pelicans and behind them the flat waters of the Coorong where *Stormboy* was set. I guess this was the equivalent of a *Hamlet* buff seeing Elsinore.

***

Then back to Melbourne with Jay, newly-wise, telling the man sitting next to me on the plane that I had said that I was no more worried than other passengers, but just expressed it differently.

He may have politely smiled and nodded, but I bet he had some very real reservations, because I do not remember enjoying that flight any more than the first one!

Christmas this year was Val's turn to cater. With admirable good sense she organised us to go to a seaside pub where Hayley's children could run amok in an indoor playground, and, by manoeuvring me into a corner seat, Jay could sit and give some approximation of being a family elder.

***

Then came departure for Seattle, and LO was determined to see us off. I was desperately offended that none of the family realised that this trip was my great odyssey come true, and had not cancelled their holiday plans to come to the airport!

Jay might not think that the idea of Auditory Training was any more than a *Readers Digest*-driven craze, but I was certain that my life was about to change. (So in fact it was, but not in the way I expected).

I administered a good dose of emotional blackmail by typing, with the result that Val and Rolf gave up a day's golf to join the party sitting in the departure lounge, brimming over with their own news that they were pregnant.

Normally I would have gone into a gooey aunt-to-be mode, but I was not in the mood to share my big moment. In fact, I felt completely upstaged!

***

The United Airlines flight from Australia terminated in Los Angeles after crossing the Pacific non-stop from Sydney, a thirteen hour marathon.

The first potential cause of drama was the toilet on the plane as, of course, I was not going to be enclosed in that shrieking, creaking, closed box by myself, but to fit the two of us in there was more of an exercise in problem-solving than I was prepared for.

In addition there was the sucking roar as the toilet bowl emptied, and the complexity of making sense of the bifold doors. A good exercise in endurance, and I survived, though the nearest toilet to our seats had its entrance in the front of the bulkhead supporting the television for the whole rear part of the plane, so, as the two of us burst out through the quivering door, there was a barrage of perplexed eyes pointing in our direction.

***

The main feeling that I remember was exhaustion, which was not surprising as I refused to close my eyes the whole way, even when the cabin lights were turned down for several hours for the passengers to sleep.

That gave rise to a problem. As usual I used my companion (in this case my mother) as if she were a reflection of myself.

This assured me that what I understood my body to be doing was exactly what it was doing, just as I liked to be sure that I was an actual part of the person whom I was using to model my own existence, by insisting that the other person and I performed similar actions.

***

This occasionally appeared in everyday life by my either eating and drinking to catch up exactly with the other person or, more inconveniently, by my insisting that he or she emptied her glass or cleared his plate to exactly the same point that I had reached if I were ahead.

It was only by seeing what I had done actually happen that I could be sure that I was doing it. So Jay had to make sure her eyes were open too every minute of the flight from Melbourne to Los Angeles. I know because I checked regularly.

Jay discovered that if she so much as blinked, I would start to chant 'Ronald McDonald!', bite my hand, or draw breath to fuel a scream of terror. She stayed rigidly awake!

***

So we both staggered off the plane equally zapped out, and through endless corridors and escalators into the immigration and customs area. All went well, and we crawled out of the building and eventually found transport that delivered us to a shiny and impersonal hotel portico.

A night and a day in that Airport Marriott room, zonked out but happy, then taxi to the Amtrak station to go to San Diego to meet with Dr. Rimland.

Of course we could have simply gone from the hotel to the airport, and on to a plane. Oh, no! We travelled by taxi, fought the idiosyncrasies of the luggage-trolley dispenser which would not digest our crumpled dollar note, and queued to take tickets into what, for me, was a noisy, people-ridden void.

Jay for some reason thought that catching a train in a foreign country would be a good experience. For whom? I ask — I had other things on my mind.

Actually she was right, as the lovely old concourse at Los Angeles Station and the busy snack bar were full of people just belong there — young in jeans, old with bags on little wheels telling friends they were going to see grandchildren, people seeing off other people, a family waiting with a Spanish speaking lady who worked for them — this was the American equivalent of Spencer Street Station in Melbourne, and these were the same kind of people who used inter-city trains at home; the differences in accents between Australian and American English were not obvious to me. This was something Jay did not realise.

***

The trip south was between barren hills and the Pacific Ocean, that same Pacific that I had raved over at Eden four years before.

The houses that extended endlessly south from Los Angeles seemed unexciting, and were interspersed with the usual spread of heavy to light industry and car yards, gradually fading to suburbs of family dream homes. Steep dry hills, and then the Spanish style station at San Diego, where ships tied up on a wharf opposite our hotel.

At night one could stand carefully just outside the hotel (not too far, in case of muggers) and look at the lights festooning the masts, or look out of the window of our room because there, almost as if one could touch the flight path, came the planes, sloping steeply to land in an airport that I thought was perilously close — and noisy.

***

San Diego Zoo is the model on which the century-old Melbourne Zoological Gardens has based its redevelopment. As a prelude to eventual retirement, LO had enrolled in a trainee programme for volunteer zoo guides in Melbourne. That was rapidly snowballing into an obsession with anything sporting fur, feathers and scales. So we were absolutely committed to seeing San Diego Zoo.

I never see the point of little mementoes, nice though it is when people remember me, but I nodded enthusiastically when Jay said we should buy a card (which she forgot to post).

The zoo at San Diego was incredibly attractive, and did something to take my mind off the looming appointment that I had so lightly engineered three months before.

We ploughed up and down the scenic walks as Jay unravelled her varicose veins that I assumed had been quietly grumbling to her right through the trip, and ended with a wonderful display of snow leopards, who so obviously were comfortable in their surrounds that I almost reviewed my anti-zoo stance.

***

The meeting with Dr. Rimland was, of course, doomed to start late with me in a state of vibrant anxiety. The effect of embarrassment, misunderstanding over meeting times, and the rather confusing atmosphere of the office of the Autism Research Institute had an inevitable effect.

However, in between hand-biting, saying 'No', being taken by my mother for a walk while he answered a telephone enquiry about the causes of autism for a court case, and standing behind some storage shelves so that trying to listen was less stressful, I did manage to type a few comments without Jay having to touch me.

AUTISM AND OTHER ADVENTURES: LUCY'S STORY

The impression I had of the whole episode was that I had messed up totally, but, on reflection, at least I could not have been said to have been an easy subject to work with. There could have been no misunderstanding that I had such difficulty with conventional expression that the Canon was truly a last resort.

***

Then back to Los Angeles by train, and a rush in a decrepit taxi with no demister, ploughing through torrential rain to the airport. The driver, friendly and with little English, was from Sri Lanka. He tried to carry on a conversation with my non-sporting mother about the current Australian international cricket team, while swooping among other vehicles and commenting at intervals that Californians did not know how to drive in heavy rain.

As we were completely surrounded by drivers who were presumably from Los Angeles, that was a little terrifying. I was so amused by Jay's reaction to this farcical situation as we travelled in the fogged-up heap that my worry-machine was switched off.

I did not even realise that the driver had never been to the airport before, had no idea of how to reach the domestic terminal and could not read the signs through his now opaque windscreen.

***

The flight to Seattle gave brief glimpses of distant buildings on the Pacific coast, expanses of farmland, and far-away clouded mounds that I guessed were the Rockies. (Wrong — they were the Cascades, which did not feature in Australian Year 9 and 10 Geography texts).

We decelerated into Seattle airport, and while my system was still decompressing my behaviour totally disintegrated.

Jay could not produce the tags for our carouseling luggage. She was trying to make polite noises in the direction of two tall strangers who had greeted us. One was Mike, but I barely remembered him from our brief meeting.

Her hands started to scuffle in her bag. That was the spark on the fuse that was laid by her broken-up voice and the total noise environment. The cases travelled round and round, clearly identifiable by the blue bows that Jay had put on the handles so she could track them with an appearance of confidence at each stop.

With a crash my world view imploded. My hand snaked forward and made contact with the fuzzy hair above the suddenly decomposing collection of features. The fury of lost confidence erupted, and I shut my mind as I felt the person on whom I relied for reassurance shake from side to side under my urgent, vibrant hands.

***

The welcoming party swiftly took control once they had stopped gaping. One leapt over the barrier and grabbed our cases over the protests of the security guard, and the other (Mike) made welcoming noises, and then led us to the car park.

Later he told me he had said to himself, 'Hello, what have we here?' but I would guess that his reaction was a little more censorable than that!

After all, he had only seen me once, six months before, sitting still and typing comfortably in a quiet room. Not quite the harpy he now had seated in the back seat of his car!

Chapter 17
Earphones and Reggae, January 1992

Vashon Island turned out to be a chunk of green countryside, complete with a small town, lots of farms and clusters of houses that were either holiday homes or occupied by very dedicated commuters.

Access to the mainland was by car ferry, and if one missed a scheduled sailing, one joined a long queue of cars waiting for the next.

The McCarthys were setting up practice in a new addition to their home, that faced over the silky grey of Puget Sound towards a bank of clouds that one magical day lifted briefly, so that the cone of Mount Ranier floated, disembodied and snow covered.

For a couple of weeks Mike juggled his first four clients between picking up his kids, reorganising the new office, and talking to me about sensation. Once the practice became fully operational, his wife, Marcie, also a psychologist, was to join it.

The second man at the airport, Dr. Jack McNabb, was at that time an associate of the practice. We were to stay in a log-cabin style youth hostel, currently vacant as mid-winter is scarcely backpacking time in the North West of the USA.

***

To summarise the theory of Auditory Integration Training at that time, the filters on the equipment are set to train the ear to ignore those frequencies which are the most sensitive, as shown by the subject saying whether or not she hears faint tones delivered through enormous earphones. The audiogram is a chart on which these responses to almost imperceptible sounds are graphed.

The first step was this damn audiogram. We were all on tenterhooks to see how I would manage this. What use my typed responses would be in charting the faint tones of the upper reaches of my weird hearing, goodness only knew.

This audiogram was to be a threshold audiogram. That is, rather than finding out whether the subject can hear in the normal range, the audiologist is discovering at what points he or she can hear outside the normal range.

***

This would not be like criticising a Shakespearian sonnet. It was to be the unbelievably incomprehensible and abstract task of transferring a sensation into a word-thought, and then removing it in time into either speech (which I could not do), or into a finger-thrust towards the 'Y' key, which was as much a matter of luck as anything else — and he wanted me to 'say' when I heard nothing!

That was something no one had ever asked me, or, if they had, I had not made an accurate response, so it was unprecedented in my experience.

***

'Well,' chirped Jay. 'Here we go!'

Mike handed me a pair of earphones. I grabbed one of the string-like cords to take them from his hand.

'No-o!' he squawked, with the first crack I had seen in his professional exterior. I don't suppose he had thought that one of his first clients would rip his equipment asunder before she had heard a single tone.

AUTISM AND OTHER ADVENTURES: LUCY'S STORY

With a new tenderness, which I suspect was as much for his investment as for my skull, he settled them on each side of my head, and sat down opposite at a little console which pretty well hid his hands and wrists.

I was still worried, because I suspected that I would pick up the flicker of his tensing and relaxing fingers in the shape changes of his upper arms. However I did not have to worry. The three of us were to have a pretty torrid time, but this was not going to be one of our problems.

***

There I was with earphones on, and Jay holding the Canon and not able to hear what I could hear. The first audiogram was terribly difficult, but then so were all subsequent ones!

We found that working with my own typed language was closer to what the other two used their speech for than my own voiced words would have been. It had the potential to be accurate, but what pitfalls there were.

Typing made me concentrate both on why I had to express what I heard, and on whether what I was expressing made sense to Jay, who relayed my answers to Mike in total ignorance of whether they were right or wrong. She had no more idea than I of what sounds and silences he was playing.

As the electronic tones peeped through, I started to respond. Mike's face at the console was no help, and he was craftier than me in the business of double bluff.

I did not realise that the movement that his hand was making was not on the key which gave the tone. That key he had under his other hand in such a way that I could see neither his wrist nor any of his hand, and his arms seemed motionless under his sleeves, even to my normally cue-sensitive glance.

***

This appallingly perceptive man was playing not only soft and loud sounds, but also spots of silence.

'*YES,*' I brought myself to type as a faint tone whirred into my ear.

'*NO,*' when he signalled that he had pressed the tone button, and I had heard nothing.

'*YES,*' I typed, and '*YES*' again, though in my ear was nothing but the hollow sound of the cup of the earphone. Perseveration had come to the party!

He double-checked all my responses several times. Then he glared at me.

'What do you think you are doing, Lucy?'

Strangely that gave me confidence. Mercifully he had cottoned on to the fact that Jay's rather abrasive, tongue-in-the-cheek approach had resulted from my adolescent-autism-with-attitude response to all more conventional forms of encouragement.

***

I became more verbose as, without being asked, I fell back on my experience in answering multiple-choice questions in Economics at High School.

The way we had solved the perseveration problem then was to make me answer each question in a full sentence, giving a reason. So my forefinger started to chatter. This put more pressure on Jay to make Mike take time.

She had also to insist that he wait, and not interpret my answer before it had run its course. For example, the expression, '*NOT THAT LOUD, BUT CAN HEAR IT*' had to be allowed to continue to the end if it were not to be translated as '*NOT*'.

AUTISM AND OTHER ADVENTURES: LUCY'S STORY

***

Essentially the whole thing was a microcosm of all the skills I had used over five years. The biggest hurdle was that I was responding into a vacuum.

What a funny way of describing the problem that I have with answering questions without the reassurance that other people will not let me get it wrong!

Someone who has used spoken or sign language all their lives might interpret that as my saying that I have so little confidence in my ability to be right, that this uncertainty was because of a need for emotional and empathetic support.

That is not what I mean. It was to be yet another two years before it struck me what made this so difficult. In spite of sitting exams and school, and reading accounts of validity tests for augmentative communication users, I still had not instinctively grasped that only I knew whether or not I heard each tone or pulse as it sounded.

***

Of course Mike knew if I were answering inaccurately when I typed '*YES*' at a time when he was making a dummy move on the controls and there was no tone.

However only I, Lucy, knew if the sounds which he did make got through to my consciousness, but Mike continually made my errors unimportant by checking and rechecking.

In spite of all this, I did not realise that he was a little puzzled by some of my consistent negatives at points which, in some cases, were well within the decibel level of a shout.

That is, some tones, especially on the speech frequencies, were impacting on my hearing when they were very faint, but the same sound played within the normal human hearing range was completely inaudible as far as I was concerned. He sought a second opinion, and, yes, this was possible, though believed to be uncommon.

***

Later, when I knew about this and had started to interpret sound marginally better in the aftermath of AIT, I began to wonder if some other substantially communication-impaired adults have a scenario not dissimilar to mine, in which the instability of early childhood remains as strong as ever as a barrier to interactive normal speech.

I suppose what really started my thinking this way was the frequency with which the function of language cropped up while I was trying to express my feelings after auditory training, and again and again while I was writing this book.

In my case this sensory colander also contributes to my difficulties with cause and effect, and to my own difficulty with understanding what is required when I am set a task which has a 'social' component.

Perhaps that explains my earlier fascination with how my nieces, Hayley's Munchkins, slowly developed their understanding through using language as a way of manipulating their environment.

***

It seems to me that there is a difference between telling someone something to show one understands a concept, which is what one does in many High School assignments, and saying something which has no prior significance to the listener.

To pass on a piece of information which is not common to both parties I find almost impossible. The reverse is also true. I still need to know what topic is in the pipeline before I can internalise the message.

Like people who assume that those around them have the same values and, unless they have lived in a pluralistic society which has many different points of view, are shocked to find this is not so, I could not separate myself enough from others to understand that there is not a commonality of experience.

What I am trying to say is that expressing an unknown fact in very clear terms that are unambiguous, and not dependent on the two people having a common ground, is something learnt slowly and through experience in early childhood. That is why a five-year-old is not allowed to give evidence in court.

***

So I sat there, while Mike and Jay struggled to work as a team on the strength of one meeting. Apart from my difficulties with discrimination and expression, the sounds at the more extreme frequencies actually made me confused.

They may have guessed this, but could do little to help me overcome it. However once they were completed, those 'intake' audiograms were as accurate as I think they would have been had I had normal spoken expression. I had managed to complete my contribution to whatever it was that would happen next.

This turned out to be another large set of earphones, through which I could hear strange sawlike sounds. I found it difficult to believe these came from the reggae CDs that Mike had slid into the player.

The change was apparently effected by a flat black box with shining knobs and flashing lights. The music was weird — totally weird in a science fiction sense. I was seating in a canvas director's chair, which unexpectedly was to become a passenger seat as I went into orbit on a heeling flight path.

As soon as I was anchored in that chair, deluged by this flowing, abrasive cacophony, I rocked, wriggled, and went through a whole lot of self-stimulations that I never normally used except when feeling very ill, but here they appeared in another context as I sat in the chair listening to the mutilated reggae. They were not only very pleasurable, but helped me to fade out the music.

***

The whole scenario was enlivened by my occasionally flinging my head from shoulder to shoulder, much in the way that had convinced Jay that there was something very odd about my sense of balance the previous year.

At one particularly grating lurch in the 'music', I levitated uncontrollably from the canvas under my backside, and came down with a very sudden thump, marked by a splintering crack as the brand new heavy-duty director's chair split down one of its legs.

'Mmm!' said Mike, wincing.

So they really had to sit with me. As soon as they had got me to control myself (as they put it), they had another surprise. I started singing, or rather chanting my ritualistic favourite nursery rhymes.

Then I flapped my hands. Both of these activities seemed to be on the veto list. With my hands down, all should have been well. However that was not what these new allies felt.

'Hey,' Jay growled. 'Lucy stop it!'

My hands had gone right to my throat, my fingers digging hard into the soft tissue behind my collar-bone. Then I grasped the balls of my elbow-joints, by this time alive in the way that my thumb joint sometimes felt when I had the urge to bite it.

By this time my vision was fragmenting, much like it did when there were a lot of people chatting to me. I pushed hard at my eyeballs.

AUTISM AND OTHER ADVENTURES: LUCY'S STORY

'You can stop doing that as well,' said Jay, and sat down facing my left arm. She swung her leg across the wooden arms of my chair, much like a rail across the seat of a fairground ride.

'Put your hands on my shin,' she said.

So all I could do to counter this intrusion into my own sound-enclave was to swallow convulsively, which Mike and Jay only saw in its final manifestation.

My upper lip flared, my tongue flicked forward, and my nose wrinkled in a porcine sniff.

'What a pig of a kid,' said Jay with maternal candour.

'Lucy,' said Mike. 'Don't sniff.'

***

That night, as on each night of our stay, after the treatment we went back to our beautiful enormous and silent log cabin where I would type. One night, frazzled but happy, I wrote to John, so far away and so wonderfully disassociated from all I had suddenly realised was at stake:

This is the fourth day that they have hooked me up to the headphones and made me concentrate on the strange collection of sounds that are now known to be a constant problem to me because I carry too much sensitivity to them.

The sound is almost like light, because it is flashing in my hearing, but there is also an awful physical feeling that was the reason for some of my strange actions.

These are still with me, but feel that there has been an improvement in very slight ways in just how the background sounds come in ... This is another of those times when I am talking to you as a clearer way of directing my thoughts ...

***

The previous night we had been sitting watching television on the little borrowed portable black and white set. I suddenly bit my hand.

'What is it this time?' Jay's voice cut across the load of rubbish pouring from the screen. Back to the Canon.

I had been irritated by the stupidity of the content of the scripted dialogue, rather than the speech-sounds that were being blurted out.

Previously it would have just washed over me, while indirectly sprinkling into my thoughts. It was the first time I had heard television-sound as being what I now thought was a component of the visual image being presented.

I thought this was how other people understood the whole nature of the social world. This was a wildly optimistic assumption.

As these various new experiences came to be part of my total understanding, they lost the impact of freshness, and I realised that I was still severely impaired.

***

However, I suppose it would be true to say that, by measuring my improved understanding against what I had lived with all my life, during the next few years I learnt to gauge something of the way in which other human beings had learned and interacted with their own individual environments.

This strikes me as much like the way that an ancient mathematician was able to calculate the circumference of our round world by measuring the distance of the Sun's declination.

A pity he and Ptolemy had not been able to bridge their respective generations and get together in the bar after work — it would have saved a lot of trouble later!

***

AUTISM AND OTHER ADVENTURES: LUCY'S STORY

I had first noticed a new awareness of sound which might now be described as a loosely crocheted mat made up from previously loose threads. I could hear rather more sounds in each collection of words.

There was what I think would be best described as a greater stability in human sounds. That is, I suddenly realised that what I had been hearing as voices was the sort of speech pattern that most people associate with Bugs Bunny.

It was pure chance that made me pass that thought on while it was still in my mind. After the episode with the little television in the cabin, Jay and Mike suggested that I kill some of the wintry hours between morning and afternoon treatments watching shows which were syndicated in Australia, to see what differences I noticed on the colour television in the McCarthys' living room.

Of course there was improved clarity in how I heard the sound, though the most startling change in me only became obvious after we got home.

However that afternoon I was riveted by Daffy Duck & Co. Alone of all these familiar programmes, in the Bugs Bunny Show the voices were barely different.

I started laughing. Jay promptly hauled me from the sofa to the computer, and was less than impressed with what I typed. I could picture a cartoon strip of this episode.

'Attention-seeking little——!' the balloon above her head would have read, under a glowing light bulb. I guess she thought I was lying in an effort to show improvement, to justify what might have been a voyage to nowhere. Mike just sat there with a grin on his face.

'I guessed that was coming. That's what her audiogram showed,' he said.

***

There was another and more obvious change in how I processed speech. As early as the fourth day of treatment I could hear the consonants at the end of words better, and for a short time some of my own terminal consonants were clearer.

However in the short-term that was the only lurch that I made towards that elusive goal, conventional speech.

There was one frustrating rent in the veil between me and real conversation. I had a brief and tantalising urge to speak. My sceptical mother did eventually believe me, because for some weeks I would walk towards her, my mouth would open slightly, and I would make a spontaneous short grunt in my throat.

I felt my head lift and my muscles twitch in the mouth and temples. According to Jay's notes, I had never before looked at another person like that.

After a while this social spark disappeared, to reappear in a couple of years, though rather diluted.

***

Later, when I came to terms with this disappointment, and was beginning to come to terms with the imperfections in what I affectionately called New Lucy, I came to believe that, had I had more useful speech from early childhood in terms of pronunciation (if not content), I might have had more experience in using spontaneous reciprocal speech with other people.

That might in turn have created some rather more effective neurological experience (or whatever the correct term is) to develop this new urge into something close to normal speech.

However my nineteen years with toddler-like mouthings had not laid the right tracks.

***

AUTISM AND OTHER ADVENTURES: LUCY'S STORY

However the isolated words that had been drilled into me in childhood in the hope that I would speak enough to express my immediate needs, eventually tended to mean what I intended them to mean.

It took three or four months before I recognised this was happening, and it is still occasionally unreliable. This more conventional speech is not terribly useful, because the words are still very blurry.

Also, if I am confused, or the background is 'noisy' (in my sense of the word), I may be compelled to use some kind of ritualistic pattern from earlier days.

***

The most wonderful thing had happened, though. I could not speak myself, but for the first time I now could understand what speech was. (I do not mean that I understood the content of speech better. That did happen, and was a consequence of the hearing changes.)

The phenomenon of speech as a human attribute suddenly became explicable, in the way that swimming may make the phenomenon of gravity explicable.

Each great discovery has its own catalyst. This was no exception, and was preceded by another rather strained exchange of views between Jay and myself.

One evening I started rocking, growling and biting my hand, an almost constant punctuation to the discoveries that I was making at this time.

'Not again! What is it now?' She thrust the Canon under my nose (snout?). I typed that I was very frustrated that I was experiencing something so momentous, and all she could see was me looking pretty much as usual. I was a little less elegant than that, but that is the general idea.

To my hurt and astonishment, Jay sat at the table laughing until I could see tears wetting her cheeks.

'Poetic justice!' she finally spluttered, her face by now almost scarlet.

I guess this was sweet revenge indeed for the months and years she had been trying to explain that the Canon was my voice, but that she had absolutely no idea as to how I could transfer my internal thoughts into typed language, and yet could only speak nonsense words.

***

In memory I was transported timetravellerwise to that small storefront communication centre, where a strange bossy woman first constrained me to use language of my own making outside my adolescent body.

Suddenly I realised that in some respects there were similarities, because there was again a sense of being redefined.

Then, even letter-by-letter, and dependent on the goodwill of another, my embryonic expressive language had been a rudimentary tentacle that had unexpectedly come into being, where previously there had only been a stump.

Flaccid and twitching fitfully, language had not only been an organ of self-expression, but also one of exploration.

Now five years older, in my new understanding of the world of human sound, I could envisage briefly the negotiation and manipulation involved in even the most cursory interchange involving functional speech.

This was a shock which was at least as disorientating as the feeling that has swept over me when I found I could make words that meant something.

Sadly, as at any time when I was stressed, I had months following of behaviours which were to make things very difficult.

AUTISM AND OTHER ADVENTURES: LUCY'S STORY

***

It was while I was listening to my prescribed sessions of modulated and filtered music that I had realised for the first time that many of my 'autistic' feeling-movements were triggered by sound.

These not only included the ones which had so irritated Mike and Jay, but things like sudden grimaces, noises and eye-movements. The corollary was that I noticed that sound and stress often had exactly the same physical effect.

Later I slowly learned to analyse my weirder activities. However then I was not in any shape for analytical thought, for this modulated music gave me some very specific sensory experiences during each of the half-hour sessions that occurred twice a day for ten days.

It could have been that I was sitting still and concentrating on the sound, but I think it was the processing, because I had had times before when I had listened with headphones, and I had never had any sensory challenge that approximated this.

That was before I realised the links between behaviour and sensation in all its forms.

***

I also did not realise that some of these defensive behaviours were specific to certain frequencies. Once we got home, Jay was very discouraging whenever I rocked or head-waved, because these almost disappeared for the first few weeks.

If she had let them re-establish, they would have become attached to other sounds. However, I suspect they would not have served their original purpose, because overall I can no longer tune out in the same way, but am still sound-sensitive in comparison to most people.

I worked this out through direct experience. Life with me was pretty noisy in the months to come. Lying in bed at night, I would suddenly surprise myself by curling up and screaming. I think it must have been a temporary reflex to my sense of balance adjusting slightly.

It was different from my lifelong feeling of falling as I dosed off. That continued to be a separate problem. These screams and other tantrums hurt my ears. I wrote in my diary that my own screaming sounded louder.

***

The peaks in the audiograms came down. However the deep troughs on the jagged line of the graph that Mike had laboriously marked out over a marathon stretch of several hours, had begun to fill up a bit when he tested me for changes after the first five days of treatment.

I could hear my own screams, and they were mammoth. However, for a couple of years until I started to sort out the chaotic fear that came from visual processing, I continued to utter shrieks that were an expression of total frustration that no one else could understand my horribly jagged awareness.

I was only grateful that right through this time I had an obligation to write for Mike, because it gave the self-awareness to realise that there was a pattern to all this, and that eventually things would fall into place.

***

A few days into treatment, another minor miracle happened.

'You know, Lu,' Jay's voice lilted excitedly as we slid over the grassy bank which led to the stony beach. She was still wondering what on earth we were doing there, and trying to persuade herself that something was changing. 'You are moving quite differently.'

I grinned. I had noticed this already. My body felt quite different, as if for the first time it had been tailored specifically for me. The ends of my fingers and toes felt real. The whole of my body made sense.

Jay noticed my ankles flexing more when we walked along the beach. She asked me why, and all I could 'say' was that I felt as if my feet belonged to me. I suppose to an observer it would seem that I no longer skittered loosely, nor stomped as if balanced on two strung tin cans.

The most disconcerting immediate effect was an occasional feeling that the whole writhing mess that my world had always seemed to be was becoming a little more real, in the sense that it was less fractured and mobile. After we arrived home, I found out what this foreshadowed.

***

At the appointed time my exam results were faxed through. I was reasonably happy with them, though I thought they might not be quite high enough for the university that was my first choice.

This attitude rather disconcerted our new friends, who were still getting used to the sight of me typing quite conventional comments at the same time as I was chanting such things as, 'Just Jeans', or singing songs embedded in my memory from music programmes.

They probably had thought that I would be delighted just to pass! But we all rejoiced together, and I simply hoped for the best.

At least I knew that I was likely to have an offer of a place at Deakin on my score. Those offers of university places were to come out early the following month.

***

For me there was more than my own new awareness to rejoice about. Though I had seen other people type, I had never seen a first assessment.

One day I walked into the office, and watched a rebirth. I saw a thirty-five year-old-lady from California type her first sentence. She stooped over a keyboard, flanked by her parents who looked as stunned as my family five years before.

I felt the timeless wonder of grandparents when they hold their own children's children in their arms. She, half a generation older than I, was to tread where I had, and stumble no doubt with as little grace as I, but at least she was on the threshold.

***

The treatment was over. For ten days I had been housebound. We did a little shopping and sightseeing in a wintry Seattle, and Jay bundled together copies of my various complaints and observations for the McCarthys. Mike looked at them with interest, though of course he had read them as they had come off my finger.

'Don't forget to keep up the diary, Lu,' he said. I suppose he saw his laboratory rat whisking her long pink tail, and sailing off into the Pacific sunset with a skinful of unprocessed data. I thought he deserved a little bonus, so, after Jay had packed and I sat down at the computer, instead of my usual monologue, I launched into a 'thank you' letter.

****

Dear Mike,

AUTISM AND OTHER ADVENTURES: LUCY'S STORY

This really has been an extraordinary experience, and that is saying a lot because my whole life has been extraordinary. Auditory training has caused the world to become a different place, and that is very difficult to explain.

The television program that I am listening to is not the same as it would have been. The screen is the main information, and the sound can direct my attention to the actual reality that they are trying to create.

Before, the commentary was interesting but parallel, as if they were not connected, but as if one had to refer to a footnote in one's mind.

One way that I learnt to read was by the children's shows, but the way the words and pictures related was a long time coming, and I think that was because the sound as the words were read was not like the written word, and the relationship to the picture was blurred so the sound was a complication rather than a help.

This is a help in explaining what has been happening now. The way that the relationship between language and speech has become close is a great help, and that raises the question as to whether the two are identical.

The thought that language can exist without full understanding of speech is strange, but that is a probability if I remember right.

The memory I have of when I was a small child is of a big sound which sometimes made me feel good, and sometimes bad. That was when I was about two. The speech I have is not related to what I was hearing, but to what I was taught.

This year, once you started working with me to establish which speech sounds I heard, I knew there was a big gap, not only in the sounds that I heard, but in the way that they came together, so there was a possibility that the treatment might work. This has proved true.

The main reason that I know this now is the lilt I hear in the voices.

LUCY BLACKMAN

I see a different association between the spoken and visual message, and that is because the spoken message is now almost complete, and the visual message is a direct reinforcement.
Love Lucy.
(17 January 1992).

Chapter 18
An Exciting, Frightening Journey, January–February 1992

The flight home was no more relaxing than the outward one. To make things more tiring, I had insisted we go straight through to Melbourne. That meant a wait in the transit area in Sydney, by which time once again we would presumably be like zombies.

The flight from Seattle left at six in the evening, and Mike farewelled us in a much more sociable atmosphere than on our arrival.

Then into the noisy international departure area at Los Angeles, where I stared fascinated through the windows of the smoky lounge at the endless queues of planes that moved to sweep into the night sky shot through with the shattering brilliance of the runway lights.

At last we took off, and my unclosing eyes watched across the Pacific as the sun slowly overhauled the plane, so that the long wing below my porthole was no longer a black patch that obscured the white moony clouds, but a sun-streaked runway in its own right. The people on the plane seemed no different, but had more impact.

I suddenly knew why when we sat, exhausted, in the transit lounge at Sydney airport. Jay struggled to keep awake over a newspaper with the antipodean view of the early stages of the Yugoslavian conflagration prominently displayed in its inner pages:

Australians on both sides of front line

As the war between the Croats and Serbs drags on despite a cease fire, Australian hunts Australian in a lethal front line contest ...

***

I suppose it only rated any real coverage because two people born in Australia of parents who themselves had been on different sides in an earlier conflict had gone 'home' to be swept up again into the maelstrom. But at that stage no one had any idea of horrors to come.

The voices of the blonde couple sitting opposite me washed into my consciousness. There was a surge of amusement that blew to a sense of wonder, and I broke out laughing. I had suddenly, and for the first time, knowingly heard an Australian accent. My own future had started to unfold.

A year later this flight coalesced in terms of sound and faces. I could wind people into the stream of my thoughts to write a story which I called *Miriam*, and which had a very small smattering of dialogue.

***

LO was waiting for us at Melbourne airport. She tumbled us into her car and back to her house to sleep and sleep.

Then two days later I was at home in our little house, the hill behind us and the Bay showing briefly in the V between the trees in front.

But to me it was not the same Bay. For one thing it was bluer, and the trees greener in the way that coloured slides are more intense than photographs. Reality was no longer at a distance.

When I stretched out my hand, it seemed to arrive at the expected point at the same instant that I saw it do so. The depth through which I saw my hand reach to rest on an object was reassuringly close to what touch assured me was actuality.

My foot felt as if the distance through which it passed before I transferred my weight to it was seemingly the same distance through which I saw my step move.

AUTISM AND OTHER ADVENTURES: LUCY'S STORY

These two parallel distances did fluctuate, but I assumed it was the way that everyone saw, and that I would now learn to accommodate that. As I got more conscious of my place in my immediate environment, I learnt to expect this relative stability, and assumed it was now a fixture.

***

We went for several walks in the first couple of days, and I learnt that indeed waves, wind and the sound of ordinary cars did not impel me to put my fingers in my ears.

Mike had suggested that we try to build up my self-awareness by using both my left and right hands in activities that required concentration.

While we were still on Vashon, I had been nagged into using his sculling-action rowing-machine for this. This had been useful, but we were not able to find an identical model for hire in those first few weeks at home.

Jay started to get me to use a couple of tennis balls to get me to focus on my left and right hands.

The ball left her hand.

'Catch-and-throw!' I chanted, in memory slotting into playing with Jenny and Kay. The ball flew from my hand vaguely into the quadrant where I knew Jay would retrieve it.

'Do concentrate, Lu! You threw more accurately than that in PE at school.' She tossed it back at me, and my cupped hands gathered it to my chest.

'Now,' said Jay. 'Think about what you are doing. Which is your right hand? Yeah ...?' sarcastically, as I put the left one up. 'Try again!'

I fixed the word 'right' onto the hand I type with, and which I knew perfectly well was pronounced that way, and raised it. The ball by now had dropped to the floor. There had been no extra hand to hold it.

'Right!' said Jay, confusing herself almost as much as me. 'Pick up the ball in your right hand,' nodding. 'That's right. Now throw — wait for me to finish! — throw to my left hand,' and she raised the hand opposite my own raised right hand. The ball flew vaguely towards it.

***

'That's fantastic!' said my uncoordinated, *sans*-ball-skills parent. From her I accepted this as real praise, unlike how I had wrongly assumed that teachers had been talking condescendingly to me when I had shown confusion in chucking projectiles at school.

Also I realised what an effort this was for her. She was not only disinterested in most sport, but visibly curled up inside when people produced even a beach ball at a barbecue.

Ball to me — fine — then ball to her. Nothing new about this. Of course, I had heard people say how good this kind of thing is for co-ordination.

What these well-intentioned, enthusiastic rationalists had never realised was that I had had no idea what co-ordination was. The fuzzy and overlapping limits to my body had seemed to have a life of their own.

***

As the New Me reached for that virulently yellow-coloured, fluffy ball, I now saw why. I could see multiples of both fingers and palm as I stretched.

In some way, probably because I was not fighting to maintain my place in space when I sat or stood, I was aware of this phenomenon consciously for the first time. Maybe also it was slightly improved.

As I moved bits of me through space, I had slightly more understanding of what was happening, and my hands made movements that were in some ways more in sync with what I was trying to achieve.

Jay's voice would snap.

'To left!'

'To right!'

And occasionally I was told, 'Both together!' So strange to find my cupped hands not just wrapping round the ball, but my fingers starting to move, each as cooperative as a strand of sea-anemone.

***

I also started to nominate which side the ball was to be aimed. The first time Jay looked clucky in a proud-mother kind of way, and the second she beamed like a Cheshire Cat, which she certainly did not resemble — more like Hobbes of *Calvin and Hobbes* fame, I would say, endlessly floating along in the trail of my enthusiasm.

She was not very impressed though when my speech-urge lost all contact with the reality of the situation. Whatever improvements Auditory Integration Training had made to movement, hearing and behaviour, the Old Lucy pathways between speech, excitement, fear and obsessions had been so deeply planted that they were to sprout again and again at the slightest encouragement.

The link between word and movement loosened.

'Le, righ,' popped from my mouth in a chant. My catching was suddenly frantic, and drowned in the repetition rather than catching with any kind of focus on the task of concentrating on left and right when instructed to do so.

Nevertheless, we went on doing this kind of thing, but Jay would cut me short whenever I started to spin out into my own world.

***

I learnt to bounce balls with the hand that she nominated, and throw them into the air and catch with the same hand. However we found that I simply could not throw a ball from hand to hand, unless one of those hands was nearly the centre of how I saw my body.

Even then letting go of the ball was terrifying. I would *pass* it from hand to hand unless Jay screamed encouragement and extravagant praise at me. I was not aware that I could not track the ball across the midline.

When it moved into that area, it disappeared momentarily, and I think my visual memory had to reinvent it. That was not such a problem inside or in enclosed spaces, but chaos still lurked in the wider world.

***

As soon as we were in an open space, I could not do those things unless we stood fairly close.

The sight of clouds scudding mysteriously past the waving treetops and the new awareness that I got from my slightly improved reactions to Jay at close range, made me realise that the distant movement of sky and foliage were a complication in how the world enveloped me, but I did not make the connection then between capacity for action and the terror of the unconfined.

(That only came to me two months later when I started to draft the story, *Flat Reflections in the Round.*

AUTISM AND OTHER ADVENTURES: LUCY'S STORY

When I sketched the prototype of the little girl under the rotating washing lines, I suddenly screamed and shook, while Jay stared at me, completely aghast at this unheralded anguish in the middle of what had been a quiet typing session.

In the same instant I was to realise, from the upsurge of my own terror at her predicament in the expanse of the open air, why she would have been petrified — such a lovely word — as if made of instant rock.)

***

One day we interrupted our walking and juggling acts to drive to visit Hayley. There was a strange moment when I held their little tabby kitten. As usual he had been placed on my lap and my hands placed on him. I looked down into the great eyes highlighted by stripes and brought into coherence by the lie of the fur on the skull. I did not recoil and was, for a brief instant, comfortable.

Then I held Aaron face to face. Looking at his big one-year-old eyes I did not cringe, and suddenly I felt what I think could be called affection (in the sense that 'affect' is a psychological term). And once again I did not understand why. Within a few days I learnt.

***

This new understanding was preceded by a fury, which I registered as what I now know to be dizziness and confusion, expressed by hand-biting and screaming.

I have no idea whether these unpleasant episodes were a trigger for my new understandings, or whether they arose in conjunction with some kind of sensory shift, but they were almost inevitably connected with them.

LUCY BLACKMAN

***

It was Australia Day, a public holiday. In spite of its being the height of summer, the morning had been fairly cool so I wore a pullover and a T-shirt, while Jay, who was not very organised in the washing and ironing department, had dragged on her remaining clean top, a long-sleeved crew-neck sweater.

On our way home in the now brilliant midday summer sun, I must have turned an unusual shade of puce. I still had not developed spontaneous ways of dealing with physical discomfort, like changing my clothes, winding down a car window or turning on a heater.

'Just take the sweater off,' Jay reminded me suddenly. 'That will make you cooler.'

I wrapped the sleeves of my pullover around my waist, its empty envelope flapping behind my rump in the daggy adolescent way that I preferred. My bare arms dangled in front of me, both fully in my visual field. It was almost lunchtime. I was hot, thirsty, and felt slightly unwell because I was hungry.

Around us was the sound of day-trippers' cars, lapping waves and occasional motor boats and mowers. Beside me was someone whom I could use as a reflection of my decomposing self-image. Reality was within reach if she would only take off the sweater that shrouded her arms.

'Ta jarm off!' (Translated this means, 'Take that jumper off!') My hand pointed urgently at her body.

'No, Lu!' Just because it was her only top garment! As if that mattered! I was past caring. I screamed and bit my hand. As I emoted by the side of the busy tourist road, she firmly grasped my arm and marched me in the direction of home about a kilometre away.

AUTISM AND OTHER ADVENTURES: LUCY'S STORY

We had to pause on a traffic island to let a stream of cars pass, so I had a chance to collapse into a full-scale tantrum before our progress was resumed. I was aware even then that I was experiencing emotions which were new to me, even though this seemed to have been triggered by the usual terrors.

***

I got my act together by the time she opened the front door. Jay firmly positioned me in front of the rather snowy television. (Snowy because we had not got round to getting an aerial, what with one thing and another.)

In the picture was a woman, speaking with humour, strength and passion on some unremembered subject. I was riveted, not by her topic but by her. I saw something that I had never consciously experienced.

This apparently irrational tantrum had not just faded away as furies had to date. Somehow it was associated with my new sensory processing, and was to act as a catalyst in my understanding of myself and the world that moved around me.

***

As I stared towards the face on the television, I was aware that there was a differentiation in depth and colour, and had some understanding of contour and the relationship between mouth, eyes and brow.

Jay happened to be looking in my direction at that instant and saw an extraordinary expression of pleasure and surprise on my face.

'Lucy, what's going on?' She scrabbled round behind a chair, retrieved the Canon and pushed the battery lead into the socket. I still have a copy of the resulting tape:

LUCY BLACKMAN

'IT IS LIKE SEEING A FACE FOR THE FIRST TIME AS THE WAY SHE IS TALKING IS THE WAY SHE IS LOOKING.'

I later expanded on that on the computer:

The face on television was weirdly different from the ones that I got the impression of before.

The way that the smile was not only the carrying of a mouth movement, but also the whole cheek and eyes, actually was not what I got from the way that I see people normally [i.e. usually].

The unlikely realisation is that I have never seen a smile before, and that is why [my] unlovely expressions are so wooden, except those which are not modelled.

***

There was another shocking discovery in the pipeline. I said in a note to Mike that it was 'as a result of a tennis ball and classical music at three metres'. I suppose that confused him, but in the event it was pretty accurate.

An hour after the great Face-on-Television episode, Jay had been throwing the ball hard and yelling at me which hand to put up to catch with, while in the background a full orchestra was featured on a cultural programme, still slightly obscured by the electronic blizzard we had been watching.

I brought my vision to focus on the projectile which moved towards me at head-height over the few feet separating us.

Startled I became aware of the depth of my mother's face as a factor that gave a slightly more three dimensional nature to her moving skin and muscles.

***

AUTISM AND OTHER ADVENTURES: LUCY'S STORY

Actually, I know now that the difference in my perception was very slight, but at the time the novelty was an enormous shock.

I could integrate the sight of an intricate and interactive shifting expression that incorporated eyes and mouth with the magical overlay of cheeks and other very slightly moving parts. I was aware that this gave me an instinctive and yet new response.

That was the first time that I realised that I had not interpreted the human face as all others.

So, although it rarely appears and I am still rather wooden in my expression, and much of my facial emotion reflects my non-social world, at the age of twenty I learned to smile at a person spontaneously.

***

I was dreadfully confused by all this. Well into the night, I would suddenly shriek, thrash around and yell for Jay. She found that the best way to relieve the real discomfort that I was feeling was by making me get up, sit at the typewriter and 'say' what I was thinking.

Not only did this help me organise my thoughts, but focusing on the purposeful and intelligent movements of my right forefinger somehow alleviated the rigidity and the spasmodic movements in my arms and back, which resulted more from terror at being still and quiet than anything else.

After these typed conversations, I usually could sleep if they went on long enough.

***

Jay was never at her best after eight at night, and was almost comatose when, a few days after Australia Day, at 2.30 a.m. I crowned a thoroughly miserable and particularly noisy night by unburdening myself to John:

Dear John,

This is the best and worst week of my life, and this is the letter I am writing to the friend who has made me feel a real person for so long

The way that I was, was a person with very poor understanding of how sound and vision were the keys to really being human. Unbelievably the seeing of other people's faces properly for the first time has made me so angry that I feel as if I want to kill myself.

The thing that has happened is that the treatment that made my ears hear my mother's voice for the first time also seems to have done something to make my eyes actually distinguish depth, and for the first time I can see the planes of a person's face.

This means that the expression [that I see on people's faces] has become just about the same as other people see, and that is a horrible thought that all these years have been wasted.

Now I can see the integration of eyes and mouth and cheeks, both of others and of myself in the mirror, and feel so much joy and so much anguish.

The sight that I have presented over the years is ludicrous, and in fact queerly obscene, and that was the, in fact, hardest thing to realise.

There is so much further to go and this is only the beginning. There is a new world at the brink of this one and the new sights that are forced on me are so strange and disconcerting.

The trees and the roads and the sea are the amalgamation of perspective and feeling as the new start of my floundering comprehension is the daring and frightened exploration that I am forced on.

The sound is far less worrying, and I feel great most of the time. Now I know that the disability that I and so many others are condemned to is mainly sensory as I wrote to you before, but now I see

AUTISM AND OTHER ADVENTURES: LUCY'S STORY

that I only just scratched at the surface, and that the whole thing is an awful warping of the way that I can interact.

The best way that I can talk about it is in terms of integrated sound and sight. The previous sound was rather resulting from peaks in certain frequencies, and holes in uncertain places, so that the speech that I heard was rather like the Bugs Bunny cartoons in some ways.

Then the sight was not the whole that you get, and that meant that the two actually were not totally in sync. The way that I saw may have been in segments and the image reassembled in my brain. At the moment I am not the person you know, and that is why I feel as if I have lost a friend.

Good night my friend,
Lucy.

***

PS (Next morning) The letter that I wrote to you was really a pretty self-indulgent exercise, though the really weird good fury was probably real. This is an awfully new experience, and so I am struggling a bit.

(1 February 1992).

He answered, thank goodness. I needed some kind of lifeline from afar.

Dear Lucy,

What an exciting, frightening journey you've embarked on. I envy you because it's like you're able to experience a birth, an entry into a new world, yet you're doing it with the mind and perceptions of an aware intelligent person ... Why is change just about the most frightening thing for human beings?

Love, John.

***

LUCY BLACKMAN

The offers of university places were published in the newspaper on 5th February. I had been offered a place at my second choice, Deakin. So we were to go to Geelong, which is directly over Port Philip Bay as the seagull flies, so I could enrol in the first-year registration day.

We went by car ferry. This links the towns of Sorrento and Queenscliff, which shelter just inside the converging Heads through which the great ocean-going ships are piloted from the Great Southern Ocean over the Rip to reach the enormous, relatively calm, circular expanse of Port Philip Bay.

Several millennia ago there had been a lush valley where the Bay now is, with a great river meandering down to finally tumble to the sea over a rocky lip between two cliffs.

Then the sea rose and drowned the valley, so that now the main shipping lane to Melbourne which follows the old river channel, zigzags backwards and forwards over featureless water.

The ships that came past the beach at Dromana seemed often close enough to touch, and then would slowly move west on the safe route to Melbourne, just visible to the north on a very clear day. That had fascinated me for years:

Needlessly battering soft sand shores
Sea surging grey and dirty white
Across the all enclosed bay.
Once a winding river ran through gentle hills
To escape through walls of stone
To sea boundlessly flowing to the Antarctic wastes.
Now the bulky shapes of ships red with rust
Loom at sky height above school and swarm of fish
Floating where once men caught their kin.
So a cataclysm can but change in kind
A world so sunk.
(Port Phillip Bay. Winter, 1988).

AUTISM AND OTHER ADVENTURES: LUCY'S STORY

An all-embracing sense of continuity, invisible but there.

***

The Rip is the movement of the sea where the old river created an indentation beyond its leap from its valley. The ferry moved slightly more as we passed inside it, and real movement again impacted on my sensory processing.

The little buildings on the shore and up the hills south-east of the ferry suddenly came to have a new quality. Fortunately Jay caught another goofy expression of surprise and delight as my awareness jelled.

Forward came her hand with the Canon, and my finger stretched to the keys before all dissolved into inexpressible memory. I would have been stammering if I were able to use speech. Just about able to type, I tried to explain my new understanding.

'CARTOGRAPHIC.' Just the one word, which in my excitement was all I could produce. I was referring to how I had previously processed that kind of view. Later I wrote:

We were swaying on the small car-ferry. This was when I saw the coast as the others see it, and Jay saw my face and asked me to explain. The nearest that I can come is the kind of old drawing of colonial settlements like Melbourne, drawn partly as maps and partly as sketches of landmarks.

Actually what I meant was that previously the background had looked two dimensional, with houses sketched in, half in perspective.

I realise now that not even then was I processing depth normally. Reality for me evermore was to be based on my realisation that measurement of my world in vision, space and sound was unreliable and idiosyncratic.

***

The second shock of the day hatched out, feathers bristling, in a most unlikely incubator.

Enrolment was carried out in the sports centre, an enormous hall full of the mutter of voices, the hum of personal computers and the whoosh of air conditioners, and now filled with disorganised queues.

Just at that moment I simply had to — no, not 'go', but *move*. I broke out of the line, and charged up and down the side of the hall, deflecting the impact of the view right in front of me by cocking my head on one side, and navigating by peripheral vision.

That felt so comforting. That was how I had moved in the hall and classrooms at school, but since our return from the States I had not been in that kind of environment. At this point in time my overall improvement in less difficult places had caused me to believe that self-control had been achieved.

Now I realised that the problem of compulsive movement, at least in part, was still with me and was linked to my sensory processing.

My new awareness of perception, and my changes in feelings that are governed by the vestibular system, gave me a sudden insight.

I was moving, not because I had a need for exercise, but because reality ceased to exist more than a few feet away, and to feel a real person I had to move because I was in an unstable world. Strange but true!

***

So the pleasure of enrolling for university courses, which five years before would have seemed like a slice of paradise, was completely overshadowed by my new discovery.

I had begun to crack the mystery of my 'behaviours'. I now realised that many of the strange actions that disqualified me from so many activities were not only started by sound, but also by visual processing, and I eventually came to believe by such things as skin temperature, or even my sense of my place in space.

In my mind's eye I also saw a difference in my contemporaries:
Dear John,
This - the actual day added to my measured life as a person who just about has all the view she needs of the basic relationship given to humans - is a milestone.

The actual sight of the students at Deakin was so happy, because there they were as people, and not moving uncaring shadows, or cutouts in polystyrene ...
Love, Lucy.
(11 February 1992).

***

Back at home I continued to learn on my feet, literally. Apart from typing, Jay's only real answer to keeping me occupied and motivated over the years had been long walks, and she clung to the familiar with a vengeance.

Twenty kilometres, ten there and ten back along the highway to the nearest large shopping mall was her idea of a short stroll.

***

The way that I had been moving had changed slightly. The steps were more even and I could feel myself moving through space towards the distance, rather than walking for walking's sake.

At intervals I still had an irresistible urge suddenly to lurch into a run, but when I was called back to the spot on the path where my immediate personal area had suddenly melded with some part of the distance, I found that I could run a flickery mental videotape to recap both my activities and the sudden change in stimuli that had precipitated them while I went through the motions of rewalking the few meters I had previously bounded across.

That had never happened in the period the previous year when we had used this tactic on the walks we had taken each evening after school.

***

I occasionally was aware from the lack of reaction from passers-by that I blended better into the background.

This was an effect I had also noticed on the plane home from the States, when I had felt the flight attendant was slightly less solicitous and wary.

I have no idea why before Auditory Integration Training I had not developed this relatively conventional walk, with relaxed shoulders, naturally swinging arms, flexing ankles, and my head poised rather that swaying.

This new effect was certainly a result of some kind of difference in myself, because I had been walking long distances for many years, and the sensory impact was now quite different.

This good feeling about movement came from a combination of new sensations. Now I had the new flexibility and tactile comfort, together with a new understanding of the whereabouts of the interlocking sections of my body.

In addition, in a small way I could not only imagine myself, but on some occasions know if I were putting my body into a certain position.

***

As I was still typing daily observations that were being bundled together and sent to Vashon Island in Batches, this motivated us to make sure that I had to comment on what I was experiencing as soon as possible after I had pulled a funny face or rushed off on my own.

Of course I was still doing some very odd things while we were walking along (and still do under some circumstances). One of these was grinning into what seemed to me to be mirrors, but what really to the rest of the world were plate glass windows.

The sight of myself in any mirror was again fascinating, as now I was seeing someone there, not a pair of flat human shapes as previously I had seen my own mirror image. The thought now comes that I must have been seeing the layers of the glass separately, because the coloured cutouts were not overlaid, but moving fanlike in opposing directions.

This was not a conceptual error, but a real vision thing. I had genuinely never realised that the shape in the silvered pane was a useful reflection in which I could see myself, but more of a shadow which happened to have some colour.

***

At school when I had rocked in the corridor in front of the Deputy Principal's office I was aware of the real people on the other side of the plate glass windows, but they had meant nothing to me.

The whole of my life I had known the theory of mirrors, but never understood how that occurred in practice. Before my new perception it was the scissor action of these images which had been so bewitching, but now I realised the reflection was a person, and it was me.

So I cocked my head to one side to experiment with this entertainment, and grinned through the glass to the astonishment of waiting hair-salon clients or restaurant patrons.

I still thought then that in some way they were both so much part of me, and yet so much accessories in my world, that I was invisible to them. In the same way even now, except occasionally, people not touching me are still like those confused suburban consumers under glass.

***

Luckily we knew no one in that long strip shopping centre. Jay gritted her teeth and decided that, as I seemed to be in a reasonably co-operative frame of mind, she might as well exploit this heaven-sent anonymity.

'Lucy, don't look in the window, ... etc.!' she would hiss, a five-star cue for defiance.

So she tried the 'return-to-the-place-the-activity-started' tack. Not only a free entertainment for me the first time, but a chance to try it again!

I did improve, but only when I knew my companion was alert to jog my memory. Even today I have to be reminded to look at something else if there is one-way glass.

However, although a second successful passage past temptation did not rule my falling again at the next shop, I did become slowly aware of which way my head was turned.

That previously had not even figured in my self image, because my whole person was not something that I could conceive as occupying space, or being directed to any activity.

***

Jay also tried to make me more aware of when my more inane grin spread across my face.

'Stop smiling!' was not the most user-friendly expression, and it was downright useless if I did not know that I was smiling in the first place.

AUTISM AND OTHER ADVENTURES: LUCY'S STORY

'Put your mouth down!' It was always helpful if I was given some action to perform which inhibited whatever it was that I was learning not to do.

I was not confused by this directive now, though I certainly had not had much success before in controlling facial movement, except with someone facing me so that I could model her. Then as now, I was not really sure that I was doing something if I could not see myself in another person's actions.

However now I could feel my mouth pulling down at the corners, though I still did not feel when it relaxed and my grin came back.

***

I had another weapon, though. I could feel moving air against my pursed lips when I blew out. So those pedestrians who were not grinned at, or spellbound by a tribal-mask-style downward-crescent mouth moving in their direction, may have noticed the twosome who strode along, with one, fluffy-haired and blondish-grey, yelping at the other.

'Blow! Don't laugh. Well done — you don't look too happy; that is great!'

***

What I did learn from these ridiculous activities was twofold. For the first time, I had a rudimentary understanding of what people mean when they use terms such as, 'What on earth must I look like!'.

Up till then I had only had a sketchy comprehension of comments such as, 'Imagine what people are thinking if you behave like that!'. My new processing of my reflection, which was juxtaposed on people who themselves were now slightly more meaningful, was itself just in the germination stage. One day it might bear fruit.

Simultaneously I was learning that my body, or rather some bit of my body (e.g. my head) had a function that was controlled by controlling the movement of that body part.

If I obeyed the injunction to, 'Look in front', I moved my head to do so. I was beginning consciously to process how my body moved, and to incorporate that into my experience and memory.

This was to lead to my eventually understanding why my visual processing was such a problem for me.

***

I learnt a lot about myself through my mother's attempts to teach me how not to make a fool of myself in public. However I think that my understanding still is pretty abstract, because, although I can cope for short periods with behaving conventionally, my self-image and self-control did not follow a continual upward path, as I found out fairly soon.

Chapter 19
Mapping My Enchanted World, February 1992

The hearing differences that I was experiencing were totally overshadowed by the visual discoveries, but that did not mean they were unimportant.

We went to visit LO. As we rang the bell, she flung open the old timber fly-screen door, and as usual led the way into the cluttered, welcoming kitchen, chatting compulsively all the while.

'Lucy, dear!' I met her eye. 'There's a bowl of stewed fruit and ice cream in the fridge (she meant the freezer for the ice cream, of course). Can you find some bowls too, and you know where the spoons are.'

She turned to put the kettle on, and then moved to help me find the first item she had mentioned, the stewed fruit. She stopped, and she and Jay looked at each other. I was placing four bowls on the table. The glass bowl of fruit was already there next to a plastic box of ice cream. I moved to the cutlery drawer.

For the first time that I can remember, I had heard and retained a string of instructions that had been part of a general conversation, rather than directions which had been clearly spoken, and reinforced with gestures and prompts.

***

I now realised that previously I had not been able to retain more than two instructions because the tasks had somehow been jumbled in sequence. They now made sense.

Later, if I was given more complicated instructions, or if the background was full of noises to which I was still over-receptive, I would get the old confusion compared with my clearer understanding in places which were both quiet and familiar.

It was on that day I made a blinding discovery. Whatever my current problems with how my brain works, I was suddenly convinced that much of my difficulty in learning skills was connected with my idiosyncratic auditory processing, and not cognitive problems.

***

Then there was the very odd 'episode of the calling bird'. The frequent strange sounds that I had made all my life seemed to be beyond my control. So I had simply assumed they were the result of uncoordinated, spontaneous and irrational changes in brain activity.

But then I discovered that some at least were echoes, and that others were the response to external sound. The latter answer came first.

We were walking down a road, with the summer sea brilliant before us and the dangling red bottlebrush flowers in a garden dancing under the weight of large honey-sucking birds suspended beneath them.

'Eeraaah.' There was a sudden musical shriek almost in my ear, and to my amazement its duplicate flew from my own mouth.

'Eeraaah!'

I shook with excitement at this revelation. All my life this connection had been hidden from me, but as I thought back, and in the weeks ahead as I monitored my own responses to the environment, I learned this incident was no freak.

However I learned as well that my chirps and coos might be a response to sounds that did not impact on other people.

AUTISM AND OTHER ADVENTURES: LUCY'S STORY

In fact some may be in response to sound imperceptible to others or to stimuli that I process as if they were sound.

***

Which brings me to the 'echo' effect. This is not echolalia, which, like many autistic people, I have had since childhood, and which is the compulsion to echo another person or to insist he or she echoed me to assure me they had understood what I had said.

My 'echo' impulse is completely involuntary, and not an attempt at communication.

I suddenly find that I am ejaculating an expression or sound which was present on a previous occasion and which impacts on me as being similar or linked by association.

What I now realise, and worked out slowly in the months following the shock of that bird cry, is that my odd noises come from my sound processing.

It was in the comparative quiet of my new reality that I could glimpse through this frightening barrier to why other people do not do this, and why they assume that speech sounds are voluntary and have meaning.

***

There was an obvious and real improvement in my overall calmness.

Strangely my skin lost that eternally flushed feeling and I was more normal in my response to pain. The whole of my life Band-Aid stuck to my skin had made me sore, but thumping down if I fell had not. I now bruised more easily.

Why did I not bruise before, and why did my sense of heat and cold change?

I would attempt, and sometimes enjoy, foods that previously I had found totally revolting because of their texture, including rice and steamed fish. My defensive actions against affection became changed into a kind of still acceptance.

***

In the course of time something very odd happened, because a year later I found out that, if I made some kind of threatening move at my mother and she hugged me, I asserted the latent feeling of exasperated affection, and was able to contain my swinging hand before it made contact.

This was farcical on occasion, as on the day when we sat in a busy University office and, because there were so many chatting people, computer fans and ventilation ducts that I seemed to hurt all over, I flung myself into her arms, rather than attack her.

What a performance, but worth it! In the following year I found that I could get the same effect by imagining this belated urge for affection and cuddles.

***

This was a very long term result and years on I am still appalled by my unpredictability, but in February 1992 how was I to know that this magic was partly knowledge for its own sake (as is all magic) and not a pathway to 'normality'.

I had not lost my enchanted world. I simply was mapping it out again, though like all discoveries it was going to lead to radical change.

When I had thought about my body or the world immediately around me, I had visualised it much as I saw it, as composites of smaller composites, with a fairly arbitrary relationship between the various odds and ends.

AUTISM AND OTHER ADVENTURES: LUCY'S STORY

The notion of 'completeness' was for me a chimera, a legendary beast cobbled together from other mythical entities.

Within that definition, I began to assume that 'completeness' was wonderfully within my reach, for I was enjoying the world in a way that unbelievably I never had. I waded into the still water at our usual beach, and swam and splashed without fear of the splash, or of my own immanent disappearance in that great space between sea and sky.

***

And yet in the space immediately around me, I also discovered the secret of onset of panic and obsession. It was by chance I discovered that there was a connection between sudden fear, the onset of my demands for an obsessive object, and startling movement on the edge of my vision.

As I was less excited and was more aware of the reason for the various responses by which I had been tyrannised for years, I identified specific stimuli which had previously been lost in the welter of sensation.

I learnt that peripheral vision was the reason for some of these sudden unexpected moments (though certainly not all), because on occasions when I had to accommodate sudden awareness of brightness on the edge of where I was looking, I had that old feeling of being dropped out of full existence.

I suddenly wondered, was it the sudden flash of soundless light that always had come with the onset of fear that had made my visual response extra sensitive?

***

This line of thought originated in my attempts to walk 'normally', looking more or less steadfastly ahead, while trying not to eye strangers, or myself in plate-glass windows.

Now I could understand that I had never looked ahead with real perception. Because I was using my vision more constructively, I realised that my centre view was constantly under attack from the periphery. Previously any brightness had stunned me momentarily, and I had never worked out why.

One day while we were walking, I had real discomfort if I did not keep my eyes down.

The previous day it had been just as sunny, and things had been much better. The only real difference was that on the second day I had exchanged my black shoes for new white runners.

When I turned my eyes down, I was able to see ahead comfortably from the top, and the bottom was filled with my black T-shirt.

I was aware of the brilliant movement of my feet, but the centre of my visual field was less sensitive, and I think my brain did not pick up its signals as strongly as from the edges. For the first time I realised why other people do not use their vision in this way.

***

A few days later, wearing dark clothes and shoes I confirmed what I had discovered. I walked quite differently when carrying a white plastic carry-bag in each hand.

If we tried to make me 'look ahead', I got flushed and disoriented, much like the bad times in the previous year. Of course plastic shopping bags rustle! The next day my load was a little more eccentric. I held an identical snow-white T-shirt in each swinging fist. The outcome was the same.

***

AUTISM AND OTHER ADVENTURES: LUCY'S STORY

'Talking' this kind of thing over was so helpful, because, like most sudden impressions, the memory of what I had just felt would have died had I not recorded it by using language.

I began to realise that there was an immediate and real reason for what had appeared to be spontaneous behaviours. Some time in that week I was sitting watching television. I moved my head slightly, and, right in a straight line with my ear, was an enormous splash of white.

My eyes flicked up and to that side, so that my visual field flicked and shifted suddenly, and I was falling into a startling and unexpected sensory chasm though I was still seated firmly on the floor, my legs folded and my hands in each other's clasp.

Unbelievably the culprit was an enormous snow-white paper lantern Jay had bought the previous day and hung with total pleasure while I had watched, deploring her aesthetic sense but unprepared for the ambush that the paper monster had in store.

There was a flash of terror and urgent need for certainty. From my grab-bag of anxieties I dredged up an image, and shuffled it into a spoken question.

'Whi pan'ies? Whi pan'ies?' I stormed around the house for a couple of minutes, urgently indicating that I simply had to know, not only where these items were, but exactly how many there were. Hankies were one thing. Intimate apparel would be something quite different, especially in public. Jay swung round, faced me and roared.

'No!' Just once, close to my face.

***

This must have cut off the urge at the root because it never reappeared, or at least not in that form.

I think it was because I was so entranced by the novelty of understanding part of the mechanism that precipitated this kind of comical but frightening chaos that I recognised the stimulus, because a few months later I still had panic attacks frightening in their intensity, and I knew intellectually that they were in the same category, but, in the same way that I had been in previous years before auditory integration training, I could no longer make myself aware of the trigger.

Far into the future I learned that if I closed my eyes tight when I got very frightened, and then opened them, I could monitor my missing sense of existence. Of course, to do that I had to learn to close my eyes immediately I wanted to, and that year I was nowhere near that stage.

***

The New Me was not easy to live with. Once asleep, I was sleeping with less fear than for many years, but I was still experiencing sudden rages in the night in the period before sleep.

Now that we knew that typing helped me avoid these, Jay would insist that I catch up on my notes to Mike in these gloomy convoluted screeds. Funnily enough, these complimented the comments that popped up when I felt happy and content.

In addition to our long walks along the Bay, she would walk with me up the steep bending road to the scenic lookout three hundred metres above our house, Canon in hand. By glimpsing through the trees at the sea, the coast and the zigzagging container ships, and typing answers to her questions about what was below, I learned that I had always had real impairments in my judgement of near and far.

The whole perspective thing was fascinating me, and I was only too happy to discuss it. At night I would comment on these tapes, often incoherently and in language so subjective that today when I read the printouts, I have problems putting my observations in context.

AUTISM AND OTHER ADVENTURES: LUCY'S STORY

However at the time I discovered that I had been able to understand perspective as a theory, but had never realised it was a device for recording the real world.

***

This did have one concrete outcome. I changed a very small part of my personal universe, the one which spilled over into drawings of monstrous humanoids, suns and stars, and ranks of blue jeans.

After a while, instead of superimposing my endless drawings of jeans on top of each other, X-ray fashion, I would draw each from the bottom, from the thigh and above ranged behind each other.

I now had a clear understanding that, even if I did not show the whole of each pair, the picture represented the concept as seen and processed, rather than showing what I knew to be there. That, though, was pretty well the limit to changes in drawing in the long run.

***

From our walks up the winding road, I also discovered something about myself through this visual adventure. That solved a related mystery, though only in a theoretical sense.

If I were approaching a bend in the road where the next section disappeared from view, I could not bear to look at it. That had not been apparent before, because I had only appeared to look straight ahead steadily.

In reality I had been glancing in very quick flashes that made a composite. The fear that I now felt on making myself walk towards such a bend with my head up was caused by the disappearance of reality in the shape of the road as it swept behind trees or rocky outcrops.

My new vision had been accompanied by the disappearance of the ability to 'fuzz up' the central area.

***

There was another difference. Just as my immediate body image had improved sufficiently to allow me to understand that I sometimes was seeing my hands, and the things I was touching, as if they were multiples, rather than a fuzzy extension of my will, so had my interaction with the more distant world.

I had occasionally had an unpleasant feeling that I could now describe, in which I felt as if an image was either multiplied, or overlaid by similar reproductions of itself in duplicate.

I had realised that this occurred, and had mentioned it to LO at school. Even so, I had never thought of describing it in detail.

Now I dubbed it 'squares' and talked about it being almost like a bank of televisions on display in an electrical retailer.

It was only in its relative absence that I could see that it had existed. I wondered whether this was a direct result of my changes in balance, sight and so on, or was it at some point a result of decreased discomfort from sound.

It was only when it reappeared in a modified form a few weeks later that I discovered (naturally at a most inconvenient moment) that it was triggered by sound and fear, and also that its sudden reappearance must have been a result of a virus infection, my accommodation to Auditory Training, and sudden battering on some frequency.

***

None of these changes in visual processing meant that my eyesight had been affected. I still saw things as before, but my understanding of what I saw was marginally different, so I understood ways in

AUTISM AND OTHER ADVENTURES: LUCY'S STORY

which other people made judgements based on experience that had not been available to me.

For example, a few days later we drove the thirty-five-odd kilometres to visit Hayley again. After the first sixteen kilometres, we stopped at a set of traffic lights and suddenly I got that 'discovery' thrill again as I saw the cars streaming across our windscreen.

They ceased to be arbitrary constructions of my intellect, and were all at once driven by real people who started their journey in a real place and would end it at an intended point.

Jay stared at my jubilant face, and pulled off the road at the first opportunity so I could explain.

In that moment I started to think seriously about one's own experience outside the events that impact immediately on one's body, and the way that I had never connected the choreography of random everyday life with the theoretical narrative that churned unspoken through my brain.

***

Shay and Kara were pretty grizzly that day. They whined at their mother for drinks, squabbled with each other and, when one of their parents refused to adjudicate in favour of whichever was complaining about her sister, scampered off to find the other for another ruling.

Inspired by this, I had a new glimpse of reality. The years between melted for an instant, and, in their language exploration, manipulation of their parents, discovery of themselves and their furious tempers, I thought I could see what I might have been in a calm, coherent and stable world.

There at my feet sat Aaron, at thirteen months indifferent to my speechless sounds. When I looked at my baby nephew, and he gazed with a kind of all-embracing tolerance and absorption at my face, I wondered what was happening to the image he was processing.

I started to think about myself in imaginary conversation with this one-year-old. Later I wrote out what I would have said, and when I came to draft the short story *Flat Reflections in the Round*, I adapted this memory of Little Lucy escaping from a barbecue in a plum orchard to fit my little fictional heroine and her personal discovery of her autism.

***

I have to tell someone about this, and you seem to be the only person who understandably is going to stick around long enough to hear me out!

So, what do you see? A rather ordinary girl in jeans, with glasses and not much expression. Far more basic is the keyboard I carry on my shoulder-strap. This little box is my key, and the person over there the oil that makes it turn in my hand.

Language grows with use, so I talk to you in my head, because the time is not right for the words to be set down. The thought comes that you may not want to listen anyway.

So here I am, telling a baby a long and involved, difficult concept so I can practise my language. Well this is the story I have to tell you. I was only three years old, and there was the whole world before me. Kids are like that. I don't mean figuratively but literally.

The hills cupped the orchard and voices in the plum trees died and swelled as the pickers moved. Very soft safe thoughts were at ground level, and enveloping branches closed off the threat of unlimited sky.

That was my world, so I entered it. Brambles hid the callous barbed wire, and the bleary vision of wandering young assisted the magic of my dream.

At the end of the world was a monster. The horns were no threat, but the eyes were nightmarish in their intensity. The nose, soft to

others, was for me the beastly imaginings of the autistic mind come to life.
The hands reached from behind, and bore me back to the crowd. And that, my darling nephew, was when the knowledge came. I damn well could not speak. Far more unlikely than my telling you this with my mind, was my calling to my mother.
Or, should I say the box is a tongue and a person a key. I can love but not show it, and fear but not say it, and tell a tale to a toddler but he cannot hear it. The hand gives me the keyboard, but the message has gone. All stories are like this for me, a creation of a moment.
(Imaginary conversation with Aaron aged 13 months, late Feb. 1992)

***

I had a clear impression then that, had we been able to understand each other, he would have been completely the appropriate audience for this monologue, though I still was unsure as to the real difference between us.

I began to realise that what I had experienced as a child had to be carefully explained to other people. My attempts to explain the discoveries precipitated by my strange new sensations in turn led me to be less frightened of these fleeting shifts.

If I had had to go on day by day simply seeing myself in this new frame, but with wordless ideas whirling behind my eyes, I think I would have made far fewer improvements in my own basic understanding. Of course I made many false assumptions, so there was still to be a day of reckoning.

***

One difficulty at this time was that Nicky was away, so I had no one except Jay to use as an audience to whom I could try to explain how things were going.

Writing to Mike kept me reasonably disciplined, because I did realise that my internal impressions were not reflected in sudden massive improvements in speech or independence. I knew that most professionals working with people with autism measured progress in these terms.

So, if I commented that I understood something better, I was obligated to point out, in whatever way I could, that I did not really behave very differently, because he was drawing on my notes in combination with his own observations of other clients as part of his research into Auditory Integration Training.

***

I was pleased that we could report that 'reality' had impinged on my relationship with my housemate, Jay. Suddenly I was able to imitate or model rather than mirror her actions, and — guess what! — I had a real instinct, as deep-seated as scratching an itch, to share with her.

So, if I went to the kitchen to get a snack for us both, I neither grabbed, nor did I insist she eat exactly as I did, but offered her some by thrusting it in her direction.

'No!' she said, and she dodged a mushy half-orange, which was weeping juicily as I pushed it into her face — and I was not distressed.

***

However I had to relearn some skills, like crossing a road or walking a correct distance from elderly people, because my visual concept of distance had changed.

Unfortunately the same thing happened with my hand movements on the typewriter.

Whereas my mechanical reflexes were much more precise and my speech-instinct seemed to be about to blossom, I was finding it much more stressful to make my hand follow the path between the language symbols on the keyboard.

When she left work, Jay had bought an Apple Classic computer, because it had a keyboard short enough for her to lay along the flat of her forearm between elbow-fold and curled top-finger joint.

By the time we flew to America, I was using it much as I did the four-inch Canon when she held it, relying less and less on my arm or body being touched.

In the twenty-four hours after the first auditory integration training session my hand became much clearer to me in some ways, but I was confused by the precise movements required to pick out meaningful sentences on a big keyboard.

Somehow we struggled through this, first with my hand held in hers, then back to elbow, and by the end of February I was both typing fluently on a keyboard held for me with no physical contact, and also noticing that, when I was not upset or tired, my language was more disciplined than it had been before — just in time for the next drama.

Chapter 20
The Lens Of the Kaleidoscope, March 1992

By a fortnight after my ferry trip to Deakin, I was very concerned about any suggestion that I could behave predictably on that campus. Of course my attendance at Registration Day had done nothing to change my mind.

The much older university that I had selected as my first choice, largely because I had thought that its varied architecture would be less visually exciting, had a Special Admissions Scheme to which I had also applied.

My eligibility was not as a result of disability only, but educational disadvantage due to my only having had four years mainstream schooling. That application was still under consideration. I suppose in all justice I should have left well alone.

I already was enrolled in a university, and there were many people who applied for the scheme who could not be given a place.

Jay had long conversations with overworked academics at a particularly difficult time of the year. At one time there was a log gap between calls, and I stressed out with increasing frequency.

The phone rang, and I listened from the bedroom.

'Oh, Hello!' Jay's voice. I could not quite make out the other, but I gathered that in his measured phrases were terms like 'supervision', 'educational outcomes' and 'research'.

Anxiously I shot towards the living room. As I got there, Jay's voice picked up the conversational baton, but somehow in the switch between the one speaker and the other, I lost all self-control. I was so giddy with anxiety that I dropped to the floor.

AUTISM AND OTHER ADVENTURES: LUCY'S STORY

***

In anger and terror I lay on my back and rocked from head to heel — and sat up in shock. The movement had been meaningless. I no longer found a river rushing through my head to drown my discomfort.

I also realised that, although I had lost this powerful inconvenient remedy, I probably did not need it any more. For the first time I could understand what was happening; my feeling of terror was just that — terror!

Jay went on trying to maintain the conversation, while the would-be BA student sat on the floor with a stunned and bewildered expression that she, Jay, was dying to investigate.

'Bye,' she said at last. 'We both really appreciate how much trouble you are taking.' But on that occasion she lied. He never knew how close she came to slamming down the receiver.

***

There was a long meeting on that campus, then a three-hour drive across the city to another institution in blistering summer heat that sorely tried our deteriorating car, which required several bottles of water for radiator top-up during the trip, and which alarmed me by grinding somewhere under the bulge down the centre whenever we stopped at lights.

Here I 'chatted' to a researcher into hands-on typing, but he could not make any suggestions which I could have coped with, and which would have reassured the staff of the university that I wanted to attend that they should make me an offer, even though I had not achieved the required exam result for admission.

At this point time ran out on me, and the orientation weeks of the various institutions began and ended without a resolution to the problem.

I knew I would have to practise moving around the Deakin campus, and so I asked to start my studies off-campus, with a commitment to travel at regular intervals to Geelong later in the year to work on campus.

***

I had not recognised the early stages of my usual virus. I thought my increased irritability was just anxiety. I had not admitted to myself that I was again noticing some sounds at a lower threshold.

Motor mowers had always battered me, but I had learnt to mow the lawn years before. I could recall that I had done so in a kind of sound-induced frenzy. Now when I trundled that same old brum-brum contraption around, it was nothing like as shocking, but the sound triggered the visual incoherence that was no longer an inevitable part of my life.

After a lifetime of unknowing endurance, I now had much less discomfort overall, and had identified the crossover of discomfort in various senses.

A whole range of sounds did not worry me as badly as they had, though some were still a problem. I noticed in the years to come that these noises were far more intrusive in those weeks when I was not well.

The physical signs of this altered sound processing were identifiable now to me as being changing eye-contact, sudden panic, loss of my feeling of well-being, and setbacks in some of my new but limited sensible word use.

Funnily enough, I could also see that my obvious sensitivities to sudden loud noises were less at these 'nasty' times, so I assume that my entire auditory processing was shifting around, which would explain why I had found things so confusing day by day during my teens.

AUTISM AND OTHER ADVENTURES: LUCY'S STORY

***

Even in those bad times I was different from how I had been before our US trip — lousy but different! Jay sat at Hayley's kitchen table and enthused.

'Haven't you noticed that she doesn't put her hands in her ears when the girls talk, or try to go home when the baby cries? She doesn't even start saying 'bye bye' as soon as I want to have a long chat on the phone!'

'For goodness sake!' snarled my eldest sister. 'She is just getting a bit more mature.'

Our parent looked mutinous and changed the subject. She was not in the habit of flogging dead pit-ponies. When we got back to the typewriter this topic came up again. I typed:

The sounds that you mention are now part of everyday happenings, so I can hardly remember how it was. I would go crazy if that sound sensitivity came again.

***

However most of the time doom and gloom was the order of the day. After being driven on a wet road, I acknowledged to Mike:

The whole awful confusion came back, and so did the lack of control.

I spiced this kind of thing up with sudden squeaks and flickering glares, which made Jay pretty nervous. That was a bonus from my point of view. Misery loves company.

We were only just beginning to notice that soft air- and machinery-noises were as difficult for me as the sounds that Jay could hear.

This new knowledge was really an outcome of my attempts to learn certain speech sounds, because we noticed that I could not repeat consonants accurately when the computer, with its noisy fan, was running. Then we also realised that the fridge motor and even windy weather did the same.

***

I was entranced though infuriated by what I was now discovering, because with hindsight I saw what I should have understood years ago. My blurry, incomplete, unpractised speech sounds reflected what I had heard as a small child.

I thought this through and realised that this vibrant anger was my reaction to learning to live without some of my worst demons.

On occasion the situation would not have disgraced silent-screen slapstick. We attended a seminar connected with one of the university courses that I was to attend. One of the lecturers, a lady with loosely arranged hair and a European accent which blurred her consonants, did the rounds of the students, chatting to each while a whole ceilingful of fans whirled above our heads.

She got to me, and we started the usual rather awkward three-cornered conversation. The whole of my being was stretched on barbed wire, and I felt my right hand start to lift as if it were a separate entity. In sudden alarm Jay's own hand came up and clasped mine.

Disaster averted — and the other party chatted on in complete ignorance of what she had escaped.

After that I was very unsure of how other people would affect me. I had not yet recognised that the whirr of overhead fans in that room had been a factor.

***

One day we went to eat in a food-court in a big mall, and Jay started to talk in waves as she had sounded when I was younger, while I was aware that her eye contact with me was wooden.

AUTISM AND OTHER ADVENTURES: LUCY'S STORY

Afterwards I realised that this was a sign my face had become rigid, and was not giving the other person any stimulus to interact. However at the time I was very upset, but when we got home this 'waves' effect disappeared, which it had not done in the times before Mike had treated me.

It was only later when I was sitting in our quiet living room that I worked out that no one talks in waves, but that my brain had processed the sound so differently that the human voice was continually distorted.

I had now realised that I had heard in surges and troughs, which were further distorted by the intrusion of background noise. I had been so swamped in sound that short term memory and language fragmented so that I could not make sense of my own thoughts.

***

The next few months I used my good times as a measuring stick against the noisier ones to work out what my environment had been during the formative years of childhood.

I suspected I was even transposing some sounds from the moment at which they flowed from another person's lips.

From my new way of looking at faces when all was quiet and calm, I had learnt that mouth movements should invariably synchronise with spoken words, but that was not always so for me, even with my improved sensation.

The sight of someone trying to be friendly, chatting away with the relationship between the features slightly awry, speech noises a little blurred, and having no idea myself at what instant my own feeling of anxiety would transform itself into a full panic was not new.

I simply had not realised that most people did not have this experience. Now I recognised that there was a reason for my confusion, and consequently for my terror.

In itself this was an enormous breakthrough, though my reaction to this kind of thing changed very slowly.

***

As far as my own speech was concerned, even as I learnt that those speech sounds that I developed through my childhood were those I could hear, I also realised that at times I was not aware of my own formless vocalisation, even when it was very loud.

I simply felt the vibration at my throat and the movement that my mouth made. On a small scale I knew from the audiograms we had done on Vashon that there were lots of gaps in how I heard human speech-sounds, and that this accounted for my strange inflection, as distinct from the conversational phrasing that most people put into even a two-syllable word.

***

When I read my chaotic and distressed midnight ramblings from the months just after the shifts in sensation took place, I now see that I still have holes in place and in time and in sound, some of milliseconds and some of over a decade.

My own racing childhood thoughts would leap the gap in time, and my adult voice would follow.

I visited the Autistic Centre a couple of years after all this happened. Through a window I watched a little group of students clambering onto a bus under the eye of the same driver who had been part of my universe.

From my lips, fourteen years later, came my little-girl chirp, 'Bye-bye!' thrown through time from another existence.

AUTISM AND OTHER ADVENTURES: LUCY'S STORY

That effect is rare, and, though scary and embarrassing, not a major problem.

However the short term sensory inconsistencies are, especially those which involve sound, because, like water splashing on a pier, sound leaves no mark, and I do not know either in what order speech should reach me, or exactly in what order it spurts out.

**

It was also about this time that I suddenly registered in my own mind that it was easier to see and track my own finger movements when my arm was held.

I was also more aware of exactly what point in time my finger was likely to touch the key of the computer. Here was part of the solution to why touch and typing had gone together.

These days Jay only had to grasp my wrist when I was too distressed to type in any other way. For the first time I was consciously aware it was because at those times my visual processing was even more broken up than usual. I learned this by comparing how I felt when I prodded the keyboard while someone held it for me in a 'good' session.

I had changed so much in these two months that I was far removed from the rather fuzzy perception I had previously had of my hands.

Though it was much better than before, for the first time I realised that my knowledge of my own touch was, and that it always had been, corrupted in relation to when my finger hit the key. No wonder I could only type in the company of someone who knew me very well. Eureka!

***

That was when I had realised that I did not always process information at the moment that my skin, balance, sight or hearing presented it to me, and that sometimes touch and sight were not in sync.

Once again I learned this by comparing the Old and New Lucy. I was less hesitant about moving down slopes, and remembered then that when we had walked after school the previous year, sometimes my feet had hit the ground while my sight had told me that I still had several inches in hand.

No wonder I had psyched myself up by bouncing around. (In generalising this discovery, I had a great feeling of relief. I realised that sometimes I had not reached the bathroom in time simply because I had not known that my body was giving me a signal.

In hearing I realised that a temporal gap substituted for this difference between body movement and visual measurement. This time lapse could be minuscule or quite substantial so, like the three-ring effect in sight, spectra of sound could arrive simultaneously and drown each other out.

***

I had discovered a trigger for both my echolalia and why I threw up apparently nonsense words. So the way that I used speech was a reflection of what I gleaned from my hearing! This was apparent to me only because I was learning to accommodate to a new and slightly less distorted environment.

However I had changed from one set of problems to a different version of the same.

Now each time I was overwhelmed or speared through or scoured by sound, I could appreciate that it should be an avoidable problem, but I had no real answer to the riddle of how to avoid it.

Of course with sound came stress, and with stress came visual incoherence, and with fragmentation of the visual surround came my urge to fly at the person who filled the tunnel of my view at that moment.

***

The shifts in sound processing had given me an understanding of my 'behaviours', but not yet a means of self-control that also let me tolerate that distortion. I hoped that I was only in some kind of limbo that my own eventual maturity might end:
Dear John,
... the last year has been like a kaleidoscope, with me falling with the beads in the lens. The first time that I realised feelings were partly reflected by bouncing speech off other people's reactions was recently.
... the wonderful thing about poetry is the compactness of thought when so much can be said in so little, but that is not something I am sure about any more.

*

For past failings, the sound ran like a chaotic sludge.
That is the way I feel about language.
Chaotic sludge transforms to clarity in intent, but not the sight.

That was the last attempt I ever made to write a poem.. My inside language had changed completely. *[Editor's note: until joining Brotherhood of the Wordless, Queensland, in 2003).*

***

I was so excited because I was learning so much about what speech was from analysing what mine was not.

It was after that letter that I started to work out that the speech that I had developed spontaneously from childhood had been very impromptu, in the sense that the word popped out in response to my internal challenge, and with no link to my thoughts.

Once people realised I had language problems, I had been slowly trained, or had learned, to say words to have some chance of getting what I wanted.

So these laboriously acquired responses had sunk into, and melded with, the chaos of my infant language. This had put two urges into play.

To complicate things, I had had the problem that I really did not know what speech was for, as I had so recently discovered. Reading written dialogue had been a theoretical exercise in some foreign environment.

***

I typed about this in yet another midnight monologue, with the cicadas whistling and shrieking in the cracked clay soil that lay under the grass behind the house, so that the sliding doors were closed to keep out the noise. My hand on the keyboard was the only thing moving in the house:

The real world was a theoretical place where wonderful ideas took over because of an emotion I did not totally understand. The books that I analysed for Year 12 were so wonderful, but not the same world.

The poetry I then wrote was so very compact, averaging a thought a word. Now that would be impossible.

***

'Do you think you can sleep yet?' growled Jay. That night, yes, but I spent a lot of time at odd moments trying to explain this in writing to her, and it was in this continuous waffling that I managed to work out why all the speech therapy and encouragement that I had been given had only caused more problems.

AUTISM AND OTHER ADVENTURES: LUCY'S STORY

So interesting because I could suddenly see that language was an enormously complex activity which was far more than typing or making noises.

I read my own words of the past five years, watched myself type and cook on videotape, and looked at how other people interacted with me.

I knew then that language itself was a limb and a sensation, and a kind of osmotic process which I had lost at some unknown point, and only now was learning what it was.

***

My stressed reactions to the uncertainties of when and where I would start a university course curdled horribly with my careful explorations of my new universe.

Nicky was still away so I asked to see Dr. Weybridge, who was now working at another hospital, because, after weeks of talking about my different sensation, I was longing to see if there was any obvious change to an independent observer. We drove up the Bay through torrential rain.

That noise, the car's vibration and the shriek of the rubber windscreen-wiper blades started to make me a little wild-eyed. We were driving through a busy commercial centre when the skies opened even more, if that were possible.

Thunder, lightning and the whole spectrum of storm noises combined with the tearing, cascading, whooshing sounds of hubcap-deep wheels motoring between echoing frontages. My new-found containment began to crack, but the breach still held.

We found the hospital car park at the third attempt. When we scrambled out, Jay realised we only had one large white handkerchief! That obsession was flaring like an invasion beacon at that time.

I not only had to have two large men's handkerchiefs, but so did Jay, and I also wanted these to be in certain colour combinations. After that drive I desperately had to have some kind of security, and I was looking urgently and noisily in our pockets and bags. Disaster loomed.

We had twenty minutes to spare, so we trotted down the street to the little strip of shops just in sight. There was a choice of food and liquor shops, and I think such things as hardware. And no supermarket or haberdasher. Blast!

But there was also a Salvation Army second-hand clothing store. The volunteer storekeeper was a little surprised when we purchased the entire stock of hybrid hankies/table napkins, seven in all, mainly bottle green.

I was still feeling extremely shattered, but could just make a connection between these travesties, and the reassurance of the real thing.

***

We hurtled to keep our appointment, with Jay trying to hurry me and not realising the room we sought had to be reached through a large and busy building. A quick foray into the wrong reception area, and out!

Muttering, she hurried me through the next entrance to a gleaming, busy foyer. Air conditioning steamed away. Also the automatic doors ground backwards and forwards in their satin-smooth lubricated grooves. The receptionist gave clear, but what to me were invisible, directions to Jay, whose face took on an expression of concentration.

I flung backwards to run in circles. Because my wrist was attached by my mother's hand, I ended in a writhing, hand-biting, snarling heap on the shiny floor. Jay abruptly rejected well-meant offers to call for help.

AUTISM AND OTHER ADVENTURES: LUCY'S STORY

We somehow ended up with me vertical and having walked through endless corridors and across a construction area to the correct department. Dr. Weybridge walked into the waiting-room, hand outstretched.

'Hello, Lucy. Nice to see you again.'

A voice and a face which I was delighted to see, but which, though familiar, was subtly different — but not so different that my time-lapse effect did not come into play.

I fell into the chaotic vortex of memory, and became again the fifteen-year-old so dependent on her incoherence, as I had been the last time we had been near to each other.

***

I was shaken, not by this second tantrum (because I had had plenty of those in the past weeks), but by what seemed to be a complete dissolution of my new self.

I had a full attack of panic, complete with flushed skin and fragmented visual awareness that my mother only realised because she had to lead me into that room by one wrist.

Under my distress I rejoiced. I was aware that I was experiencing something that was related to my new view of the world. So the strange sensation that rushed over me was for the first time clearly recognisable, though still indescribable.

As I emoted I had another revelation. All my life the trigger to my sensory distress operated the same way, whether it was activated by sound, fear or memory.

***

The other two talked, and I typed urgently and emotionally. As I did, my focus and my better understanding of what my hand and my brain were doing seemed to reduce the giddiness of my fear. As Jay wrote that night to Mike, something was different:

Lucy had some difficulties; however when we sat down I insisted on her typing on the Canon. That fairly soon overcame the 'autistic' speech, and the rest of her anxiety subsided.

I took note of the time I started to make her do this, because about 15 minutes is the usual time I have always allowed for a 'fury' to evaporate if she types.

However on this occasion, after about two or three sentences she was operating at her usual 'new' level.

***

As we drove home, new 'reality' began to reassert itself. On one bend in the road going round Olivers Hill, commanding a sweeping beach backed by a pier and the main shopping street of suburban Frankston, I started to chuckle (which is not the same as giggling). The car pulled into a layby and I typed:

'*I SUDDENLY IN FACT DAMN WELL GOT A FEELING OF THE PERSPECTIVE THAT HEIGHT GIVES IN A GOOD SENSE.*'

Once again by briefly making a language sketch of what my world-view had been, I was starting a discussion within myself that would make sense later. Later that afternoon I was to continue on the computer:

Has the sight of a drop a pleasant side? The view down the possibly scary cliff was suddenly more weirdly delightful. When I was small the height was fine, not scary, but the drop just had unpleasant sensations even then.

My new view was not lost. I had a crack through which to look at a world which was new to me, and also could use it as a view-finder to partly understand why I was a little confused by my new universe.

AUTISM AND OTHER ADVENTURES: LUCY'S STORY

***

The real changes in my auditory processing were still there. I moved through space with the same ease that I had experienced only in the past two months.

Although imperfect, my new hearing was still unfolding the sound of human speech, and the faces around me were at one with mine.

I had learned that there were good reasons for my sudden distress on this occasion, and was beginning to guess that there were equally good reasons for my becoming the kind of person that I am, even though I suspected that I had only scratched the surface of this mystery.

***

When we got back to the house, I had to step over a book-shaped bundle on the veranda before I could get to the front door.

Then I squinted back at it, and saw the Deakin logo and a computer-generated delivery label which said *HUL 101 — Literary Studies — Narrative Situations A*.

When I unwrapped it, the first page of the 'Unit Guide' flapped open as the plastic wrap was dragged down. Words flashed at me briefly:

This course is based on a recognition that story-telling, in many and varied forms, is one of the most fundamental ways in which individuals and communities try to make sense of their experience.

I had been given a new tool.

Afterword to Lucy's Story. 1999/2001 edition
Tony Attwood, Ph. D.

What can we learn about autism from Lucy's autobiography? We already know that it is a complex developmental disorder that affects the person's communication skills, social reasoning, behaviour, cognitive skills, sensory processing and movement skills to varying degrees with each individual. Lucy had difficulties in all of these, and through her autobiography we can achieve an insight into the effects on her and how she coped. The following are my personal thoughts on some of the significant points that have enhanced my understanding of autism.

Communication Skills

It appears that Lucy has not developed the ability to speak fluently for two reasons, namely a disturbance of the perception of the speech of others and a movement disorder that affected her expressive communication. The following extract from her autobiography illustrates the perceptual problem:

Because of my auditory peculiarities, I had never used sentences or other verbal arrangements in my speech. Also I had somehow never recognised or processed this when other people spoke to me, so that their words kind of splatted over the griddle of my consciousness, sometimes sunny-side-up, sometimes easy-over, and, more often than not, with a broken yolk and very uneven edges. They arrived in a random order and often overlaid each other, so I had not established any real pathways to process my own verbal thoughts. (Ch 6).

She was also not aware that her attempts at speech were unintelligible to others, for example:

The language that I developed internally could not get past the barrier of what speech I did have. I did not understand that the words

AUTISM AND OTHER ADVENTURES: LUCY'S STORY

I did produce were unintelligible to others. I thought I was sounding as they did, but of course I was not. (Ch 3).

It appears that her internal language was achieved through acquiring the ability to read. We have known for some time that some children with autism can acquire literacy skills despite a very limited spoken vocabulary. Lucy describes how she acquired the ability to read:

Although I was not to make my first total sentence till my teens, and that on a keyboard, the safe and coherent language of the written word was with me from an early age.

This started as the other girls brought home simple reading from schools. I must have been very young because I think I could understand some of the words in Jenny's very first reader, and she started school when I was two and a half.

A picture of a ball and the four letters that were below it came together in a completely synchronised way, but I know that until I was a lot older I never connected those symbols with the huggable plastic sphere I could hold in my hands.

I never developed the urge to follow a written or symbolic instruction, and I never became automatic in speaking a written word. So no one knew I could read. (Ch 4).

Why was she unable to express her thoughts in speech? The problem appears to be with the link between mind and body. The thought could not be expressed in oro-motor movements or conventional body language. One may consider this as a form of dyspraxia and this could explain the personal benefits Lucy receives from Facilitated Communication. Lucy describes that:

I was not learning to type. I was learning to help other people to enable me to stumble around the keyboard so that I could use my underdeveloped internal language in the way I thought speech and writing were used by everyone else. (Ch 7).

Lucy has experienced many years of intensive training and practise in learning to use a keyboard, with continual emphasis on becoming more independent, such that:

After five years she did not have to touch any part of my arm or body while my finger chattered on about those topics which occupied my brain at that particular moment. (Ch 9).

This autobiography describes Lucy's development up to 1992. Since 1995 she has typed freehand but still requires someone to help her control her autistic behaviour and to provide verbal feedback, i.e. to read aloud her completed text.

The question of who is typing is no longer an issue. However it is inevitable that this book will be considered in the debate and argument regarding the validity of Facilitated Communication. My opinion is that this autobiography is about Lucy, an exceptional young woman who has been through exceptional circumstances.

Social Reasoning

We know that people with autism have considerable difficulty with social reasoning and empathy. Lucy described how, 'My autism was not caused or aggravated by lack of interaction in any way.

My own lack of interaction was innate.' (Ch 1). She also explains that, *'Because I had no instinctive urge to cooperate, I could not reach out halfway to take a glass or a garment from someone's hand unless I was told to do so.'* (Ch 5). It is interesting that Lucy *'did not realise that I was expected to enjoy cuddles.'* (Ch 2).

The emotional behaviour of others was initially a mystery to her, as illustrated in the following quotation:

When Michael, who was a little older than I, cried, I did not see him as sad but that his face had changed and that his noise hurt my ears. *I did not understand that he was experiencing what I did when I was upset. I felt disoriented rather than sympathetic.* (Ch 2).

She was also unable to 'read' a face, illustrated in her description of her mother becoming anxious and the effect on her own anxiety:

This anxiety was compounded by her face foreshortening as her head bent forward, so that all the shadows and curves of her features made a different pattern, and the person who I was relying on decomposed in some way. (Ch 5).

As a young child she was not interested in socialising or able to fully understand the thoughts and motives of others. However, she eventually acquired these skills. This was not achieved by special remedial programs but by natural observation and intelligence. Despite her initial confusion, she has developed the ability to self-reflect and to understand the perspective and thoughts of others.

John Marsden is correct in describing Lucy as someone with *'sensitivity, creativity, eloquence, warmth'* (Ch 10). I would add that she has a sense of humour as illustrated in her comment that *'there is no fun in being frustrated by oneself'.* (Ch 12).

Behaviour

On first meeting a child with autism, you realise that such behaviour is either a constructive adaptation to the disorder or an inability to provide a conventional response. On reading Lucy's autobiography, one is aware of how confusing the world is for her. As Lucy states:

Because I lived in an uncertain world, change of any kind was so incomprehensible that when anyone said, 'I think that I might ...' or 'I wonder if it would be best to ...', my four-dimensional world unfolded like a paper streamer. (Ch 10)

Perhaps as a result of such apparent chaos, she was fascinated by order and symmetry and imposing control. For example:

Lego blocks were not a tool from which I constructed something which my mind had pre-planned. As a small child, the feel and symmetry of these plastic interlocking blocks was all absorbing, and all I understood of their function was that they made patterns in long rods. (Ch 2)

The determination to have symmetry was one explanation of some quite unusual behaviour:

At one stage I would not allow the driver to leave one hand resting on the gear knob and the other on the steering wheel, because this position was not symmetrical. At times I thrust and pushed at Jay while she was trying to steer us through traffic because the wind-up knobs for the front windows had about a sixty degree difference in alignment, which meant that when the windows were symmetrical, the knobs were not — and vice versa. (Ch 9)

From Lucy's perspective, her actions were logical and a means of coping, but the logic was not always apparent to other people.

One aspect of autism is that unusual behaviour can be a means of expressing a particular thought or feeling. Lucy illustrates this with her explanation of her self-injurious behaviour, namely hand-biting:

...my own anger found an outlet in biting down on my own hand just above the thumb joint, a wonderfully comforting kind of pain, and made me feel in control. (Ch 4).

I have decided that my hand-biting was an unrecognised sign that I was developing an urge to use more spoken words, because when I was an adult I discovered that biting my hand nearly always occurs when I would have wanted to make a forceful comment (usually of the four letter word variety), or a casual observation, such as, 'That was not a bad idea!' or 'Luv ya!' (Ch 4).

<u>Cognitive Skills</u>

A major problem in cognitive skills is apparent from her autobiography, namely a difficulty in sequencing and learning cause and effect. This is illustrated in her attempts to learn how to make her bed.

I could not string the preceding segments of how to make a bed together, and I really think that this was because I could not process 'cause and effect'... (Ch 1)

What appears to have helped with this problem is an environment that was structured and predictable. As Lucy states,

'The environment of the Autistic Centre was so structured that for me problems with cause and effect were minimised.' (Ch 8).

<u>Sensory Processing</u>

Lucy has significant problems with auditory and visual perception. Her sound sensitivity explains some of her unusual behaviour.

...so I relied on activities such as swaying, humming and running in circles, which defended me against uninterrupted exposure to my sound-environment. (Ch 3).

Even today continuous motor noise makes it impossible to interpret my environment or the people in it. Hearing certain sounds gave me more of a skin- than a brain-response. (Ch 1).

She also has problems with depth perception and processing anything close to her centre of vision. She *'basically emphasised folds and depths'* and seemed *'to have lived in a world where depth was not a factor'.* (Ch 2). She reports that she has benefited from Auditory Integration Training, a relatively new technique that has yet to be established by research studies as an effective therapy for sound sensitivity.

Subsequent to writing her autobiography, she has benefited from the use of Irlen lenses. We have only just started to define and explore the problems people with autism have in sensory processing but we do know that it does have a profound impact on the person's daily life and behaviour.

Movement Skills

Lucy has always had significant problems with movement skills. It is also of note that *'the continuous clamour of everyday life was only relieved by movement'*. (Ch 4). Thus some movement patterns may be an attempt to cope with specific aspects of the environment.

Are there any other factors that contributed to her progress?

There are certain medical factors, for example, the discovery that [some foods] influenced her health and behaviour and anti-depressants *'caught my panic attacks before they got out of hand'* and made *'...my sensory integration a little more efficient'.* (Ch 11).

Time and academic study have also been important factors. I have noticed an improvement in her writing style and 'signature' as she has matured from a younger teenager to a woman. Her degree in Literary Studies has improved her language and writing skills.

Thus no single strategy or treatment can be credited with achieving the outcome that appeared inconceivable when she was first diagnosed as having autism.

She still cannot speak in clear sentences and requires considerable support in daily living skills and managing her behaviour. However her autobiography is proof of her intelligence and literary ability. She has autism, but she has also achieved her ambition — she is an author.

Glossary

<u>Some terms used in *Autism and Other Adventures: Lucy's Story* relating to Autism Spectrum Disorders. (A general guide only)</u>

Echolalia = Repeating the speech of others in an apparently parrotlike way.

Irlen Lenses = Tinted lenses invented by Helen Irlen and which some people with Autism have found useful

Operant conditioning = Teaching through reward and punishment; in a modified form these principles are widely used with young children with Autism either as part of a more general programme or as intensive behavioural therapy (ABA)

Perseveration = Locking into a specific series of actions or a special theme or interest.

Proprioception = Awareness of the position of one's body in space

Yoked Prisms = Prescription glasses designed for developmental vision problems.

<u>A little Australiana</u>

Fairy floss = Cotton candy
Kinder = Kindergarten
Nappies = Diapers
Take-away = Take-out
'Tea' = The evening meal, often the main meal of the day, not 'high tea' in the sense sometimes used in Britain.

At the Author's request the words *'biscuit'* and *'pavement'*, which in the original were used in their Australian and British meanings, have been replaced by the almost universally understood

American 'cookie' (except for its use by 'May' in Chapter 12) and by 'footpath' for the benefit of North American readers.

Most of the book is set in and around Melbourne, capital of the State of Victoria which forms the south-east corner of the Australian mainland. It is on approximately the same latitude as San Francisco, but the coast faces south towards Antarctica.

In Australia, Education and Disability services for children vary from State to State. Also there have been lots of changes since the period covered by *Autism and Other Adventures: Lucy's Story*. Many Australian children with Autism will have been diagnosed and educated in settings which are different from those described in the book.

Editor's Note

Except where otherwise indicated, the text of this book was created by Lucy Blackman between 1992 and 1998, i.e. during several years of writing and re-writing. The original manuscript was slightly shortened and some punctuation added by Mary Jane (Jay) Blackman under Lucy's direction, before professional pre-publication editing, which mainly involved further revision of punctuation.

The only changes made to the 2024 edition have been to a couple of words to allow for differences in commonly used vocabulary over the past 25 years, and alterations to pseudonyms at the request of the people concerned.

www.ingramcontent.com/pod-product-compliance
Lightning Source LLC
Chambersburg PA
CBHW032037090426
42744CB00004B/45